Putting Up with
the Russians

EDWARD CRANKSHAW

Putting Up with the Russians

Commentary and Criticism, 1947–84

Elisabeth Sifton Books
VIKING

ELISABETH SIFTON BOOKS • VIKING
Viking Penguin Inc.
40 West 23rd Street
New York, N.Y. 10010, U.S.A.

First American Edition
Published in 1984

947.085
Cra

LIBRARY OF CONGRESS CATALOGING IN PUBLICATION DATA
Crankshaw, Edward.
Putting up with the Russians.
1. Soviet Union—Politics and government—1945–
—Addresses, essays, lectures.   2. Communism—Soviet Union
—Addresses, essays, lectures.   3. Russian literature—
20th century—Book reviews.
DK274.C697   1984   947.085   84-40260
ISBN 0-670-58330-8

Printed in the United States of America
Set in Baskerville

Contents

143641

Acknowledgements

I cannot begin to thank all those in so many countries who over the years have helped me pick my way through the Soviet minefield, enlightened and instructed me in innumerable ways and helped me to preserve such sanity as I may lay claim to. They include scholars, historians, diplomatists, authorities in every field from oil to cattle-breeding, government officials in many lands, fellow journalists. I thought of individuals to single out, some obscure, some with resounding names. But there were far too many. It was brought home to me as never before how much the work of one person, for better or worse, owes to others even, as sometimes, in sharp disagreement.

So I will remember publicly only two, in fact the first two, neither appreciated by the world at large: my friends A. T. Cholerton, the brilliant correspondent of the *Daily Telegraph* who first opened my eyes to Soviet reality even as I was staring it in the face uncomprehendingly, and Llewelyn P. ('Tommy') Thompson, later United States Ambassador (it sometimes seemed to all the world), kindest of friends and to my mind the wisest and most perceptive diplomat of his time: he must have found Mr John Foster Dulles an even heavier cross to bear than Mr Molotov.

I should also like to thank David Astor who, as Editor of the *Observer*, gave me much rope and the wherewithal to travel almost at will, although I was never a formal member of his staff. And a special word of gratitude to my friend and colleague Lajos Lederer, with whom I made many journeys and whose constant stimulus and flow of news, sometimes speculative, sometimes quite startlingly accurate and unexpected, have been equally invaluable.

Thanks too to Miss Lalage Johnson for her patience in transcribing so many yellowing and tattered pages, and to Mrs Jean Malins, as always, for transforming chaos into some sort of order.

I also owe an especial debt to my publishers and editors who worked very hard to help me put this volume together when I was out of action through illness: my friends A. D. Maclean, Lord Hardinge of Penshurst and Mrs Hilary Hale.

E. C.

The author and publishers are grateful to:

The Atlantic Monthly
Books and Bookmen
William Collins Sons & Co. Ltd.
Granada Publishing Ltd.
Hamish Hamilton Ltd.
C. Hurst & Co. Ltd.
New York Times
The Observer
A. D. Peters & Co. Ltd.
Simon & Schuster Inc.
The Spectator
Thames & Hudson Ltd.

for their courtesy and co-operation in the preparation of this book.

Introduction

The articles, essays, lectures, prefaces, reviews, etc. collected
here extended over a period of thirty-seven years, from 1947 to
1984. For the greater part of that time I kept up what was in
effect a continual running commentary on what I thought the
Russians were up to at home and abroad – above all in the
Observer and its globally syndicated Foreign News Service, but
very much also in the *New York Times Sunday Magazine* and in
lectures and broadcasts all over the place. This selection is a
very small fraction of what, looking back, appears as a rather
horrifying outpouring adding up to millions of words (not
counting a number of books). At the time, however, this
effluxion seemed the most natural thing in the world.

There were a few things I wanted to say and go on saying
with some urgency about the Soviet Union, the character of its
peoples, the nature of its government, its designs on its neighbours and its attitude to the outside world in general. I had little
competition in those early days; very few people knew the
Soviet Union at first hand, but I had served with the British
Military Mission to Moscow for nearly two years during the
war and this experience had filled me with the determination
to know more, going back far into history. Thus it was that
after demobilisation David Astor half-flattered, half-bullied
me into diverting a recently resumed and quite harmless career
as a critic of the arts, and I found myself committed to the
hilt.

The Soviet Union has to be treated not as a monstrous,
unfathomable apparition to be contemplated helplessly, but as
one country among others (with startling peculiarities, of
course) and part of the general global mess. I wanted to show
that while the Bolshevik regime was even more vile than it was
possible for anyone who had not experienced it to imagine, that
although it would make mischief on every possible occasion and

xi

find it hard to resist every opportunity for easy expansionism and subversion, there was next to no danger of the Kremlin launching a formal war and it could always be stopped by a firm and clear declaration of the line it must not cross – backed by sufficient force to make that declaration credible.

It may seem odd for a journalist to resurrect pieces written years ago for particular occasions. Let me say that nobody could be more surprised than I myself. The reason is quite simply that I find myself being asked questions by younger generations which I imagined had been settled for ever; more particularly that we, and especially Washington, seem quite suddenly to have forgotten what we have learnt. There are disconcerting signs of a drift back to the old panic fear of the Communist menace, an ideological crusade and the more absurd attitudes of the cold war. There is a general loss of a sense of proportion. Nuclear overkill runs wild. An American President appears to see nothing demeaning in proclaiming to the world at large that the fate of his great, magnificent, rich and so powerful country depends on the outcome of this or that squalid civil war in Central America – and this after Cuba, 1962! Many years ago I wrote that the Kremlin's one great achievement was turning itself into a bogy to give us an excuse to stop thinking. Is this to happen all over again? Nothing, nothing at all that has happened in Afghanistan or Poland or Angola, or in the way of a shift in the balance of armaments, in the least way changes the picture of Russia built up over the past forty years – an intolerable, a disgraceful regime imprisoned by its own past, an imperial power run by men who got where they are by conspiracy and still think of the world in terms of a gigantic counter-conspiracy. (It might be pointed out that the Russians have just as much right – and just as little – to make themselves felt in Africa or the Indian Ocean as the Americans or ourselves.)

The pieces here are not chosen for their 'crisis' interest. So many of these dramas, from the Berlin blockade to the invasion of Afghanistan, have come and gone as part of the eternal superficial flux. I was never a reporter, except for special occasions, and I did not regard myself as a Kremlinologist until driven to behave like one by the stimulating vagaries of the Khrushchev era: it did not seem to me to matter in the least which of Stalin's circle the great leader might next murder, and the differences between Brezhnev and his colleagues seemed of no more interest than the differences between a number of stale buns. So, although the *Observer* had its excitements (it made journalistic history, for example, by scrapping almost its entire contents at the last moment to print verbatim Khrushchev's 'secret' speech denouncing Stalin in 1956; it printed circumstantial – and accurate – details of the Sino-Soviet quarrel long before the Chancellories of the West acknowledged its existence), these are not reflected here. What I have tried to show is the continuity and the predictability of Soviet policy – and the advantages of seeking to penetrate attitudes and motives rather than speculate about individual puzzles.

It is impossible to tell a great many things about the Soviet Union. It has only itself to blame if we conclude the worst on every possible occasion, since the leadership devotes so much energy to concealing not only from the outer world but also from its own people and, indeed, itself the truth about its simplest activities behind a smoke-screen of mystification (a national inheritance) and by the propagation of systematic or institutionalised lies (Lenin's personal contribution) developed to such a degree that few Communist Party functionaries would know how to recognise the truth even if for reasons of expediency they found themselves speaking it. Nevertheless it would be a mistake on our part always to assume the worst: for our own sake, for the sake of the rest of the world, including Russia, we need to understand as clearly as we can what it is we are coexisting with. Of course we can never completely understand. I myself, after forty years of trying, find myself still faintly wondering when faced, for example, with the Kremlin's imbecile behaviour after the shooting down of the South Korean airliner in the summer of 1983, or its ludicrous prevarications about the health of Mr Andropov, dead to the world for months on end. One can understand the historical causes of this nonsensical way of carrying on and yet still stand amazed and flummoxed by its more bizarre manifestations.

Leaving aside such elements of fantasy, there is still a great deal to be understood. Our great and continuing failure in this respect has been not to ask the right questions. Perfectly simple questions. For example: what do the Russians hope or intend to do? And why? How does this compare with what they say they hope or intend to do? How do these intentions or aspirations, real or pretended, deceiving or self-deceiving, compare with what they are doing in fact? And so on. There has been plenty of scope for sober consideration here but too often our politicians and soldiers have preferred wild speculation based on the unsupported proposition for a war of conquest with an eye to global hegemony. Further, even less excusably, they have taken at its face value the Kremlin's insistence on the monolithic unity of the Communist world – and by so doing succeeded in welding the very disparate parts more firmly together. In this way the so-called 'Communist Menace' was conjured out of almost nothing, facing us with a grisly monster of our own imagining.

There was and still is indeed a menace of sorts, and one to be taken seriously and quietly: our old friend Russian imperialism, given a new cutting edge by modern armaments and driven by a combination of fear and greed and a cock-eyed political philosophy. Of course the Kremlin uses Communism as a stalking-horse, but it was Russia in arms, not Communism, which occupied half Europe in 1945 and proceeded to impose upon it her own totalitarian system. It was not Communism which tried to drive the Western allies out of Berlin, but a naked military threat which drew back in the traditional Russian manner when robustly countered. We did not profit by that lesson as we should have done. So obsessed were too many of us with the chimera of Communism as opposed to the reality of Russia as a power that we refused for a long time to believe in Tito's quarrel with Stalin, which should have exploded once and for all the myth of Communist unity. Worse, by insisting that the Chinese Revolution of 1949 meant the apotheosis of global Communism and the virtual unification of China and the Soviet Union, the USA brightened itself into fits, allowing its entire outlook on the world to be dangerously distorted and precipitating the disgraceful and morally ruinous phenomenon of McCarthyism. Ten years later, with a decade of unassimilated, undigested experience behind it, came Washington's almost unbelievable mishandling of the Cuban Revolution. If anyone was pushed by inept behaviour firmly and inescapably into the arms of Moscow, it was Fidel Castro. And now we have

El Salvador and the astonishing contribution of Dr Henry Kissinger. . . .

I have called it *Putting up with the Russians* because that is what we have to do. The Soviet Union is a fact of life like the weather. We have to live with it. Soviet leaders go on about 'peaceful coexistence' as though it were an original idea they had dreamed up. It is not an idea at all. We do in fact coexist and will continue to do so whether we like it or not unless and until we blow ourselves off the face of the earth. The adjective 'peaceful' simply begs the question. We have different ideas about its meaning. For us it means, or should mean, live and let live. For the Government of the Soviet Union it embraces the concept of an unceasing 'ideological struggle', aiming at the salvation of humanity through the substitution, by all conceivable means short of war, of the Soviet political and social system for every differing system in every country on this planet – a process dignified by the name of World Revolution. It is impossible to tell how much or how little the Soviet leadership still believes this antiquated rubbish, but it is certainly influenced in its behaviour by at least the habit of belief.

E. C.
February 1984

PART I

Russia's Weakness and Our Duty
1947

One of the most damaging illusions of modern times is the belief in Russia's invulnerable might. The Russians themselves, at tremendous cost, have done all they can to encourage this belief, which is half their strength in the conferences of the world. If they had proclaimed their weakness at the end of the war, public opinion everywhere would have demanded the alleviation of the sufferings of a gallant people tortured by long adversity, but Mr Molotov and Mr Gromyko would have found it harder to get their way in the poker play of post-war conferences.

The Soviet Union, for all the magnificence of its achievements, is not a brand-new realm. Under entirely new management it is still Eternal Russia. The peasants have at last been trained to use machines, and countless thousands of them have been herded into the new factories. But they are still the peasants of Chekhov and Gorki – or their children. Mechanisation and Communist drive will modify their character, but it is uphill work, and the new Party intelligentsia (the most important product of the Revolution) has not yet by any means succeeded in turning the one hundred and seventy million Russians and their twenty-odd million square miles of territory into a giant version of, say, agricultural and industrial Britain.

In imagining the Soviet Union as an orderly, drilled and mechanised embodiment of power we do injustice both to the Russians and ourselves, and we introduce the distorting element of fear into our thinking about the future of the world. If the present regime can stay the course for another ten or fifteen years the picture will be different and the Soviet Union will begin to appear as a highly organised power. For the time being she is nothing of the kind, and we have to use those years to find out how to live with her. We shall do this more readily if we

3

refuse to allow ourselves to be hypnotised by size, and think more in terms of human beings.

Had there been no war the chances are that the Soviet Union would have been hardening into a truly formidable power just about now. But there has been a war, and it has thrown the harsh and painful pattern into chaos. The success of the Red Army blinded us to its weakness. It was the most wasteful and sacrificial victory in the history of the world. Before the suffering of the Russian people in that conflict we can only bow our heads. But even with all their immense sacrifices they scraped through only by the skin of their teeth. And still today they are holding on by their teeth.

Their present wretchedness is more than the weariness and disillusionment of an exhausted people who hoped too much of victory. It is the exhaustion of an undernourished people with a largely disrupted economy. And now comes the bitter blow of last summer's drought. Instead of fearing Soviet Russia, we should be wondering whether to help her – or how to help her, in spite of her Government's attitude. The withdrawal of the United Nations Relief and Rehabilitation Administration from White Russia and the Ukraine is a sad beginning.

The drought has struck cruelly. It came at a moment when great tracts of the Ukraine, White Russia, and the western parts of Great Russia still lay waste, and when every grain was needed to feed the industrial workers and sustain the current Plan. Even if the Plan succeeds it can mean no more than a relatively scanty increase in the all-important light industries which are the gauge of a nation's standard of living. The people of the Union will still be miserably short of those consumers' goods which they alone among all the peoples of Europe outside the Balkans have for so long gone without.

If the Plan fails they will have to go without still longer. And it may fail. The Russians can endure everything and anything; they can work like men possessed, even in the depths of privation, for long stretches. But even a Russian cannot work steadily at the pace demanded of him by the Plan, year in year out, without enough to eat and with nothing to show for it but impersonal trophies – schools, civic centres, silos. He sometimes wants something for himself. And already certain industries are falling behind the production schedule for this year.

4

If industry is shaky, agriculture, upon which Russian industry utterly depends, is catastrophic. During the war the
grimly desperate achievement of collectivising the peasants was
largely undone, even in areas where the Germans never pene-
trated. Peasants filched land from the collectives and no one
stopped them. Managers of collectives sold land to individual
peasants and gave them certificates freeing them from communal work. The Politburo set in motion a strenuous purge but
this seems to be making heavy weather. In the Black Earth
areas the representatives of the Extraordinary Commission
report that it is not always possible to make resisting peasants
give up their illegal gains. And this means that the state is
powerless to collect its grain and to enforce efficient methods.

This sort of thing is taking place in the heart of Russia proper
– for example, round Tambov. In the peripheral Republics the
ravages of armed bands of deserters, separatists, recalcitrant
peasants, renegades, and the rest are now added to war devastation and post-war drought.

That is a crude sketch of the sombre and tragic background
against which we must see the Kremlin's foreign policy. It
appears to have two main and mutually contradictory elements: fear of the West, and a desperate need for material
assistance from the West. Fear of the West dictates every
conceivable expedient to break the power, the sense of direction
and the unity of the West, at whatever cost in human suffering.
Need for material assistance dictates concessions to the West,
concessions made if possible from artificially inflated demands.
The two motives do not go well together. And in the conflict
between these motives lies the key to the understanding of the
vagaries and contradictions of the Russian line – complicated
by clumsiness, muddle, and ignorance of our ways.

There are other motives, too. There is the dream of world
revolution, which may survive many years of cold storage. And
there is the historical expansive drift along the line of least
resistance, which it is easy, if troublesome, to stop by firmness.
But fear and need are the two main motives. Neither is new, but
both are aggravated by the conditions of the moment.

The one certainty is the truth of Stalin's recent statement,
that 'not a single Great Power, even if its Government is
anxious to do so, could at present raise a large army to fight

5

another Allied Power'. This will remain true of Russia for some years to come. Her weakness leaves us with an immense responsibility. Unless we, together with the Americans, are prepared to attack her now, which is unthinkable and would mean the disintegration in wickedness of Western civilisation, we have to find a way of living side by side with her. Russia will not help us much in this, at any rate for the present. It is our burden. And it does not mean appeasement. On the contrary: it means checking the expansive drift by standing firm, and at the same time making it clear that we are ready to assist and co-operate with a non-expansive Russia to the fullest possible extent.

There is no other hope but this. If we fulfil it we shall ensure the salvation of those Western values by which we set great store. And we shall gain most valuable time, before the Soviet Union rises to full strength, in which to convince those who rule Russia, and those who will rule her tomorrow, that they can live peacefully and prosperously in the same world with us.

The Living Image
1948

Unless he is taken on a conducted tour, the first impressions of the stranger to Russia are likely to be harsh, and especially if he enters the country by the northern sea route and in wartime. Archangel is one of Russia's back doors; and there is a good deal to be said for the back-door approach to anywhere: by the time you get round to the front you know the worst, you know the sort of ideas that have gone into the making of the façade, and you can also judge the amount of effort that has had to be put into the task of keeping up appearances, which is not a thing to be laughed at.

In Archangel there are no appearances. Archangel is a sea-port, ice-bound for half the year, and in peacetime mainly concerned with the export of timber. It is nothing but timber. Far out into the White Sea the water is streaked and dotted with the logs that have floated down from Archangel. The Dvina river itself, when at last you cross the bar, spawns logs and the steamer pushes them aside. The right bank of the winding estuary is composed for mile after mile entirely of timber, timber in unimaginable quantity, in the water, half in the water, out of the water; inert in stacks the size of churches, which look as though they have rotted there for generations, or half alive in the form of wooden wharves and roads and sheds and houses. Immense irregular rafts of timber, a quarter of a mile long, and with little houses built upon them with smoking chimneys, are lugged down the river by Dvina tugs, or self-propelled by some kind of outboard engine. It is impossible to tell where seasoning timber ends and building timber finishes. The people live in the timber, build their houses, their roads, their boats of it, burn it in their engines and their stoves, and load the surplus into ships. Archangel itself, when you reach it after traversing interminable timber flats, is nothing more than a sudden outcrop of highly organised, and sometimes carved and painted, timber in the shapes of houses, streets, and public buildings. And then, on the confines of the city, it sinks down again into timber in the mass. And everywhere is utter flatness. There is not a living tree to be seen. The only life comes from the intoxicating quality of the hard northern air with the tang of the distant sea and the distant fir-woods in it, and from the luminous brilliance of the pale blue sky, which, at sunset and sunrise, produces the majestic effects found only in the desert or at sea.

Against this raw, astringent background the people pullulate in tattered furs.

My own first impressions were as they should be. It was October 1941. Russia had been at war for little more than three months; but already Moscow was directly menaced, and already Archangel, capital of one of the biggest consumer provinces, was being starved. Except as a port for the unloading of war materials from Britain and America, she could play no part in the war effort. So she was treated as a port. Arrangements were made to man the dock facilities at full strength; but nothing else was to matter at all. The Government could not afford to send food to people who could do nothing to help with the war. So the people of Archangel got no food.

When I arrived it had been snowing, but the snow had melted into slush, mixing with the accumulation of summer dirt into a thick, porridgy mud which made the steeply raised wooden pavements as slippery as ice and filled vast pot-holes in the streets with greasy water. Urchins rushed up with strident cries, brandishing five, ten, twenty rouble notes which you were supposed to take in exchange for a couple of cigarettes. Over all was a reek of sewage and sickly-sweet *mahorka*, the Russian equivalent of shag, smoked as a rule in a roll of newspaper. I wanted to telephone; but the only call-box in view had been used as a public lavatory; and when I looked in at the public lavatory, belonging to the brand-new and shining river-steamer station, it was easy to understand why. That river station, a resplendent café which was closed (but which reopened later), and a large and imposing new theatre were, apart from the pleasant Admiralty building in the old Moscow style, apparently the only sights in Archangel, through which hunched, grey-faced figures, swathed in black shawls or greasy, ragged sheepskins, plodded their way through the slush with the air of ghouls.

I had come across from Bakharitsa wharf on the other side of the river in the launch of a Russian trade-union official. There had been no time to look at Bakharitsa, and the journey across the water, alive with dozens of remarkably smart-looking launches, and all dominated by the dazzling white paintwork and Italianate lines of the Admiral's streamlined barge, had not prepared me for this; but by the time I had wandered round the town and fought my way back to the public ferry to return I was ready for anything. The ferry, a sizeable steam-packet something on the lines of a Mississippi steamer, was packed. But the people who formed the jam, and who ten minutes before had been picking their way through the slush and the pot-holes with the appearance of ghouls, were suddenly amiable and expansive, no longer a scattered, misanthropic mob, but a noisily and gaily chattering crowd – the very mixture one had expected, of ebullient peasant youth, pig-tailed small-town flappers, raw privates in new uniforms, a scattering of amiably condescending Red Army officers, green-capped frontier guards very much off duty, and the age-old patience of peasant old-age. Humanity showed its face. But only to hide it again immediately.

For soon the ferry approached what was meant to be a landing stage – a heavy platform of waterlogged timber, just awash. At the landward gate leading on to this platform a grey and hideous mob was waiting in silence. In a moment the self-respecting peasants on the ferry were themselves a grey and hideous mob, heeling the ship over in the silent and unanimous surge to the landward railing. I was interested to see how the numerous blue-coated militia, both on the ferry and on shore, and all with rifles on their backs, would handle these rival mobs. I reckoned without the evident desire of the militia to see how the mobs would handle themselves. For instead of letting the passengers off in a thin stream, and instead of holding back the waiting crowd until the ferry was cleared, they treated me to my first Russian inspiration. At a prearranged signal the gates in the side of the ferry were swung open simultaneously with the gates on the landing stage. Five hundred people on the landing stage lurched forward towards the ferry, completely submerging the floating stage. Five hundred people in the ferry swept

9

down the lowered gangway. A thousand people in two opposed armies milled about up to their knees in water. Old women with unimaginable bundles quietly wept. Children screamed. Soldiers and dockers shoved and cursed. Young women spat. The battle went on for a long time. The militia looked on, contributing energetic shouts of 'Davai!' an extremely Russian form of exhortation which can mean 'Come off it!' or 'Get a move on!' impartially. Swept out of the ferry and on to the landing stage in the first rush I managed to edge out to one side and stood with my ankles in the water, clinging to a rope which depended from the ferry, until the riot had sorted itself out. Then, at the height of the mix-up, I was aware of larger shouts. Two tallish soldiers were focused in the very centre of the mob, and they were forcing their way towards the ferry with the aid of what looked like a battering ram. But the battering ram, now swung up on high, revealed itself as a stretcher covered with an army blanket from under which two booted feet protruded. Above all other smells there was suddenly the sickly smell of death. But nobody paused because of it. On and on the soldiers shoved, pressing back the people who were trying to get to the land. One at last got a foothold on the ferry. The stretcher was now raised at a fantastic angle above the heads of the crowd, who paid no attention, but went on pushing. Until finally, after a number of false starts, the other soldier, with the aid of two dockers who caught the stretcher on their shoulders when it looked like falling and discharging its burden into the water, managed to climb into the ferry too and the corpse was deposited on the ferry's deck.

By the time I touched dry land, twenty-five minutes had passed. Reflecting on the lessons of these twenty-five minutes, notably the utter contempt of the ordinary Russian for the ordinary police, whatever he might feel about the secret variety, and the dramatic and immediate transformation of a pleasant and cheerful boatload of people into a blind and bitter mob, or pack, I ran into a group of soldiers on the main wharf trying to back a horse and cart on the slippery boards. They went about it with that sort of inefficiency which in the warm and sunny South occasionally exasperates but always charms. It does not, however, accord with the savagery of the northern climate, where you have to watch your step. The little horse was slipping about all over the place. With contradictory ejaculations of 'Davai!' the four soldiers pushed it about and would not give it a chance to find its feet. They were ordinary peasant conscripts, small, wiry, bullet-headed and cropped. They were not being cruel. They were being helpful. I watched with my heart in my mouth as the wretched, rough-coated little animal slipped and slithered about on the edge of the wharf. A final, triumphant push sent the back wheels of the cart over the edge; the front wheels followed, and then the horse itself – a ten-foot drop into the icy water which was just beginning to freeze. In due course, after various flounderings, assisted by 'Davais' and futile tugs and a soldier who went down a ladder to try, ineffectually, to unharness it, the animal drowned and lay half in half out of the water with its rough hair streaked and matted and a red discoloration where it had cracked its head. The soldiers were still looking at it when I went away. Next day the cart was gone. It could be used again. But the little horse was still there, and there it remained for many days afterwards until the ice completely covered it. It could not be used again.

By now I was feeling very sick and very angry. So sick and angry that my first sight of a convict gang being led away from the docks did not move me at all and the stupid sentry who stood at the gangway of the ship and whose immediate reaction to the production of your pass was to make an impassive, threatening lunge with his immensely long spike-bayonet, seemed to stand for all the blank and mindless inefficiency of a country which could not afford to be inefficient. I did not know it at the time, but in that one short afternoon I had been granted the most valuable introduction to Russia that could possibly be desired. And that is why I have done my best to share it with the reader, who might well prefer an evening at the ballet.

You do not see every day a corpse used as a battering ram even in North Russia, even in wartime; nor do you see a horse being foolishly drowned before your eyes. But you are very much hemmed in by the attitude that finds its ultimate expression in such fantasies, and the demonstration of its logical conclusion helps to fix it in your mind. What it helps to fix is the muddle, the carelessness, of a country in which efficiency has never paid full dividends because people and space have always been 'expendable', and the automatic and instantaneous transformation of the kindliest people in the world into utterly self-centred and oblivious beasts when it comes to survival in even its most trivial and impermanent aspects – such as who shall get the last place on the tram. You are very soon aware that physical survival is by no means a *sine qua non* in wartime Soviet Russia, where the devil really does take the hindmost. The Russians are aware of this all the time, and this awareness shows itself in odd ways. Once the point of the moment is carried, once victory is assured, once they have got their foothold on the last step of the tram, or picked up their bread-ration, or corralled their share of timber for the stove, they relax into immediate affability and will go to great lengths to help the next man get his, even to giving up a large part of what they themselves have just won. But it is the winning that seems to be the thing; and since, particularly in wartime Russia and above all in the north, the greater part of life is taken up by precisely the primitive activities I have listed above – the struggle for food, fuel and transport – the impression of the Russian street crowd is apt to be disconcerting, and it is a long time before you realise that what Maurice Baring, and many others, have said about the Russians is quite true: namely, that they are the kindest-hearted and most generous people in the world . . . . But they need a base for their generosity. You can't share your last crumb of bread unless you have got it. And getting it has for a long time been difficult. So we have, repeatedly, these extraordinary transformations from man to beast and back, best expressed, perhaps, in the attitude of a Moscow shopper, who will divide all she has with the neighbour who was unlucky in the scramble but whom, in the course of the scramble, she would cheerfully have slain.

But at first you do not know about this. You see simply the grey-faced, ill-dressed masses, skulking about like lone wolves, then converging in hostile packs, then separating again. They look neither to left nor to right, but straight ahead and slightly downwards, shuffling along in their shapeless felt boots with that peculiarly Russian gait, body bent forward, arms hanging down and slightly in front of the body, and, apparently, haunted by the fear of showing interest in anything at all. So that in hard times one of their number may drop exhausted by the roadside and die there in the snow without anybody stopping to help or to enquire.

Another thing you become aware of in the north, and which dominates your ideas, is forced labour in its many different forms. As you sit at breakfast in your hotel you hear the dreadful sound of a woman wailing, half hysterically, in the street outside. And looking out you see thirty or forty women and girls being marched along the frozen street by guards with fixed bayonets, each woman with a small bundle. You do not know where they are going; but you know that they are being marched away against their will, that the call came suddenly and roughly, and that behind them they are leaving homes which are, as it were, still warm, while they trudge through the snow with nothing but their bundles. Most are stony-faced; but one is weeping loudly.

This is the beginning of one kind of forced labour. But they do not know which kind. These stony-faced women may be petty criminals being marched from one prison to another; or they may be minor political offenders, sentenced to hard labour for foolish indiscretions: or they may be women who have evaded conscription being taken off for enrolment in the women's forces; or they may be housewives turned out of a block of flats, at half an hour's notice, because it is wanted by a government department engaged in fighting the war. You do not know. All you know is that it has, whatever it was, happened roughly and suddenly and without appeal, and that the women are now in the cold, being marched away under guard. And you are harrowed by that wailing, which is like the end of the world.

For forced labour in Soviet Russia, you very soon find, is a term which may mean almost anything, from the sentencing of violent criminals or 'political' offenders to a lifetime of brutalisation, the effective length of the sentence varying with the endurance or stamina of the individual prisoner, to the drafting of one member of every household in a given street to live for three months in the forest and cut wood against the winter. It may, when you come to think of it, equally include the drafting of a dozen newly graduated doctors to a remote Siberian township where doctors are urgently needed – but the newcomer to Russia only knows what he sees. Entering by the back

13

door and in wartime he almost certainly does not see the worst, but he sees a good deal.

He sees, for instance, toiling in sixty degrees of frost on the construction of a new wartime port – a raw and terrible affair of manhandled timber baulks and splitting ice – a gang of fifty alleged human beings, evidently brutalised beyond description, probably by their features not political offenders but criminals of the lowest order – one gang of fifty among a dozen such gangs used on this urgent and appalling job with no regard to anything at all but the most rapid completion of the job, as men were used by the builders of the pyramids – he sees this gang being marched back to quarters by a strong guard with fixed bayonets and rifles *at the ready*. Marched is not the word, convoyed, perhaps; they shuffle desperately along the ice-covered wharf, black figures with greasy fur-caps hiding half their faces, in the shadow of the rustling walls of merchant vessels iced up for the winter, each with its growing piles of garbage thrown out from the galley on to the winter ice to wait until the spring thaw carries it away. And while the onlooker is speculating on these sub-human figures, speculating on their value as workmen, speculating on how they live when off duty, he observes the furtive glances charged with animal greed which they cast at the heaps of frozen garbage, and he hears the guards shouting to them roughly to keep their eyes to themselves; and then suddenly, unbelievably, one black, stooping figure has detached itself from the horrible procession; like a broken-winged crow it flaps two or three paces out of the line and grabs at a chunk of bread which has rolled away from the nearest garbage-heap; and in that moment, and to the accompaniment of an ear-splitting detonation, vicious in that still and unspeakable waste, the figure pitches forward into the thin snow.... The other prisoners shuffle on without a glance at their late companion. The guard who has fired the shot walks up and stirs the black shape with his boot and, satisfied, stumps on after the others, working the bolt of his rifle with a metallic rattle. The indistinct grey twilight deepens into night. But next day the black shape is still there; and for many days after, embalmed in that frigid air, it lies huddled beneath the dead side of a British steamer, gradually becoming greyer, then whiter, with each fresh fall of fine, fragmented snow, until there is nothing but an uneven hummock in the smooth surface of the snow.

14

Cold War or Hot?
1950

The appalling menace of the hydrogen bomb has brought new fears of sudden war. If the United States can make it, we are told, any industrial power can make it; and a submarine in the Hudson River could blast New York City off the face of the earth. But if we look into the matter more closely, it seems to me that the effect of the new bomb may, in fact, reduce the risk of war.

Nobody in this world wants war for its own sake, or even as a means of getting his own way. But one power, the Soviet Union, has so far been committed to the belief in the inevitability of a series of wars on the march toward the ultimate victory of Communism. This conviction has conditioned the whole of Soviet policy since 1917. It has nothing to do with wanting or not wanting war, which is seen simply as a part of an inevitable historical process, much as the Day of Judgment used to be seen by millions who did not in any way look forward to it.

In trying to evaluate the chances of war between Russia and the Atlantic powers, it is necessary to understand this attitude. And the importance, first of the atom bomb, and now of the hydrogen bomb, in this context is that it may cause the Bolsheviks to think again. It was all very fine and easy for Lenin to talk about Communism rising like the phoenix from the ashes of war in the pre-atomic era. But we have now reached the stage where nobody remotely in his senses could imagine that reciprocal destruction, on a scale now freely envisaged, can prepare the way for the organised dictatorship of the proletariat or for anything but universal ruin. And if Stalin is forced to modify Bolshevik teaching on the place of war in the Leninist-Marxist system, he will be forced sooner or later to modify other important aspects of that teaching.

When we speak of war between Russia and the West we mean total war. In the eyes of its rulers, the Soviet Union has been at war with the non-Communist world for over thirty years – since Lenin made Russia the base for his own private war against that world, which at that time was the whole planet, except for a hundred thousand Bolsheviks. This state of war has existed ever since, though concealed at times in one way or another, for purely tactical reasons. After a brief offensive in the early days, Russia went over to the defensive with the slogan of 'Socialism in One Country'. The main objective was to turn the USSR into an invulnerable base for world revolution.

The principles of this war were laid down in Lenin's innumerable writings. The main body of his teaching, in this sense, has been rehashed by Stalin in *Problems of Leninism* and *A Short History of the Communist Party of the USSR*, both of which are compulsory reading for all Communists. As manifested today, the principles call for the strengthening of the Soviet Union as a defensive base for Communism, the weakening by all possible means of non-Communist powers, the prevention of anti-Communist coalitions, and the fostering of revolutionary movements in other lands, in so far as these can be subordinated to the Communist party of the USSR.

Nothing could be more lucid in theory or more complicated in practice. The complications arise from the fact that there are frequent contradictions between the internal needs and the external policy of the Kremlin, i.e. the desire to exploit a revolutionary situation abroad may conflict with the need to build up strength and morale at home.

If the theory is lucid, the practice is tortuous and involved. The methods called for are in essence the tactics of the Trojan horse, ramified in every conceivable way and complicated by an instant readiness to sacrifice the whole apparatus to the enemy should such an action seem expedient. The general line is conveniently outlined by Lenin himself in his celebrated pamphlet, 'Left-wing Communism: An Infantile Disorder', written shortly before his death and dedicated in an ironical spirit to David Lloyd George, then the British Prime Minister.

Lenin says:

It is possible to conquer a powerful enemy only by exerting the most intense effort, by taking thorough, attentive, meticulous and skilful advantage of each and every split among the bourgeois of the various countries, and by taking advantage of every opportunity, even the most trivial, to gain a mass ally, though this ally may be temporary and unstable, vacillating, conditional, and unreliable.

The most recent statement of Soviet war aims was made in a special *Pravda* article by Lavrenti Beria, one of the new triumvirate now ruling the Soviet Union under Stalin. The article was written for his master's seventieth birthday.

Stalin has laid down a programme of action for Communists. They must (1) exploit all differences and contradictions in the bourgeois camp; (2) take concrete action to unite the working classes of the economically advanced countries with the national liberation movement in the colonies and dependent nations; (3) complete the struggle for unity of the trade union movement; (4) take active measures to bring together the proletariat and the small peasants; (5) support Soviet rule and disrupt the interventionist machinations of imperialism against the Soviet Union, bearing in mind that the Soviet Union is the base of revolutionary movement in all countries.

Thus, in practice, the present aims of Soviet foreign policy, which is a belligerent policy, may be summarised as an effort to achieve without war certain objectives of a kind traditionally achieved by war: the ruin of Western economy; the integration of the satellites with the Soviet economy; the penetration of Asia; the overthrow of sovereign governments in non-Communist countries. A principal way of achieving this is to weaken opposition and divide it. Particular activities, like the Communist offensives in Italy and France, the Berlin blockade, the Partisans of Peace movement, the attack on colonial empires, attempts to intimidate Turkey and Iran, the betrayal of the Jews, the disrupting of the United Nations, all fit themselves into one or another of the main objectives.

But our real question is whether, in the next five years, or fifteen years, or ever, total war is likely to seem to Moscow a better means toward the ultimate objective than the sort of policies preached by both Lenin and Stalin, and, until now, practised with steadfastness and restraint.

To anyone who knows Russia and the Russians, the idea of Moscow starting, or deliberately and consciously risking total war – which means, in practice, a shooting war with America and the British Empire – within the next five years is so absurd that it is impossible to consider it seriously. The Soviet Union would be quite incapable of sustaining an aggressive war against the United States and the British Empire in the next five years because it is too weak materially and too divided internally – to say nothing of the fact that it is engaged in holding down by force, or the threat of force, a ring of satellites looking for war as the signal for revolt.

Materially, the USSR has a population of close to two hundred million, at least a third as much again as the population of the United States. This vast population is scheduled this year to produce 250,000,000 tons of coal as against America's 1949 production of 435,000,000, and 35,000,000 tons of steel as against America's 77,868,000, 35,000,000 tons of oil as against America's 315,000,000. These moderate figures show a strong recovery from the post-war position and an increase on the 1940 level. They absorb the whole energies of government and people, the immense mass of the labouring classes working for a bare subsistence under conditions of extreme harshness and privation in order to fulfil the Plans. In 1940 the figures were: coal, 164,000,000 tons; steel, 18,000,000 tons; and oil, 30,000,000 tons. With this level of production, and materially assisted by America and the British Empire, Russia only just managed to pull victoriously through the fight with Germany, at the cost of untold devastation, sporadic famine, universal undernourishment, the total dislocation of her whole economy and the active revolt of millions of her minority nationalities.

The farthest Russia now looks ahead is to 1960. Five years ago Stalin gave as the target for that year 'at the earliest', 60,000,000 tons of steel, 60,000,000 tons of oil and 500,000,000 tons of coal. 'Only under such conditions,' he said, 'can we regard our country as guaranteed against any accidents. This will require perhaps three new Five-Year Plans if not more.' All the signs show that it will require more.

The Russian people have been driven too hard for too long, in exchange for too little. Even the mass of Party members are no longer pulling their full weight in the struggle for production, and recent purges of local officials have been on a scale unprecedented since the Thirties. The faint flicker of post-war optimism has given way to a sort of dreary apathy which has resulted in lowered production. This applies to the USSR as a whole. But both unofficial reports and official admissions, oblique or direct, show that in the minority republics, Azerbaijan, Uzbekistan, Kazakhstan and the autonomous Tartar Republic, opposition to Kremlin rule has spread to the highest Government circles. In the Ukraine, there is still resistance to the Moscow Government.

In a word, Russia is not strong enough to launch an aggressive war for many years to come and, even if she were strong enough, the Russian people are in no fit state to fight one, while many of the minority nationalities would actively revolt. We should never forget that the White Russians and the Ukrainians welcomed the Germans as liberators in the first months of the last war until Hitler showed his true face, while the mass of the ordinary Russians west of the Volga put no heart into the fight until they had experienced for themselves the wickedness of the Nazis.

As far as numbers go, the Red Army could overrun Europe. As far as armaments and aircraft go, it could swamp Western defences. This has been true for the past three years. But in view of retaliation from the air, the potential armed might of the United States, the shaky state of Soviet morale, and the colossal problems of holding Europe down by force – as well as the whole of the USSR – that sort of adventure can have few attractions for the Kremlin.

However, Russia has been an expanding power since the foundation of the Muscovite state in the fourteenth century. This instinctive expansionism has always been characterised by two peculiarities: a defensive attitude, shot through with a certain missionary zeal, and an easy readiness to stop when it finds itself up against a firm barrier. These profound Russian characteristics fit with remarkable exactitude into the Bolshevik theory of action. Left to herself, Russia would expand right around the globe. The Czars were hedged in by great powers: Prussia, Austria and Japan. Stalin is not. But he has America to cope with, which the Czars did not have, and what is left of the British Empire, which is still a force.

An extremely important point – indeed, the supremely important point – about this expansionist impulse is that it has been Russia's ruin in the past and seems likely to be her ruin in the future. By spreading her people and her resources too thinly over the ground, the Governments of Russia have prevented the standard of living, and with it the productivity of the people, from rising.

But the point we are discussing is whether this lust for space goes hand in hand with the waging of aggressive war. The answer is that it does not. The traditional Russian campaign is the spacious defensive campaign, followed by pursuit of an exhausted enemy.

And this fits in with the Bolshevik philosophy, as outlined not only by Lenin, but also by Soviet military strategists. Only when the Bolsheviks are quite sure of easy and overwhelming victory will they permit themselves to attack openly with guns – as in the case of the Finnish campaign, which was considered afterward an error of judgement. And what most people do not seem to realise is that the Soviet Army itself is imbued with this doctrine. In his book, *The Brain of the Army*, the Soviet ex-Chief of General Staff, Marshal Shaposhnikov, makes it quite clear that the enemy is to be defeated by political means before a shot is fired, so that when the troops are finally deployed, all they are required to do is to push over a tottering edifice.

It is plain that this attitude makes perfectly good sense if one is convinced, as the Communists are, that history is on their side; that sooner or later capitalism will collapse under its own weight and as a result of its own internal contradictions, and that all the good Communist has to do is to trust in Marx and keep his powder dry. Sooner or later a clash must come: the supreme objective is to ensure that the citadel of Communism is in a fit state to profit by it when the day arrives. Soviet Russia, far from being in a fit state to profit by war with the United States and the British Empire, is, as we have seen, not even in a fit state to profit by war with Yugoslavia.

That is why I do not expect the USSR to initiate total war for a very long time to come, if ever. Such an onslaught on a strong position has no place in the Leninist-Stalinist philosophy. And

20

the idea of some people that Stalin is going out for world domination as such (as distinct, that is, from presiding, if he is spared, over an expanding Communist empire) will not hold water. According to all of Stalin's teaching, the world revolution is not a steady process, but proceeds in intermittent leaps. The first big leap was in 1917 and after. The second was in 1945 and after. And just as, according to Stalin's own theory of ebb and flow, the capitalist world managed to stabilise itself in the Twenties, so what is left of it will manage to stabilise itself in the Fifties.

Meanwhile, the Kremlin has China to think about, China, which I, personally, see as the beginning of the end of Muscovite power. China will occupy the best brains and resources of the Communist Party of the USSR for some time to come. The building up of the Soviet Far East, for example, is not at all pure gain to Moscow. It is being done at the direct expense of European Russia – just as, in a far lesser but still fatal degree, it was done before in the time of the Czars.

There is one other bogey which worries a great many people. If Stalin feels himself slipping, they say, isn't this the very thing to drive him into some wild adventure to divert attention from the shortcomings of the Soviet regime? I see no danger of this at all. In the first place, I do not believe that Stalin is a megalomaniac in the Hitler manner. In the second place, the Russian people for centuries have regarded war as an unmitigated evil.

It is my firm belief that if Stalin plunged his country into war it would be the end of his regime. He knows that his own overthrow was missed only by a hairsbreadth in 1941, when innumerable Russians in the west were welcoming the Germans as liberators and when, for a few months, practically the whole nation, even those who fought bravely, saw the Government's failure to keep the country out of war as the ultimate betrayal.

But even if the Kremlin does not want war and will not start one for many years, this does not mean that there will be no war. The Leninist campaign of disruption outside Russia may be so successful and may call for such sustained and concentrated effort to counter it that sooner or later the West may be forced to conclude that it can no longer go on squandering its substance in maintaining a state of constant preparedness for attack. Then it might conceivably be necessary to say to the Russians, 'We have so far been containing you, can continue to do so, but the cost is more than we are willing to pay. We are sick of living in an armed camp at the expense of all decent living. If you persist in your absurd and evil course of trying to break us down internally and of tyrannising over half of Europe we shall have to take decisive action – namely, to wipe you out by means of total war.'

This sort of situation, it seems to me, is the only one in which there lies a real danger of war. If the Kremlin continues on its present course and the rest of the world allows it to do so, it will become more probable day by day. But there are many stages between our present passive resistance to Communist expansion and a final ultimatum. And if our statesmen can bring themselves to think aggressively instead of defensively, then there is every chance that we shall be able to do without an ultimatum at all.

But we have to remember that statesmen do not function in a vacuum. They are sustained and upheld by public opinion. With the people in a defeatist frame of mind, our leaders will never get around to thinking aggressively. To produce the suitable mental and emotional climate for a new sort of approach to the Russian problem we have to get back our own nerve and stop being hypnotised by the sheer vastness of Russia. To do that, we have to take a great deal more trouble to understand both the Soviet Union and Communism, their strength and their weakness.

If we do this, we shall be amazed that we have allowed ourselves for so long to be reduced to panic and stampeded into so many retreats. This new mode of exasperated confidence will soon find ways and means of expressing itself in action of a kind that Stalin understands. But without it we are helpless.

Not Ideas but Force
1951

One of the sacrosanct assumptions of our time is that you can do anything with propaganda. This seems to me one of those half-truths in which so many people develop a vested interest that they are taken for whole truths, with no questions asked. Elaborate systems of thought and conduct are based upon them; and soon the whole of life is twisted out of shape to accommodate an overblown idea which has never been critically examined. Thus, when George Orwell produced his nightmare vision of a world conditioned in every way by the propaganda of a centralised tyranny, very few people questioned his basic assumption that it is possible to kill the human mind, to eliminate the capacity to think and reason, by sheer weight of propaganda and force.

I do question this assumption; and I think it is time we all began to question it. For if it is valid, then the view of humanity upon which all our values are based must be false; and if it is not valid, then by accepting the assumption we are in effect abandoning those values.

The whole issue is brought to a head by the fact that we are now confronted with a power, or the Government of a power, the Soviet Union, which has staked its existence on the strength of propaganda backed by force. Stalin and his friends apparently believe that you can condition human beings into believing anything you tell them – at least the vast majority of human beings; and they have harnessed the whole apparatus of modern publicity and mass-suggestion technique to the business of making their regime appear other than it is, both at home and abroad: to the business, that is to say, of disseminating a colossal and complex lie which comprehends the whole of human existence.

We stand appalled by the apparent power of this terrible machine, and we ask ourselves in dismay what answer we can hope to find. What oppresses us above all is the thought of the young, cut off from the outside world and all standards of comparison, their minds filled, directly or indirectly, with the lies of Kremlin propaganda, every moment of their waking day.

But need we be dismayed, if we really believe in the human spirit, as we say we do? And if we do not believe in the human spirit and see in the mind no more than an aggregation of conditioned reflexes, then why should we worry?

One of the first things to be clear about in our minds is the difference between propaganda and force. We talk freely about the power of Soviet propaganda inside Russia and behind the Iron Curtain generally in conditioning the minds of the people along certain lines; but, as I shall try to show, what we are really thinking about in many cases is not propaganda, but the power of the state, through the Communist Party and the secret police, to impose its will by force. Surely, best evidence of the failure of the Kremlin domestic propaganda to do the work required of it is, in fact, the perpetually increasing apparatus of force; the growing power of the police; the vast network of labour camps; and the relatively small size of the Communist Party; that is, of people who can be trusted, and the reiterated purges within the Party itself.

I should not dream of underestimating the power of propaganda to fill human beings with second-hand ideas and to enervate the power of original or logical thoughts. We have only to look around us, at our own civilisation with its tremendous emphasis on advertising, with its docile crowds all doing the same thing and pursuing the same pleasures, not because each individual has thought out his conduct for himself, but because it is the accepted thing – we have only to do this to see the power of propaganda to fill the mind with second-hand ideas. But that is not the same as killing the mind. The mass of people depend absolutely, and must depend, on second-hand notions: it is the rare individual who thinks out all his actions for himself.

On the other hand, I have yet to meet a person who is completely made up of second-hand ideas. In every individual there are special interests, however small, which defy all the attempts of propaganda to iron them out, whether in the form of mass-suggestion, herd-consciousness, the blandishments of commercial advertisers, or the official manipulation of truth.

24

And this seems to suggest that all propaganda can do is to fill up with its own ideas areas of the popular mind which are open to second-hand ideas, while having only a very limited and uncertain power over the active areas of the mind which may reject second-hand ideas of whatever kind. In other words, it cannot basically change the human mind; it can only exploit its weaknesses.

This idea is borne out by watching the effect of the Kremlin's propaganda inside Russia. And what happens there is what one would expect to happen after watching the effect of propaganda in other countries, say, in the United States or in England. For we must not forget that we too, each of us, are subjected to a barrage of propaganda from the cradle to the grave. We take for granted all manner of things which, if we thought for a moment, we might sharply reject – from the proper way to rear our children to the proper way of disposing of our bodies when we are dead.

And the things and ideas we accept seem to be, as a rule, either things and ideas about which we hold no firm view, or else the things and ideas which we more or less strongly want to accept. Propaganda which tells us to do things or accept things that we actively dislike seems to have very little value – unless it can so twist the truth that it appears to be offering the reverse of what in fact is being offered.

Thus, for example, most Americans accept the American way of life in detail, without subjecting it to critical examination, just as most Englishmen accept the British parliamentary system. We nearly all accept the idea that it is a good thing to have a motor car and a radio and that we should spend as much as we can afford, if not more, on the education of our children at schools and colleges. An astonishing number of us accept the idea that money is the criterion of worth. Americans and Englishmen each accept conventional views of the respective histories of the United States and the British Empire, views which differ widely from each other and are neither of them much concerned with truth.

It is perfectly natural for us to accept these ideas because they accord with our own natural inclinations. Also, as we all know, 'there is no pain like the pain of a new idea.' And, up to a point, the propaganda which ensures that we shall not ask too many questions saves us from anarchy. We have to live by an accepted code; and it is only the born original who insists on questioning that code not only in detail but also in its basic assumptions: it is he who keeps the code alive and flexible. On the other hand, there are very few individuals, if any at all, who accept without question every item of the accepted code. On the matters that touch his heart most closely each individual reserves the right to decide for himself, and does so. In such matters he is immune to propaganda.

It is very much the same in Russia, with the difference that the born original is liquidated. With the difference that in Russia all propaganda is sharply centralised and so often goes against the inclinations of the people that it creates areas of immunity which are probably more marked and extensive than you will find in the average Englishman or American.

On the other hand, the single-mindedness behind all the propaganda which does succeed makes for a remarkable community in credulity. The total effect is a curious mixture of credulous ignorance and stark scepticism – scepticism which nothing in the world can touch, and certainly not the blandishments of direct counter-propaganda.

Thus most Russians, including those who actively detest the Soviet regime, believe certain things they are told every day of their lives, some of which are true, some untrue. They believe that Russia is a great and glorious country. They believe the Russian has something which the foreigner has not got. They believe that the Soviet Union has good friends in Eastern Europe, although they regard these allies with mild and unthinking contempt.

They believe that the Soviet Union wants peace (they themselves are peace-loving, and it is to them inconceivable that their Government should go to war unless attacked) and that therefore any talk of war must originate abroad. They know there is talk of war, and they are told by Stalin that the peoples of the West want peace; therefore, they are ready to believe him when he tells them that the Governments of the West want war.

They believe the masses of the West are downtrodden and oppressed because, from their own experience, that is what happens to masses; they know that their own Government is harsh and tyrannical and false, but they are inclined to think that this is in the nature of government everywhere. They hold officialdom and the secret police in utter loathing, but they do not see how a country can be run without officials and secret police. They are inclined to think that Stalin and his colleagues exert a mitigating influence, which would be much stronger if the officials and the police were not so numerous. And so on.

They believe in these things because they are the natural things for a Russian to believe. Just as they believe in the uniqueness of the Moscow Underground and the magnitude of Soviet constructional achievement, because they are their own achievements.

But when it comes to believing in the Communist Party (six million among nearly two hundred million), or direct government statements, or the collectivisation of agriculture, or Stakhanovism in industry – that is quite a different story. Nothing in the world will ever convince a Russian peasant that he is better off under collectivisation than with his own uneconomical small holding. The general attitude toward the Communist Party is illustrated with fine simplicity by the spontaneous and perfectly matter-of-fact answer of a Georgian villager who was asked whether there were many Communists in his village. 'Good heavens, no,' he replied, 'we are all poor down here.'

The attitude toward direct government statements (which are invariably discounted as propaganda) is illustrated by the way in which for some time after the Battle of Stalingrad I myself found it impossible to convince ordinary Russians in Moscow that they had won a great victory. They looked at me pityingly: they had heard that one before. But they discounted the official communiqué, with no particular resentment, as a piece of inevitable government bally-hoo. They discounted it with no more resentment, for example, than an Englishman feels when, with prices rising on every side, he is told by the official spokesman that the cost of living has not gone up, or than an American feels when he is told by his official spokesman, of whatever party – well, any of the things which official spokesman are paid to say in flat contradiction of observable fact.

Probably, indeed, the Russian feels less resentment than the Englishman or the American. Because although these, like the

Russian, know very well that it is one of the duties of official spokesmen to tell lies, unlike the Russian, they have a tradition of turning the government out when it has told the same lies for too long.

So what you find in Russia is not only much the same reaction to propaganda as you will find anywhere else, but also a more thoroughgoing scepticism toward recognisable propaganda of all kinds, good and bad. This scepticism is born of the fact that for too long the propagandists have been trying to make the Russians think and feel and do things which they have no desire to think and feel and do. In a word, it is not so much the power of propaganda which is terrible; propaganda often defeats its own ends. It is the spirit behind the propaganda which is terrible.

For government propaganda is always with us. It may vary in any decently governed country from deliberate over-simplification to what one might call temporary lies of expediency. But there is all the difference in the world between the statesman who lies or oversimplifies only when he is driven to it by the clamouring pressure of events, and the Soviet leader who lies as a fixed principle of government.

There is one further point to be borne in mind in thinking about the Kremlin's propaganda and that is that some ideas which we think false do not seem false to the Russians. It is not, for example, propaganda which reconciles him to single-party elections so much as the deep immemorial instinct which suggests to all Russians that since there must be a central government it would be the height of foolishness to allow a licensed opposition to sabotage its efforts. The propaganda at election time in Russia, which is strong, is designed to stress the points at which the people may feel a sense of community with the government.

Again, we should not be deluded into thinking that it is only ignorance which prevents the Russians from rising up against the Kremlin and demanding chromium-plated bathrooms. It is an illusion that the Russians in their poverty would be dazzled as one man by a glimpse of the material wonders of the West. Many, very many, after a moment's reflection would say rather smugly: 'Yes, no doubt you have the best plumbing arrangements in the world; but life consists of more than bathrooms.'

28

And they would go back to their outside sanitation with a strong sense of moral rectitude. Bathrooms, too, are products of propaganda; and so, I suspect, is the general vague idea that the majority of American homes possess one.

As for the very young in Soviet Russia, I think there is little doubt that most of these at first swallow pretty well everything they are told by their school teachers, by their radio, by their newspapers, by Stalin. But there comes a time when the realities of life in the Soviet Union are seen unmistakably to conflict with what they have been told; and then there is a swing over toward scepticism of that uninstructed and unselective kind which, in the West, afflicts the adolescent reacting from his parents' teachings. In the West many people (but by no means all) recover from this reaction, because the school of parental teaching is replaced by the school of personal experience; whereas in Russia the teaching of the state continues throughout life, perpetually stimulating the sceptical reaction.

The reaction in the Soviet Union manifests itself in any of several ways. Either (and this is the commonest way) the individual becomes apathetic and disillusioned and capable of no initiative; or he becomes cynical and corrupt, actively devoting himself to getting what he can and to the acquisition and use of *blatt* (the most significant word in contemporary Russia, which occurs in no dictionary, and means in practice the cultivation of special influence with the largest possible selection of officials); or he begins seriously to question the foundations of Soviet rule. The members of the last category, which is larger than most people believe and growing rather than diminishing, finish up sooner or later in a labour camp. That is a victory not for propaganda but for superior force.

This kind of questioning is occurring increasingly among the children of the new middle class, which is going to be the real danger to Stalin's regime. The middle class was called into being, and must continue to grow, because the whole movement toward a modern industrialised state depends on it. Among its children, boys and girls who have learned nothing at all beyond what they have learned at Stalin's knee, there is a great deal of questioning.

But these children, freed from the urgent necessity of slaving to help the family keep alive, have time and energy to question.

29

And their example is spreading. The current outcry against the shortcomings of the Komsomol, the Young Communist League, is an indication of that; many of the best youngsters are not joining; others join simply for the sake of social standing.

As long ago as 1947 I myself was extremely impressed to find children who, when I had last seen them (four years earlier in the middle of the war), were living for the day when they could join the Komsomol, suddenly rejecting it. Two gifted young sisters of fifteen and seventeen were very interesting on the subject. Their parents were not Communists, but for the sake of the future, they had encouraged their children to go with the tide, which they gladly and intolerantly did. But as the time to join the Komsomol approached, something happened. One refused, while the other was preparing to refuse.

They were modest about it, and deeply concerned and perplexed. 'Obviously,' one of them said, 'Comrade Stalin is a great leader, to whom we owe everything. But we feel that the Party has drifted away from him. We see it doing things which Comrade Stalin, if he knew, could not possibly approve of. We see it doing things which seem to us in direct contradiction of everything he stands for. We do not understand this. But we feel quite certain of one thing. And that is that it would be wrong for us to join an organisation which we cannot believe in, even if it should be our fault that we can't believe in it.'

That, I believe, is a by no means uncommon attitude among the best adolescents in the Soviet Union today; and it is the beginning of thought in the teeth of every attempt to kill thought. It indicates the limitation of propaganda as such. A further example of these limitations is found in the number of obedient Communists in certain lands, who, after years of apparently total subservience to the Moscow line, at last break away and show by their conduct that their brains have been in no way blunted by their long acceptance of ideas imposed upon them from outside.

Indeed, why should we expect anything else? Propaganda is nothing new. It has been a necessary instrument of government, both spiritual and secular, since the beginning of time. Certainly in our time the central agency has at its disposal apparatus and means undreamed of by the witch-doctor of the Congo or the princes and prelates of medieval Europe. But this very apparatus has been called into being by the growth of the minds of the masses, which is in itself a mark of the failure of propaganda in the past.

What is really bending the people of Russia to Stalin's will is not propaganda but force. Stalin may believe that one day he will be able to condition the minds of those who survive in the Soviet Union so completely that the sanction of force is no longer necessary; but at the moment, and after more than thirty years of Bolshevik power, he is strengthening the police as never before. At the same time he is increasing his propaganda. Each action is a confession of failure in the other. Force begins, when propaganda fails; propaganda begins when force fails.

I would go so far as to say that there is only one thing that propaganda can achieve – and that is to induce a disbelief in everything. This is certainly the problem that will have to be faced in Russia one day. It is one point to bear in mind in our own efforts to tell the Russian people what is going on outside their borders. Another is that the final and victorious foe of all propaganda is the unquenchable impulse to ask questions, so that the best service we can do the Russians and ourselves is to stimulate that impulse.

Another point is that propaganda is only effective when it confirms people in what they want to believe. Thus the Kremlin's peace propaganda is much more successful than its propaganda for Communism: people want peace. Thus the nationalist propaganda in Asia is successful because it coincides with the deepest impulses of the Asian peoples.

It is the unscrupulousness of the Kremlin's propaganda which makes it hard, if not impossible, for us to counter it on its own ground. Much our best hope, I should say, would be to build up a picture of ourselves, admitting the bad, claiming credit for the good, which has a genuine ring of truth, and so not only encourage the questioning spirit but give those who have lost all belief in public utterances of all kinds a new basis for comparison. And if we are really serious we might even start practising at home.

Coexistence? By All Means, but How?
1951

The world outside the Soviet bloc has been given its battle instructions by, of all people, Syngman Rhee, President of the Republic of Korea. They are comprehensive. 'We are all,' said Mr Rhee, 'caught up in a gigantic global struggle between communism and democracy. Coexistence of these two ideologies is impossible. Either one or the other must go. This is the great and tragic historical fact that our generation must face and understand.'

This apocalyptic vision, is the logical end of a confusion of ideas (it can hardly be called a train of thought) which is rapidly gaining ground in the West. It is a confusion that leads straight to war. Its proponents do not define democracy: it would spoil the look of the argument. They talk today as though this battered planet were nothing but a grand arena for a straight fight between Communism and democracy – democracy including, presumably, Franco's Spain, the wreckage of Hitler's and Hirohito's empires, all the republics of the South American continent, Egypt, the Arab kingdoms of the Near East, the Iran of Mr Moddadegh, the Dominion of South Africa within the British Commonwealth, the supporters of Chiang Kai-shek and others.

By this definition, democracy means nothing at all but anti-Communism. This is not the definition of democracy we learned at school. On the other hand, if one excludes from the democratic brotherhood those peoples who do not believe with passion in trying to achieve some sort of approximation to the old-fashioned democratic ideal, then plainly the world is far from being divided into two opposing armies of Communists and democrats. But this whole view of inevitable conflict is stated without definition – Communism is not defined. Nor is coexistence. And it is this word, it seems to me, which is at the heart of the confusion.

Coexistence means existing together, or side by side. Thus, when Stalin grandiloquently declares, with the air of a man bestowing a priceless concession on humanity, that coexistence between Communism and what he calls capitalism is possible, he is enunciating a self-evident truth: they do, in fact, coexist. On the other hand, when people who ask for a preventive war say that coexistence is impossible, they are flying in the face of manifest reality. Plainly, therefore, to talk about the possibility of coexistence as though it were an open question is absurd. What we want to know is whether it can continue.

One thing seems to be clear from the history and that is that there has been a great deal of coexistence on this planet between incompatible ideas and hostile powers and systems. Over considerable periods of time, for example, France would have cheerfully assisted at the annihilation of England and vice versa. It might have been said that there was no room in nineteenth-century Europe for four such great and predatory powers as Austria, Prussia, Russia and France. But they did exist side by side, without wiping each other out, although they went to war among themselves. Or, to confine ourselves to what we nowadays call the ideological sphere, it might have been said that there was no room in Europe for Catholicism and Protestantism, but in spite of the Thirty Years' War and other holocausts, these two forces did exist side by side and they continue to do so.

Communism and anti-Communism (I think we ought to leave democracy out of this) we are told are different; they cannot exist side by side; one must be wiped out.

But how does one set about wiping out an idea? The instigators of religious wars have tried it down the centuries – in vain. For centuries, too, Jewry has been persecuted – in vain. One man at last decided that persecution was not enough; there could be no coexistence between Jew and Aryan. He set about his business logically and systematically and began to kill off every Jew. There is no other way of banishing Jewry from the face of the earth. And there is no way of killing Communism except by killing Communists wherever they may be found until there are no more to be found. Even then, it seems to me, the memory of Marx and Lenin (perhaps, who knows, even of Stalin?) would linger on earth, glorified and transfigured, to

33

form a rallying point for new generations of Communists revolting against the policy of extermination, who would themselves have to be wiped out.

The real trouble is, of course, that so many of us are afraid of Russia, or if you like, of Communist Russia. People transfer their fear of Russia to one of Moscow's most potent weapons, its fifth column, the Communist Parties of all lands. Their argument, if it means anything at all, means that there can be no coexistence with the Soviet Union. But even if the Stalin regime could be, like magic, wiped out, there would still be Russia – a Russia which, for the last hundred years, has been actively and often aggressively interested in the Far East, in, above all, Korea. Would the disappearance of Communism from Russia really make very much difference to Moscow's Far Eastern policy?

Stalin, when he talks of coexistence, is speaking as the ruler of a great empire who also has a stake in the world outside his empire. Sooner or later, according to Leninist theory, and after much bloodshed, the capitalist system will collapse and be replaced throughout the world by Communism. This will result not from the action of Russia as a power, but from the workings of the inner logic of history, which only a Marx and a Lenin could understand. Russia, as the headquarters of this remarkable revolution, may assist this transformation with her own might, but it would take place one day even if Russia did not exist. Stalin has inherited his view.

On the other hand, Stalin also knows that Communism will not sweep the world tomorrow. He knows further that even if Russia could conquer the British Empire, all Asia, Africa and the Americas, with the Middle East and Western Europe thrown in, the peoples of these very considerable territories would not embrace Communism of their own accord, looking to Moscow for orders. He knows as well that it is one thing for him to dominate his small neighbour states by force and intimidation and quite another to dominate by these means the rest of the inhabited world. Thus he must resign himself and his system to sharing the world with other authorities for an indefinite term of years – in a word, to coexistence.

And so he seeks to make a virtue of necessity. Stalin, with his mumbo-jumbo about peaceful coexistence, has never yet suggested that Communism and anti-Communism should settle down into non-competitive stagnation, to a freezing of the status quo. His conception of coexistence means, at worst, that Russia is not yet ready to conquer the world; at best, that she has no desire to. While preaching it, he adopts in his actions a highly aggressive, competitive policy which would do credit in its ruthlessness and unscrupulousness to a nineteenth-century oil king.

Nothing is safe from his attentions; nothing is immune from his attack; no holds are barred. By fair means and foul (the latter are usually more convenient) he persists in every conceivable course calculated to weaken the world outside the Soviet bloc and to strengthen Russia, either for the sake of Russia as a power or for the sake of Russia as the base of world revolution, or both. Seeing this, we move too easily to the conclusion that Stalin is lying when he says he believes in coexistence. But he is doing nothing of the kind. He is stating a self-evident proposition. It is we who muddle ourselves, as he intends us to, by reading into a drily technical term meanings which do not belong to it. Coexistence on this planet means existing side by side on it.

Stalin knows this. In preaching coexistence he is telling us that he knows it. In his actions he is warning us that although coexistence is necessary, he will use diplomacy, force, fraud and any weapon that comes to hand to ensure that he has things as much as possible his own way.

There is nothing fundamentally new in this situation. Great powers have striven by unscrupulous means to achieve dominating positions throughout recorded history. But although the essential situation is not new it contains new features. And these are responsible for our present confusion. Stalin, if he is still a Leninist, is convinced that coexistence must sooner or later end. For him, it is a temporary expedient – though temporary is a relative term. The weapons at his disposal – above all the Communist fifth column, backed by all the mighty apparatus of modern propaganda – are so great an improvement over the fifth columns of past centuries that they have passed the point at which a difference in degree becomes a difference in kind.

But still more important than these are three little facts: the first is that the planet has filled up, leaving less room for old-fashioned diplomacy and manoeuvre; the second is that atomic weapons and guided missiles have put a new complexion on war; the third, and the most supremely important, is that while the Government of the Soviet Union continues the old tradition of cynical and amoral behaviour in the international arena, the chief Governments opposed to it are painfully, convulsively, and in deference to the popular will, engaged in renouncing the unquestioned prerogative of all governments in the history of the world – that is to say the freedom to work with cynicism and perfect lack of scruple in what they conceive to be the interests of their country.

In other words – and this is a paradox which we have not yet grasped, but which we simply must grasp if we are to survive – the really new element in the international game is not Communism but democracy. Communism, as a cross between a religious faith and a secular drive for power, is in essentials as old as mankind. Democracy is so new that its eyes have still to open. It is we, ordinary, decent, long-suffering, ignorant, on the whole kindly and sentimental nonentities, with no experience of governing, in Britain and America and a few other lands suddenly emerging in shaky control of our official governments, who have introduced the complicating factor into international affairs. It is really time we showed some awareness of this, and of our very great responsibility.

In the past, the coexistence of antagonistic and predatory powers was assured partly by the availability of unclaimed areas of the world and by a fluid organisation of checks and counterchecks known as the balance of power. The balance of power called for changing coalitions against powers which showed signs of becoming too strong. These coalitions, as a general rule, were the products of expediency, not of moral conviction; they were made possible by the fact that government was in the hands of experienced men of the world who were not hampered by inconvenient moral scruples. By the same token, it was not found necessary to approve of the conduct of allies in general or in detail. In a word, no power was irrevocably committed and the sort of diplomatic *tour de force* brought off by Molotov and von Ribbentrop in 1939 was a commonplace.

Russia is still playing that game – aided, as we have seen, by the new weapons of the Communist fifth column and modern propaganda techniques. The game is concerned with strengthening Russia against all comers and for future aggrandisement. We, who think of ourselves as the true democracies, are trying to stop playing that game. In fact, we play it in a half-hearted way all the time, but it is only under extreme pressure that we play it openly, admitting the fact to ourselves – as in the last war, when we allied ourselves with Stalin's Russia in face of the German threat; as now, when we are allying ourselves with Franco's Spain, and anyone else we can find, and trying to resurrect German and Japanese militarism in face of the Soviet threat.

Our heart is not in the game. We play our cards unskilfully and too late. We suffer for our convictions, and then, in a panic, throw them away, having gained nothing by them. And even then we will hardly admit to ourselves what we are doing. We pretend, to quiet our consciences, that what is expedient is good. And so on. The Russians, in their reactionary crassness, always believing that we intended to ally ourselves with Germany and Japan against the Soviet Union, and then seeing us do so in fact, attribute to us unplumbed depths of duplicity, failing entirely to see that it was Moscow, and Moscow alone, that drove us back from our new idealism into these uneasy courses.

Coexistence between antagonistic powers, of systems, remains an axiom of life on this planet. As far as Russia and we are concerned (I refer above all to Great Britain and America) it can be terminated only by a war of mutual annihilation. This may occur either because the Politburo overestimates its chances of winning or because America and Britain lose patience. It can be maintained in two ways; either by a reversion on the part of Britain and America to the old, undemocratic system of secret agreements between powers based on nothing but expediency – these would include as a matter of course the kind of agreement reached about Poland at Yalta – or by a refusal of Britain and America to be stampeded into this condition, which calls for a very swift growing up on the part of democracy. We have to distinguish between what is possible and what is impossible. We have to recognise, for example, that there are two hundred million Russians and four hundred million Chinese living under Governments which a great number of them actively detest, but which, in the last resort, are national Governments. We have to be quite clear in our minds about our ultimate aims. We should wish, for example, to break Russia's power over the satellite ring in Eastern Europe.

If, as I imagine most of us believe, the deliberate unleashing of an atomic war against the Soviet Union would create more evil than the existing state of affairs in Eastern Europe, we must resign ourselves quite calmly, and without hysteria, to building up our strength to the point at which we can call the Kremlin's hand with confidence. Similarly, in building up our strength we must know exactly what it is for: to serve the peace of the world and to limit Soviet rule to the frontiers of the Soviet Union. We must be as clear as possible in our minds as to how much strength we need, and we (and here I speak especially of America) must see to it that the great efforts required are not allowed to dislocate the internal economies of the Western allies so that, through undue and unbalanced hardship, these become an easy prey for the Communist fifth column.

The easy way for America to tackle its immense responsibilities in this matter is to give orders to the other free nations, not in the Russian manner, backed by the threat of force, but in the Western manner, backed by the threat of withholding supplies. America will find this course extremely tempting when faced with what must appear to it as the unreasonableness of weaker allies. But, if it yields to this temptation, it will put itself on a level, vis à vis Western Europe and non-Communist Asia, with the Soviet Union vis à vis Eastern Europe and Communist Asia. America may be driven to do this but it will mean the end of the democratic way of life.

What I have written is, of course, an oversimplification. But it illustrates an aspect of the truth about the world today which is insufficiently realised. Stalin is committed to coexistence, if only because he knows he cannot conquer and dominate the world. He may bring about a war through some aggressive diplomatic blunder or because he is totally misinformed about the strength of the forces opposed to him. The first seems more likely than the second.

So that when we talk about the possibility of continued

coexistence, we are really asking not only whether Stalin will make war, but also whether we, in the West, have the nerve, the resolution, the stamina and the intelligence to make democracy work in face of the attacks of jealous and powerful foes who know well how to exploit its weaknesses.

It is a tall order, but I believe that we should see the threat of Communist Russia not as a dismal fate to be warded off by every means at our disposal, including the recantation of everything we have tried to stand for, but as a challenge to bring out the best in us and help us, under fire, to realise what we stand for. And the first thing this demands is a cool and unprejudiced examination of what we really mean by democracy. We have the trappings but have we yet found the spirit? We have grasped the privileges of self-rule, but have we assumed the obligations and duties?

We have, at the same time, to realise that, however we may strive, we shall never reach perfection – which does not belong to this world. We have to recapture some of the worldly wisdom of our ancestors, who knew many things that we have forgotten. To take what may seem a banal example: if sovereign governments during past centuries had refused to trade with the potential enemy for fear of strengthening his ultimate offensive, there would have been no international trade. This is not an argument for trade with Russia or China, a question which has many aspects, but it is certainly the sort of fact which has to be considered coolly when we think in terms of coexistence.

What we have to do, it seems to me, can be quite easily summed up. We have to make every effort to break down the present paralysis of the brain which allows us to confuse coexistence as such, which is attainable, with coexistence on our own terms, which is not attainable. It is the job of our statesmen to find out what terms we can impose at any given time and push them to the limit of the possible. It is the job of ordinary people to remember that from its first beginnings the world has been full of menace.

Even if there were war, and Russia were beaten, and her Government cast down, there would still be an infinity of discord, unless America were to set herself up as the absolute, unbrookable dictator of the world. Then there would be neither Communism nor democracy, only a tyranny which, however benevolent in intention, would lead to mutterings and then to violence.

Coexistence, as I have tried to show, is more than a political conception: it is a philosophical conception. It would not be too far-fetched to see in the relations of the Stalin regime with the rest of the world a universal parable. Only the Marxist can deny its eternal validity. To deny it, and to act on that denial, is to deny the very foundations of all that we believe.

Stalin has said in effect that he is resigned to coexistence for an indefinite time to come. There seems every reason to suppose that he means this, since he cannot wipe us out. The question really is, are we ourselves resigned to coexistence? And, if so, are we, in our present confusion, applying ourselves to making the best possible bargain for our own sphere, as Stalin is for his?

The Technique of Communist 'Confessions'
1952

The ritual trial, ordered by Moscow and leading to its pre-ordained conclusion of assassination by proxy, which ended last week in Prague, has brought home to the non-Communist world the essential meaning of these strange demonstrations more sharply than ever before.

The trial of the Czechoslovak Communist leaders Slansky, Clementis, and the rest, differed only in small points of detail from the notorious trials in the Soviet Union during the Thirties, when Stalin set about systematically destroying the old Bolsheviks, and in Bulgaria and Hungary since the war. But it touches us more closely than any of these. This is partly because, for the first time, this kind of atrocity has been committed in a land with a strong democratic tradition, partly because we know a great deal more about the men who are to be executed.

The Prague trial has not been obscured by the fog of total unfamiliarity. These things have been happening in a country which a few years ago had a Government not unlike our own, shared many of our own cherished ideas, whose people are tough and not servile, and whose leaders we knew well and admired. In a word, we know that everything said at this trial was nonsense. We know the characters of Clementis, Sling and Frejka from firsthand contact. We know that Slansky and Geminder, far from being Anglo-American agents, were in fact the more dire and embittered enemies of the West. And so on.

Thus, many who in the past have been inclined to give the prosecutors in such trials the benefit of the doubt have now changed their minds. The Prague trial, a replica of so many other more obscure ones, is plainly false from beginning to end. And the whole grisly vista of Stalin's advance to power is now lit up for all to see in the sultry glare of this latest abomination. We can see the past trials for what they were, straightforward, uncomplicated, unsubtle strikes of terrorism, designed at the same time to remove men whom Stalin thought might stand in his way and to induce in the rank and file that mood of baffled hopelessness, that conviction of the futility of opposition, without which he cannot rule.

If this lesson is remembered, Messrs Slansky and company will not have died in vain. It is still being asked, nevertheless, how it is that the disparate victims are brought to the point of making, with every appearance of conviction, these fantastic and ludicrous confessions whereby they abuse and degrade themselves in the eyes of their fellows and posterity. Some of the victims, like Slansky and Geminder, are men of excessive unpleasantness and ruthlessness, their hands still reeking with the blood of others. Some of them, like Clementis and Sling, not in themselves monsters, have been led by the weakness of all politicians everywhere into this deadly impasse; others, like Frejka, fanatical idealists, have walked blindly into the trap set by Stalin for all convinced revolutionaries, who, having served his purpose, must be killed before they start asking questions. Yet, in the dock they all behave identically.

It is obviously no good talking about the Russian soul in this context. None of these Czechs are Russians. Kostov, of Bulgaria, was not a Russian. Rajk, of Hungary, was not even a Slav. Cardinal Mindzenty was neither a Slav nor a Communist, but a Catholic prelate. Yet all these widely differing characters behaved in the dock like characters imagined by Dostoyevsky. And so people talk of drugs and other mysteries.

It seems to me that one of the most important things in the world for us to realise now is that in fact there is no mystery. There is no excuse at all for any doubt as to why these strong men are broken. We have plenty of evidence that it is done by sheer fatigue.

I say it is important for us to realise this because so long as we believe that it takes drugs, or hypnosis, or some devilish art to break the human mind and spirit, we are refusing to recognise one of the facts of life which has been discovered, or rediscovered, in this twentieth century, a fact on the understanding of which the effective ruler of half the world has based his power. With a minute proportion of exceptions, whose bodies will die before their spirits are broken, men and women everywhere can, we know now, be totally unmanned and turned into one quivering conditioned reflex, jumping, not reluctantly but eagerly, to the invisible whip, by sheer physical and mental exhaustion.

We have all the evidence. There have been exceptions who have survived. There's no reason to believe that if these exceptions had been persisted with they would have remained exceptions. Some would have died, still unyielding, as some already have; others would in the end have given way. We have in an extraordinary book called *Invitation to Moscow*, published last year, the detailed account of Dr Z. Stypulkowski of the preliminary to one of these trials.

He was one of the sixteen Polish leaders abducted and taken to Moscow in 1945. For eighty days and nights he was subjected to almost uninterrupted interrogations by relays of examiners, coupled with every kind of psychological trick and threat, so that at the end, deprived of proper food and sleep, physically and mentally exhausted, convinced that he was betrayed by his comrades, convinced, so circumstantial was the knowledge of his interrogators, that every fact about his life and the lives of all his friends was known, he was brought almost to the point of confessing everything required of him. By extraordinary reserve of will he managed to hold back. His colleagues had all broken down during this time and were led to the witness box to say their lessons in perfect acquiescence.

We have glimpses of the same story in other books – notably *Conspiracy of Silence* by Alex Weissberg. And from some of the many stories of life in Soviet labour camps we receive confirmation from quite another angle; the spectacle of what happens to the human spirit and mind, the spirits and minds of millions of our contemporaries, when subjected to hunger, cold, exhaustion and total privation, endlessly and without hope. They simply break.

There is no magic in this. The human spirit has limits of resistance which can be reached without torture as commonly understood. The human spirit can effectively be annihilated. Any philosophy of life which does not allow for this terrible fact is a false philosophy. The Communists know this. It is time we knew it, too.

Lenin in 1917
1955

The most remarkable thing about Lenin was his changeless conviction that he alone among all men was right. He followed a straight line, undeviatingly, from the dawn of his political consciousness to the moment of his death. Even in the moment of supreme crisis, under overwhelming pressures, he continued his straight line and yet was not broken. Behind him, into line, he swung a vast and primitive country of a hundred and fifty million souls. Those who held out against the swing were broken. It was a one-man performance unique in the history of the world. The crisis, the testing moment, when, according to all possible calculations, Lenin had to give way or be broken, began late at night on April 16, 1917. He took it at a trot, apparently quite unaware that he was doing anything out of the ordinary.

He took it at a trot quite literally. For eight days, cooped up with an assortment of exiled comrades, he had been travelling across Europe in the famous sealed train from Zürich. For anybody but Lenin those days would have been solemn with soul searching; the professional revolutionary, trained and self-disciplined and dedicated for years to the moment of action, cast off and toiling ceaselessly in the squalor of foreign exile to keep his comrades up to the mark, was going home to put his ideas into practice. The long, fantastic train journey, arranged by the German Government, which saw in this obscure fanatic one more bacillus to let loose in tottering and exhausted Russia, was an opportunity for stocktaking of the most elaborate kind. But to Lenin it was nothing more than a slow and tedious way of getting on with the job. He had been at the job for years. He had been under pressure for years. For years his task had been not to preach revolution but to keep the preachers of revolution up to the mark, so that when the day came they would know what to do. For years he had worked in

44

exile because the police would not let him work in Russia. Now that it was possible to go back to Russia there was the difficulty of crossing enemy territory. He had thought of every conceivable means and had to abandon plan after plan, until the strange, equivocal millionaire-revolutionary intriguer, Parvus/Helphand, persuaded the German Government to put him on a train.

He felt no gratitude. Since the first news of the Revolution had reached him in his dismal lodgings in Zürich he had lived for this day, which had now, miraculously, come. Another man would have been betrayed into the expression of emotion in the first relief of tension. But not Lenin. Nobody knows what he felt in his heart; he gave nothing away. He accepted the German offer as his right: they were not doing it for love of him but out of sheer self-interest – as well they might, seeing that he was going back to Russia to end the war! And, while they were about it, there were certain conditions he required them to observe, if he was going to honour them by travelling in their train. He laid down the conditions, like a conqueror; and they were accepted.

So he embarked, with thirty-five fellow revolutionaries, as the most natural thing in the world. The train journey was simply a hiatus in his work. He was fairly certain that he would be arrested the moment he set foot in Russia; and he spent some time preparing a speech in his defence, which he discussed with his comrades. About his personal emotions we know nothing. Indeed, the deeper we go into the existing accounts of Lenin's life the more glaring becomes the almost total absence of any information that throws light on his state of mind at any given time.

It is tempting to conclude that he had no emotional life; but it would not be true. Nadezhda Konstantinovna Krupskaya, his wife, the companion of his lifetime, his fellow revolutionary, tells us what little we know; and it is enough to show that he was no automaton. From time to time in her memoirs we learn that Ilych was withdrawn, moody, cast down, or in high spirits. From time to time the two of them, usually for Krupskaya's health, go off into the mountains to be alone with nature, which Ilych loved. He liked hunting in Siberia, and once let a fox, which he should have shot, go off unhurt 'because it was so beautiful'. He would listen to music, and above all he loved the

Appassionata Sonata of Beethoven. He read other things besides revolutionary philosophy and blue books. Particularly in the last days of Swiss exile, with the world at war all around him, he gave more time to the novels he loved: Krupskaya says he had 'mellowed' at this time. Nobody knew anything about this. Krupskaya tells how when she was first introduced to Lenin she was told he had never read a novel or a poem in his life. It was much later that she discovered with surprise (the surprise is characteristic) that in fact he was as well read in the classics as she herself. He read them all again in Siberia. But the world did not know. The world knew practically nothing. As a child he had respected and admired his brother Alexander, who was hanged for his part in the attempted assassination of Czar Alexander III. That respect and admiration was reciprocated, but, said Alexander, 'We do not understand each other.' His schoolmasters did not understand him either. The headmaster of his school at Simbirsk on the Volga, none other than the father of Kerensky, whom Lenin was one day to overthrow, did his best for the boy, but complained of his excessive reserve and unsociability. He had 'a distant manner even with people he knows and even with the most superior of his schoolmates.'

Later on he was to develop an extreme sociability. But it was the sociability of the great headmaster, in Edmund Wilson's phrase. There is no record of any conversation at all with Lenin that was not about the coming revolution, how to make it come, and how best to equip the Party to be fit and well and mentally trim for the fight. So he went on being reserved. Perhaps his friendship with Maxim Gorki was his only safety valve. Only with Gorki did Lenin ever allow political differences to be overridden by personal warmth. There is also one note to Kamenev, written when Lenin had to go into hiding after the 'July Days', when the Provisional Government put its ban on him. '*Entre nous*,' he wrote, 'if they bump me off I ask you to publish my little notebook *Marxism on the State* (stranded in Stockholm). Bound in a blue cover. All the quotations are collected from Marx and Engels, likewise from Kautsky against Pannekoek. There is a whole series of notes and comments. Formulate it. I think you could publish it with a week's work. I think it is important, for it is not only Plekhanov and Kautsky who have got off the track. My conditions: all this to be absolutely *entre nous.*'

And Trotsky comments: 'The revolutionary leader, persecuted as the agent of a hostile state and figuring on the possibility of attempted assassination by his enemies, concerns himself with the publication of a 'blue' notebook with quotations from Marx and Engels. That was to be his secret last will and testament. The phrase "bump me off" [*Ukokshit*] was to serve as an antidote against that pathos which he hated, for the commission was pathetic in its very essence.'

In that little note, forced out of him by an extreme emergency – for the agitation against Lenin as an alleged German agent was then formidable and dangerous – we see perfectly expressed the familiar character, while for once we are permitted a glimpse of the human feelings beneath the normally unflawed reserve.

'All the writing of Lenin is functional; it is all aimed at accomplishing an immediate purpose', said Wilson. This was true of his whole way of living. For the sake of an immediate purpose he ruthlessly cut across old friendships without the least apparent hesitation or regret, and in his public attacks on men who had been his devoted comrades the day before, employed for the first time that crudely savage invective, the 'robber-cannibal' style which has since become the dreary idiom of the Communist Party everywhere. But Krupskaya tells enough to show that he often felt regret. His recurrent joy when Martov, the Menshevik leader whom he loved, returned to the straight and narrow path of Leninism (only to stray again), is proof of this. There is more in Lenin's welcome than the delight of 'I told you so!' He knew feelings of tenderness; what he lacked was a sense of doubt. He loved people with a perfect detachment, as one loves a pet animal. There was no sharing in his love. Never, at any time, did it occur to him that he might be wrong and others right. Various contemporaries commented on the extreme sensitiveness with which he entered into others' feelings. But it is to be doubted whether he was capable of this. He was considerate to a degree when consideration was politically permissible. There was a deep fund of kindness, which he would switch off when it was politically desirable to do so, but it was kindness from outside. It was the

47

kindness of the man who does not like hurting animals but will kill them, as painlessly as possible, if they get in his way. This has nothing to do with the kindness of understanding. He was also a romantic of sorts, and naïve. His attraction to the Appassionata Sonata is a clue to this; so is the way in which he glorified his own Machiavellianism and the squalor of the poor *emigré*'s existence. He romanticised his own asceticism. Krupskaya tells how 'Ilych was delighted' because one of their Zürich landladies, in a house frequented by thieves and prostitutes, gave them their coffee in cups with broken handles. But it is clear that, whatever the almost uniquely insensitive Krupskaya may have thought, Ilych did not like cups with broken handles. These for him symbolised the renunciation of a sensitive and fastidious soul. Once, in a way, the man behind this delicately imposed façade exposed himself. When Kollantai extolled the merits of free love she said that sexual satisfaction was of no more account than drinking a cup of cold water. When this was reported to Lenin he flashed out: 'That may be. But who wants to drink out of a cup that has been used by many others?'

By the time of his recall to Russia he was disciplined absolutely to impersonality, so that it had become his real nature. Because of this I say that he hardly knew what he was doing, or that he was facing the supreme crisis of his life. The journey in the sealed train was a hiatus. His response to the challenge of the Revolution had been immediate and direct, like a reflex action. While others rushed around with loud shouts of joy Lenin sat down then and there and composed a telegram of admonition to the Petrograd Bolsheviks. While others were seeking solidarity with all revolutionary elements, Lenin yelled across Europe the slogan of absolute exclusiveness. '*Never again* along the lines of the Second International! *Never again* with Kautsky!' he wrote to Kollontai in Stockholm. And in his telegram: 'Our tactic: absolute lack of confidence; no support to the new government; suspect Kerensky especially; arming of the proletariat the sole guarantee; immediate elections to the Petrograd Duma; no *rapprochement* with other parties.' And then again, when he heard that the Provisional Government, supported by some Social Democrats, was for continuing the war, 'the imperialist war', and calling it a 'war of defence': 'Our party would disgrace itself for ever, kill itself politically, if it

48

took part in such deceit . . . . I would choose an immediate split with no matter whom in our party, rather than surrender to social patriotism.'

In Petrograd these words seemed to Lenin's foes the shrill cries of a madman; to his friends the ravings of a man who had been out of touch for too long. What did Lenin know of the Revolution? How could he possibly understand the power and glory of the tremendous upsurge, which he was now asking the Bolsheviks to cold-shoulder? When he was safely home in Petrograd he would begin to understand and see things differently. The first task was to defend the Revolution against all attacks from outside. Then they could think again.

But Lenin was to go on saying what he had been saying for years, what he had already said in those first letters and telegrams. Already, in these, and in articles for *Pravda*, he had laid down what Trotsky was to call 'a finished analysis of the Revolutionary situation'. But to those on the spot this analysis seemed irrelevant and absurd. Of the Petrograd Bolsheviks, curiously, only the young Molotov, then in his twenties and quite obscure, had grasped what Lenin was really after. When the Revolution hit Russia, Molotov was editing *Pravda* and keeping it on Leninist lines. Then Kamenev and Stalin came back from exile in Siberia and took over from him. When, in Stockholm, Lenin got hold of some copies of *Pravda* and read the editorials he was horrified; it was indeed high time to go back. And when at the Russian frontier Kamenev and Stalin were there to meet him, all ready for an affecting welcome, Lenin's first words were: 'What's this you've been writing in *Pravda*? We've just seen some numbers, and we gave you what for!' Krupskaya was so moved by her returning home that she could not speak to the crowd that gathered round. But Lenin found no difficulty in speaking – or in cutting short his speech when the train pulled out. 'Are they going to arrest us when we get to Petrograd?' he asked. The welcoming delegation smiled. That question showed, if nothing else did, how much Comrade Vladimir Ilych was out of touch. Within three months Lenin was in hiding for his life. That showed how much the comrades had been out of touch.

Then came the great arrival. At the Finland Station the revolutionaries had taken over the Czar's waiting room. There they waited with a bouquet for Lenin, and speeches. We have this scene from Sukhanov, a non-Party Menshevik sympathiser, whom Lenin would not have allowed within speaking distance of his Bolsheviks, but whom his Bolsheviks had taken up as a friend. It was to have been an affecting scene of welcome and reconciliation – and it was to put Lenin in his place, as the respected *emigré* leader out of touch with the realities of Russian life, who would have to learn to walk all over again before he could run. The head of the welcoming committee was Chkheidze, with Dan and Martov one of the leading Mensheviks, and it was to Chkheidze that Lenin came at a trot:

> Lenin walked, or rather ran, into the "Czar's Room" in a round hat, his face chilled, and a sumptuous bouquet in his arms. Hurrying into the middle of the room, he stopped short in front of Chkheidze as though he had run into a completely unexpected obstacle. And then Chkheidze, not abandoning his melancholy attitude, pronounced the following "speech of welcome", carefully preserving not only the spirit and the letter, but also the tone of a moral preceptor: "Comrade Lenin, in the name of the Petrograd Soviet and the whole revolution, we welcome you to Russia . . . *but* we consider that the chief task of the revolutionary democracy at present is to defend our revolution against every kind of attack both from within and without . . . . We hope that you will join us in striving towards this goal." Chkheidze ceased. I was dismayed by the unexpectedness of it. But Lenin, it seemed, knew how to deal with all that. He stood there looking as though what was happening did not concern him in the least, glanced from one side to the other, looked over the surrounding public, and even examined the ceiling of the "Czar's Room" while rearranging the bouquet (which harmonized rather badly with his whole figure), and, finally, having turned completely away from the delegates of the Executive Committee, he "answered" thus: "Dear Comrades, soldiers, sailors, and workers, I am happy to greet you in the name of the victorious Russian revolution, to greet you as the advance guard of the international proletarian army . . . . The hour is not far off when, at the summons of our comrade Karl Liebknecht, the people (of Germany) will turn their weapons

against their capitalist exploiters .... The Russian revolution achieved by you has opened a new epoch. Long live the world-wide socialist revolution!"

That was the beginning. To quote Trotsky:

Thus the February Revolution, garrulous and flabby and still rather stupid, greeted the man who had arrived with a resolute determination to set it straight both in thought and in will. Those first impressions, multiplying tenfold the alarm which he had brought with him, produced a feeling of protest in Lenin which it was difficult to restrain. How much more satisfactory to roll up his sleeves! Appealing from Chkheidze to the sailors and workers, from the defence of the Fatherland to the international revolution, from the Provisional Government to Liebknecht, Lenin merely gave a short rehearsal there at the station of his whole future policy.

What was that policy?
The policy came next day, after further rehearsals. That same night he made a little speech to the revolutionary guard of honour on the platform, spotlighted by searchlights, the sailors standing at attention:

Comrade sailors, I greet you without knowing yet whether or not you have been believing in all the promises of the Provisional Government. But I am convinced that when they talk to you sweetly, when they promise you a lot, they are deceiving you and the whole Russian people. The people need peace; the people need bread; the people need land. And they give you war, hunger, no bread – leave the landlords still on the land .... We must fight for the social revolution, fight to the end, till the complete victory of the proletariat. Long live the world-wide socialist revolution!

They put him in an armoured car and drove him in triumph through cheering crowds to the Kschessinska Palace, the gorgeous mansion of the *prima ballerina* who had been the Czar's mistress. Krupskaya was overcome by the tumultuous scene. 'Those who have not lived through the revolution cannot imagine its grand and solemn beauty.' Everybody was overcome, caught up in the tremendous release of primitive power, eager to see brotherhood and concord as the future state of all those who had helped pull down the Czar. Only Lenin was not overcome. With his speech to the sailors under the searchlights on the Finland Station he had called for a new revolution: a revolution against the Provisional Government. And he went on calling. He spoke from the Kschessinska Palace. To the mob he gave no rest: they were pleased with themselves for what they had done. Lenin told them it was not enough. To his fellow revolutionary leaders he brought a shock of reality and a sense of dismay.

And next day he made a formal speech to a meeting inside the Kschessinska Palace which lasted two hours.

'On the journey here with my comrades I was expecting they would take us directly from the station to Peter and Paul [the notorious czarist prison]. We are far from that, it seems. But let us not give up the hope that it will happen, that we shall not escape it.' From savage irony, directed at those who thought they could come to a compromise with the liberals and the capitalists in the Provisional Government, he went on to the downright expression of views which seemed to his audience to have no connection at all with what was really happening. They were as pleased with their Revolution as a dog with two tails. They thought they had done wonderfully well. And here was Lenin, who had watched all from the safety of Switzerland, throwing it in their teeth – not a word of congratulation or praise, just scathing contempt like a lash. And in its place? Here again, Sukhanov:

> He swept aside agrarian reforms, along with all the other policies of the Soviet. He demanded that the peasants should themselves organise and seize the land without any governmental interference. "We don't need any parliamentary republic. We don't need any bourgeois democracy. We don't need any government except the Soviet of workers', soldiers', and peasants' deputies."

The audience felt they had been hit over the head. Next day came the celebrated April Theses. In Trotsky's summary:

The republic which has issued from the February Revolution is not our republic, and the war which it is waging is not our war. The task of the Bolsheviks is to overthrow the imperialist government. But this government rests upon the support of the Social Revolutionaries and Mensheviks, who in turn are supported by the trustfulness of the masses of the people. We are in the minority. In these circumstances there can be no talk of violence on our side. We must teach the masses not to trust the compromisers and defensists. "We must patiently explain!" The success of this policy, dictated by the whole existing situation, is assured, and so beyond the boundaries of the bourgeois regime. We will break absolutely with capital, publish its secret treaties, and summon the workers of the whole world to cast loose from the *bourgeoisie* and put an end to the war. We are beginning the international revolution. Only its success will confirm our success, and guarantee a transition to the socialist regime.

Lenin was alone. The April Theses were offered in his name alone. They infuriated the Mensheviks and drove many Bolsheviks into the Menshevik camp. He did not mind. 'Do not be afraid to remain in a minority – even a minority of one', echoes Trotsky, 'like Liebknecht's one against a hundred and ten.' And he proposed a formal break with the Mensheviks. He would no longer share with them the name of Social Democrat. 'Personally, and speaking for myself alone, I propose that we change the name of our party, that we call it the Communist Party.' Not one of the members of the conference agreed to that final break with the Second International, which had betrayed itself when its members voted war credits to their own Government in 1914. 'You are afraid to go back on your old memories?' he jeered. 'Don't hang on to an old word which is rotten through and through. Have the will to build a new party . . . and all the oppressed will come to you.'

'Have the will to build a new party', this extraordinary man demanded in the moment of the Party's triumph. Six months later the deed was done, but not before Lenin himself had been driven into hiding to escape Peter and Paul.

How was it done? What was it all about?

The October Revolution was produced by the impact of two

53

distinct forces. One was immense, undisciplined, unsettled as to purpose, and a mass of contradictions; the other compact, manoeuvrable, and single-minded. One was the people of Russia in revolt who, in March, had overthrown the Czar; the other was the extreme left wing of a single revolutionary party among many; the Bolshevik wing of the Russian Social Democratic Labour Party. At the moment of crisis this party was reduced for all practical purposes to a single individual, Vladimir Ilych Lenin, born Ulyanov, who had made Bolshevism, sustained it, preserved its inviolability against bitter odds, identified it absolutely with himself, and yet, on the eve of its triumph, was on the verge of resigning from it. The Bolshevik Party in crisis was nothing but Lenin's will, and the men who were prepared to submit to it absolutely. If Lenin had resigned after his return to Russia in 1917 it would have lost its identity, swallowed up by the Mensheviks and the 'Compromisers'. Lenin would have formed another party, but too late to win for himself the government of Russia; there would have been no Soviet Union. Lenin made his unbelievable stand when he trotted into the Finland Station in his little fur hat, found himself face to face with Chkheidze, and brushed him aside, and with him the pent-up emotional force behind the whole Revolution until that date.

The Russian people had wanted revolution. It had to come. What they meant by revolution was the overthrow of an inept and suffocating tyranny and its substitution by some more liberal system. The Provisional Government, if it had immediately sued for peace with Germany and shown more activity about the redistribution of land, could have held, leading Russia into some kind of democratic system. But because it clung to the war as an obligation, because it knew it would depend in future on the favours of the Entente, and because it was patriotic, it could not begin to alleviate the misery of the people, greatly aggravated by the war. It was this misery which Lenin deliberately set out to exploit.

He was not, he never pretended to be, an original thinker. From the moment of his discovery of Marx at Kazan University his way was clear. Russia had to have revolution. In this he was at one with the whole of the Russian intelligentsia. The only proper way to bring about revolution was the Marxist way.

Revolution in Russia would have to be made by the urban proletariat and the rural proletariat of the poorest peasants, led by professional revolutionaries who understood what was going on. All this was a common ground of all the Marxist parties. And, indeed, it is no use looking for the secret of Leninism in any particular line of theory. His whole contribution was to practice. Marx for him was a blueprint, a guide to action. The fundamental point was the dictatorship of the proletariat. The enemy was liberal reformism, which would betray the pass. The proletariat had to be educated and raised up politically to the level of a handful of professional revolutionaries, who could not possibly alone produce a revolution. Anything that in any way debilitated the strength of the professional hard core was anathema. And what debilitated was not wrong theory but mistaken strategy and tactics. The word for mistake was compromise.

Thus the criticism which dwells on Lenin's theoretical inconsistencies misses the point. He *was* inconsistent. He appealed to Marx as the fundamentalist appeals to the Bible. He had a single burning idea: to bring the Marxist revolution to the world and to Russia. His approach to this problem was the approach not of a revolutionary theorist like Trotsky, like the Mensheviks, like most of his Bolshevik colleagues (held together by Lenin's personality alone), but of the self-made, practical statesman. His political sense found the proper tactics and strategy. His knowledge of Marx then found the text to support his action. His will and personality carried him through. His quarrels with his closest colleagues of the Social Democratic Party were invariably quarrels about tactics and strategy, not about theory: how best to further the Marxist revolution, the dictatorship of the proletariat, in the shortest possible time. He found the way. But others, like Trotsky, like Martov even, were the more correct Marxists. It was Lenin's personality and tactical skill alone which enabled him, in the name of Marx, to make skilled Marxists follow him against the teachings of Marx.

He did this, in the end, by the means he outlined in the April Theses. In the suffering and confusion of revolutionary Russia he held aloof from those who were trying to make the Revolution work. He harassed them and embarrassed them with absolute ruthlessness. He appealed to the people, the workers, the soldiers, the peasants, for whom generations of the revolutionary intelligentsia had sacrificed themselves, over the heads of the men who had at last helped the people, the workers, the soldiers and the peasants to carry out the Revolution. He appealed to their most selfish instincts: the desire for bread, for land, for peace. And, in the end, he got them on his side sufficiently to overthrow the Petrograd Government. For this he substituted the dictatorship of Lenin's will. He was a man selfless and without ambition. He was *absolutely* lacking in imagination. He loved the people as animals, not as people. He pitied them, but he did not respect them. He was, in the last degree, a sentimentalist. He wanted to save the people from the dreadful tyranny of the Czars – but in his way and no other.

His way held the seeds of another tyranny. He did not see this. If he had been able to see this he would not have had the superhuman single-mindedness which carried him through all the isolation of the years in the wilderness, denouncing like a minor prophet all those, however beloved, who saw differently from him, on to the Finland Station, at a trot, to declare war, and sustain it to victory, against a Revolution which promised to give the people of Russia all that they had ever asked. His sustaining faith, his scientific base, as he would have called it, was that the world revolution, which alone could sustain the Russian Revolution, was at hand. He was wrong.

Relics of the Past
1958

Nearly fifty miles from Moscow, on a little hill, there stands the town of Zagorsk. It used to be called Sergievo, after the Monastery of St Sergius, the Troitsko-Sergievskaya *Lavra*, which was one of the most holy places of Russia – as it still is to this day for those who believe in that sort of holiness. Many do believe, predominantly the old; and Zagorsk remains a place of pilgrimage. The town is nothing except a few broad cobbled streets as wide as Trafalgar Square and a great open place in front of the fortress-monastery as wide as a desert. There used to be a famous toy-making industry there, and a handicraft museum; but all that has gone, and only the monastery remains. It is a fairy-tale monastery, a dolls-house fortress, bright with primary colours and enchanted buildings frozen into fantasticated shapes. But the walls of the toy watchtowers are thick and twice withstood the assault of the Polish invaders, who took Moscow three centuries ago. Inside the walls behind the great gates is the Holy Russia of exactly forty years ago – or four hundred years ago – untouched. For many years it was a museum piece. The monastery bells were silent, and in the Metropolitan's apartments and the vestry-room, the *riznitsa*, was displayed one of the most astonishing collections of ecclesiastical art ever to be seen. This is still there. But now the church is back again, and the monastery houses the Theological Seminary where young men in considerable numbers are trained for the priesthood.

The most spectacular building, embowered in trees, is the Cathedral of the Assumption, crowned with onion domes painted since the war in the sharpest of royal blues, scattered with golden stars. The paint is a little faded now, but when it was fresh the domes with their fretted gilt crosses made a composition of heavenly splendour. These, with the Rastrelli belfry, a sturdily elegant column over three hundred feet high, dominate the town; but they are not the holiest places. As always in Russia the holy shrines are insignificant. They are the chapel of St Sergius, with the image of the saint, and the holy-water grotto built into the wall of the Cathedral of the Assumption. It is to these, and to the small, cramped Cathedral* of the Trinity, with its superb icons, that the pilgrims come.

On a feast day the whole fabulous apparatus is going full blast. The quiet air in the monastery courtyard, beneath shady trees, is rent and riven by the sound of bells: not the remote, mathematical meditations of the English countryside, not the calm contemplative melodiousness of Italy, not the elaborate, sliding intricacies which float across the polders of the Low Countries – not anything at all that we in the West understand by church bells; rather a barbaric frenzy, with maddeningly repetitive counterpoint. Wandering into the middle of this one fine September Sunday, with the lime trees and the birches gleaming gold, I found myself in equatorial Africa. These bells were drums, endlessly beating out the terrifying simplicities of an unknown superstition. You can hear them exactly, any time you like, in a gramophone recording of the coronation scene of Moussorgsky's *Boris Godunov*. Boris was not crowned at Zagorsk. He was crowned in the Moscow Kremlin. But he lies buried at Zagorsk, and over his monolithic tombstone which stands in the open beneath the trees outside the cathedral walls there stream out incessantly the very sounds which have immortalised his sombre tragedy. Moussorgsky's tremendous, solemnly spaced chords, violent to the point of brutality, reproduce exactly the brazen assault of the great tenor bell; his violins, with the endlessly overlapping circles of shrill reiteration, are the jangle of toy bells – a flock of frightened starlings crossing and interminably recrossing the great sound waves of a Chinese gong.

There is no frenzy about the bell-ringers. When the morning service is over a greasy-looking priest comes out on to the terrace of the baroque refectory and makes a highly secular sign to his bearded mate (there is no other word for him) high in

* The Russian conception of a cathedral is different from ours. Inside the walls of the Moscow Kremlin, for example, there are several cathedrals, which are, in effect, self-contained oratories, or chapels.

the Rastrelli tower, who turns to the bell-ringers to tell them to knock off – which they do, in mid-peal, so that the silence in its suddenness itself has a quality of violence. But the business of praising God goes on. In the St Sergius chapel, under the holy icons, there is a sweating press of men and women, mainly women, mainly old, queuing to kiss the toe of the saint. In a dark corner by the image of the saint a youngish priest of extreme greasiness gabbles away at the holy office, paying no attention to the old women who seize the hem of his habit and kiss it. Little groups of women will suddenly, two or three at a time, set up a new chant, which, swelling, floats above the dark and noisome scene like a visitation from another world, such is the purity of line achieved by their quavering voices. God is in that pit, in the stink, the sweet music, the groaning genuflections; and, outside, people waiting their turn cross themselves incessantly, flinging their arms wide in the broad Russian manner, and bowing almost to the ground.

Not far off is the holy spring, and here the crush is even greater, as old women with china vases, cracked tumblers, chipped enamelled mugs and green-glass beer bottles clutched in their hands, push and struggle to reach the holy spring in its grotto, and then fight their way out tremulously folding the mugs and bottles in their shawls to shield the precious fluid, as they mingle with the tourists in the monastery courtyard. For Zagorsk is a three-star tourist attraction, as well as a place of holy pilgrimage. On that Sunday in September there were five charming Komsomolkas, young girls of seventeen belonging to the League of Communist Youth, wearing the discreet little badges of Moscow University. They had come out, dressed neatly in their Sunday best, hatless, unobtrusive; and I shall never forget the expression on their faces as they stood watching the pandemonium of religious frenzy, or black superstition, in St Sergius's chapel. Clean-limbed, slender, fair hair gleaming, carefully brushed back from the high, arched foreheads, they gazed in stupefaction at something they had never before imagined, or could now believe to be possible. They did not sneer or giggle, they simply gazed wide-eyed. And I am sure that when they went back to Moscow on the crowded electric train each and everyone of them was full of a solemn sense of rededication to the cause – to the heart-breaking task of making

59

the Soviet Union a model to the world and of rooting out 'survivals of the past'.

The other tourists were not bothering. They had come to see the churches and the treasures and to picnic in the open air on what was to be the last fine Sunday of the year. They spread themselves on the benches and the low stone walls in cheerful family parties and addressed themselves to bread and sausage and fizzy drinks in garish colours. They were entertained by everything they saw and heard: the bells; the monks, standing and conversing among themselves, aloof in the Orthodox manner from the people seeking God; the peasant women with their rags and bundles; the pilgrims; the pigeons. And to complete the picture, in the middle of this scene of bourgeois relaxation, stood the traditional Russian Idiot: a young man with a beard and a bundle, fine features and long hair, stretching out his arms to all the sights, crossing himself, turning to babble and beam at anyone who came near him, still touching by his presence the hearts of the new products of the Soviet age: the Holy Fool.

Zagorsk has television now. Every rooftop sprouts a crop of masts, one almost to each room. And into the old-fashioned houses of this empty country town come, every night, living images of the outside world, of the might and glory of the Soviet Union, its mechanical skills, its vigour and zest, its highly developed arts. But the mad bells still ring out over the tomb of the tragic Czar. And the Holy Fool, beaming and babbling, still draws the suburban stalwarts of the Five Year Plans to the deep magic of the goodness of total silliness.

Zagorsk, if you like, is a show-place: such a show-place that the Government has caused what used to be a terrible, pot-holed, rutted country road to be remade into one of the finest roads in Russia so that foreign delegations may be conveyed there swiftly and in comfort – not, as a rule, on Feast days. But it is far from being alone. I remember one day stumbling on a small church in an outer suburb, where there were no made-up roads and the ruts were two feet deep. For all I knew the church was closed, or used as a granary, or a village club-room. But the doors were open and I went up the long flight of steps under their canopy to see what was inside. Coming from the sunlight into the dark interior I could see nothing for a moment. I could only hear a wild wailing, like a wake. And, indeed, it was a wake. There, on a bier, rested a coffin, and round the coffin were a number of men and women, kneeling or prostrate, groaning and wailing, and banging their heads on the stone floor. I tried to slip away silently, but I had been seen. Three women with candles made a rush at me, and I wondered how to apologise. But I was not required to apologise. In that cavernous doorway they fell on me with rapture, catching hold of my coat, stroking my sleeves, all but embracing me and falling on their knees. One was old, but the other two were in early middle age, and one of these seemed to be in charge: 'Glory to God! A stranger has come!' she exclaimed. 'To the stranger, welcome!' the others responded. And by now the kneeling peasants had got up from their knees, except for one very old woman who remained prostrate; and all crowded round exclaiming in chorus: 'Welcome to the stranger', the women crossing themselves and bowing, the men bowing almost to the ground. I said I was sorry to have interrupted them at such a grievous time. 'It is our honour and glory by the mercy of the Holy Mother to receive you,' said the woman with the candle. 'Now, you must stay. Now, you must see . . . . Sir, here lies our beloved Ivan Serafimovitch, lately dead –' And, turning to the others: 'Make way for the stranger who has come to look on Ivan Serafimovitch!' The mourners made a lane, without a murmur, and bowed again. There, at the end of the lane, stood the coffin, swathed in scarlet bunting, and in the coffin, open to the air, lay a little waxen old man, his head and shoulders outlined by elaborately pleated white paper, like an Elizabethan ruff, or a pie frill. I contemplated the dead man and crossed myself, but without the broad Russian abandon. The mourners held their breath and did the same. Then suddenly the old, old woman leapt up from the floor and seized my hand and kissed it. 'The wife of Ivan Serafimovitch,' said the woman with the candle. 'Babushka beloved, the stranger has come to bless Ivan Serafimovitch with his kiss.'

'Ai, Ai,' moaned the mourners, in an orgy of crossing. 'Glory be to God and infinite the mercy of the Holy Mother.'

There was nothing for it. I kissed the dead man on the forehead. The old widow embraced me and I kissed her too. And then I found myself walking back into the sunlight through the lane, which had reformed and showered me with cries of awe, wonder and delight. Ten minutes later I was on the trolley-bus, heading for the city centre.

I suppose this sort of thing would be taken by some as an example of the deathless power of Christianity, by others as a proof that the Soviet Government lives up to its professions of religious freedom. It seems to me neither. Anybody who cares to call these things evidence of the Christian faith is welcome to do so; but it is the last thing that would occur to me. As for religious freedom in the Soviet Union, while making a great show of this to the outside world, the Government conducts at home a campaign of militant atheism, combined with frantic propaganda to raise the moral tone of Soviet society. The first seems to me deplorable; the second, in the context of Zagorsk, has my sympathy. Few things strike me as more odd than the concern shown by cultured and delicate-minded Christians in the West for the survival of the dark superstitions of the Russian faithful and the sleek, cynical opportunism of the Russian Orthodox priesthood. I am one of the few articulate members of my own generation never to have been a Communist, or, as far as I can make out, anything like one; but just as I felt much closer to the five young Komsomolkas – priggish no doubt, charming certainly – looking down their pretty noses at the old women of Zagorsk than to the high priests of that establishment, so I find myself closer to those Soviet Communists who are trying to make the Soviet Union work than to the leader-writers of the West who have come to equate Christianity, in spite of its origins, with what they like to call Western Values and thus exalt the mumbo-jumbo at Zagorsk, and elsewhere, to the role of a shining liberal, or spiritual, bulwark against the forces of darkness which deal in better drains.

Russia's Imperial Design
1957

The concept of imperialism is now so debased that it is almost impossible to discuss it with detachment. This is a pity; imperialism is a useful word, and no other can take its place. It should also be an evolving word, not a term of abuse.

It was designed to express a fact of life: the domination, in the international sphere, of the weak by the strong. This is an enduring fact, and it is much better acknowledged than denied. In the days of the Roman Empire, imperialism stood for the ordering of barbarian tribes by a strong, centralised, highly developed state, for the imposition of the rule of law and the bringing of material progress to dark and backward areas. In the heyday of the British Empire it meant much the same thing. Never in the history of the world has an empire-building course been started and sustained for reasons of altruism; the original motive has always been self-interest.

Self-interest may be diluted, or even transformed, by other motives. But few intelligent Americans, I imagine, would deny that the driving force behind the foreign aid programmes of successive United States administrations, which constitute the most advanced and complex form of imperialism the world has ever seen, was, and remains, self-interest (the response to the threat of Russia), although altruistic motives work to modify and transform the naked self-interest.

Since the days of the Roman Empire, the imperialist dynamic has manifested itself in three broad categories, which overlap: the strategic, the economic, and the missionary. The first is concerned with military security, and sometimes with military glory, the second with mercantile expansion; the third with the salvation of souls and the imposition of what is regarded as a better way of life on what are believed to be inferior cultures. The combinations and variations are infinite and constantly changing. Further, at any given moment in its history, an individual power will exhibit great variations in its own imperialism. The differences of approach on the part of the British to the many parts of their own empire have been wide and sharp. Again, American imperialism shows different faces in different places; the America of the Marshall Plan is identical with the America exploiting, through great business corporations, the backward areas of Latin America. The ways in which dominion can be achieved are also varied and overlapping: through straightforward military occupation, to money lending, to the rule of priests. These categories may also be divided; economic domination, for example, can range from helping foreign peoples to help themselves, so that they may grow into sturdy allies, to subsidising foreign potentates to keep them on their thrones in face of popular revolt.

To understand Russian imperialism we have to try very hard to put ourselves in the position of the Russians and look at the world through their eyes. The process which brought American dominion to the Pacific coast and beyond was little different from the process which brought Russian dominion to Baku and Vladivostok. Both these processes were similar to the process which took the British to the ends of the earth – the only vital difference being that England, as an island, had to expand across the oceans. Americans were themselves aware of this not so very long ago far more clearly than they are today; it is worth noting that in the nineteenth century, right up to the early days of the twentieth century, American expansionism was taken for granted as a strong and beneficent natural force, and that distinguished Americans regarded Russia as their natural rival.

The first beginnings of what became the Monroe Doctrine may be traced to a speech of Secretary of State John Quincy Adams in 1823: 'There can, perhaps, be no better time for saying, frankly and explicitly, to the Russian Government that the future peace of the world, and the interest of Russia herself, cannot be promoted by Russian settlements on any part of the American continent.'

Russia, on her side, was disturbed by the American westward drift. In 1860 the Russian ambassador reported: 'They have taken California, Oregon, and sooner or later they will get Alaska. It is inevitable. It cannot be prevented, and it would be better to yield with good grace and cede the territory.' In 1866 this was done, and we have a glimpse into the state of a large section of American opinion through a leading article in the *New York Herald*. Referring to Russia and America as 'the young giants' of a new world, the writer said: 'The young giants are engaged in the same work – that of expansion and progression . . . the colossi having neither territorial nor maritime jealousies to excite the one against the other. The interests of both demand that they should go hand in hand in their march to empire.'

But, of course, they did not. Soon there was a new conflict, this time in China. 'Eastern Asia', wrote Brooks Adams in 1899, 'now appears, without much doubt, to be the only district likely soon to be able to absorb any great manufactures . . . . Whether we like it or not, we are forced to compete for the seat of international exchanges, or, in other words, for the seat of empire.'

I have no idea to what extent the heady delights, and the apprehensions, of this early American expansionism are remembered in the United States today. But I know very well that they are remembered in Moscow. 'Russia and America may remain good friends until, each having made the circuit of half the globe in opposite directions, they shall meet and greet each other in the regions where civilisation first began . . .' (that is, China). These words, written by Secretary of State Seward in 1861, are better remembered in Moscow than the following, from William Woodville Rockhill (1911): 'I cannot too emphatically reiterate my conclusion that the sympathetic cooperation of Russia is of supreme importance . . . . she can never withdraw from participation in Far Eastern affairs or maintain an attitude of indifference toward them.'

When did Russian imperialism begin? It is hard to draw rational lines between the consolidation of a number of principalities into a centralised state, the expansion of the newborn state into contiguous territory for reasons of military security, and the planned or accidental extension of that enlarged and strengthened state to include subject peoples as various as the Eskimos of Yakutia, the nomads of Kazakhastan, the mountaineers of Georgia. But for all practical purposes we are concerned here not with the birth of nations, but with the deliberate attempt to carve empires out of a finite world and to secure markets and bases at the expense of other would-be empire builders. Russia did not embark seriously upon this last course until the nineteenth century. Then, however, she brought to her activities the ingrained habits of a thousand years.

The Czarist Empire was a classic example of the strategic empire. The young Muscovite state had to expand or die. Westward expansion was difficult, in face of highly organised Christian peoples (Lithuanians, Poles, Swedes, Germans). The only objective worth a serious struggle against heavy opposition was an outlet into the Baltic, for which Czar after Czar accordingly strove. Expansion eastward, on the other hand, was easy once the power of the Tartar horde had finally been broken by Ivan IV in 1583. And so Russia entered upon her long course of almost unconscious expansion along the line of least resistance – first east, then south. There was nothing to tell her where to stop – nothing until the Pacific coast was reached. And, indeed, it was not safe for her to stop until she had filled up, however thinly, the immense space of Eurasia which, sooner or later, would all too easily and willingly have been filled by others. By the time the Pacific was reached, the habit of expansion was so ingrained that it was the most natural thing in the world to cross the Bering Straits into the no man's land of Alaska.

In a century when the modern empire builders were getting into their stride and beginning to carve up Africa, seize bases in the Pacific, and compete for trade in southeast Asia and Latin America, Russia followed her traditional line: when in doubt, move forward; when you are stopped, try to flow round; when opposition is violent and strong, draw in your horns. The British were in India; the Turkish Empire, with its centuries-old dominion over the Middle East and the lower Danube basin, was breaking up. Poland had been partitioned for the third time between a newly self-conscious Russia, an octopus-like Austria, and the comparatively new state of Prussia with its inordinate ambitions.

In the drive to the east (the Pacific) and the south (the Black Sea) Russia had largely depended on the private initiative of Muscovy traders and Cossack adventurers – just as Britain had once depended on her exploring merchant adventurers and

66

pirate-admirals. But now there were tougher nuts to crack. Having secured her natural eastern frontier and a warm-water port in the south, Odessa (which could still be effectively blockaded by any power controlling Constantinople), Russia sold Alaska to America and concentrated on a southerly and southwesterly drive, having for its object an approach to India and a secure outlet through the Straits into the Mediterranean. At the same time, she had her eye on China and Japan – but more as potential threats to her own sparsely inhabited hinterland than anything else. In the same letter of 1860 in which he advised St Petersburg to give up Alaska gracefully to the United States, the Russian ambassador to Washington also wrote: 'Russia, too, has a manifest destiny on the Amur, and further South, even in Korea.'

Until now the driving power had been almost exclusively strategic. Even the need for an outlet into the Baltic and a warm-water port on the Black Sea had been more strategic than economic, that is to say, the Russian Czars needed secure and regular communications with such allies as they might acquire in the outer world for the free import of the sinews of war. Even the preoccupation with Constantinople was at first entirely strategic. It is possible to discuss without end Russia's real intentions in the matter of the Eastern Question. Did she think of the Straits as a sally port for her own warships, embarked on further conquests? Or were they, rather, seen as a danger point, narrows which could be blocked by enemies to strangle her Odessa trade or to bring invading armies (as in fact happened in the Crimean War) to the vulnerable Black Sea coast?

And what about India, a profound interest in which accounted for Russia's conquest, brutal and highly organised (no longer an affair of merchant adventurers), of Turkestan? The mad Czar Paul at one time concocted a crackbrained plot to invade India in conjunction with the French, a plot which involved a monstrous portage from the Black Sea to the Caspian. Subsequent Czars kept the British in a constant state of alarm for the safety of Afghanistan, the northwest frontier, and Punjab. But it is very much to be questioned whether any Russian Czar ever seriously contemplated a formal conquest of India – just as it is to be questioned whether Stalin ever seriously contemplated the conquest of Western Europe.

67

Rather, their own pathological obsession with security (a state of mind readily explained by the vast frontier to be defended and the vulnerability of a hinterland lacking natural lines of defence), together with their inborn and developing technique of the war of nerves (pre-dating Communism by centuries and perhaps springing from their own experiences of Tartar methods), aimed at weakening the concentration, resolution, and unity of real or potential enemies, came before any clear-cut imperial ambitions.

For centuries, Russia was separated from the main current of Western culture by her life and death struggle with the invading Tartars and by the great schism in the Church. While Europe was glorying in the Renaissance, Russia – in Russian eyes – was sacrificing herself as the shield for Europe. The Russians sought consolidation in their isolation by making a virtue of their enforced backwardness. 'You may have all sorts of things that we have not got' was the cry ringing down the ages, 'but what about your soul? We have preserved our soul. We have suffered and starved and been jeered at. But we have kept our integrity, while you have sold yours – for what? One day Russia will arise to save the world you have betrayed. And then you will see!'

After the fall of Constantinople, Muscovy began to regard herself as the third Rome. The Russians might be materially backward, but spiritually they were a chosen race, and one day they would emerge from their forest gloom and astound the world by their example.

For a long time this brooding impulse was turned inward. But with the defeat of Napoleon and the entry of Russia into the arena as a major power, it began to be turned outward. At the Congress of Vienna, Alexander saw himself as the leading spirit of a guild of Christian monarchs, whose God-given task it was to organise Europe and quell the blind, devouring force of revolution. Russian thinkers began to elaborate the concept of a Russia, backward for so long but with her vital forces husbanded, bringing to a corrupt and bankrupt world a pristine spiritual impulse.

Thus Russia's historical aspirations toward Constantinople were reinforced by a vision of Russian expansion into the Balkans and rationalised by the proclaimed intention of the

Czar to extend his protection to the Christians on the Danube basin and elsewhere still living under Moslem rule. The drive into southeastern Europe was now in full swing. Its original impulse, strategic and economic, was transformed by a powerful mixture of pure messianic zeal and a new imperial spirit of pan-Russianism to match the jingoism of the times. It was in this spirit, too, that the Russians set about the ruthless subjugation of the Caucasian and Transcaucasian peoples and the lands of what is known now as Soviet Central Asia – populated by numerous peoples who no more resembled the Great Russians of Muscovy than the Hindus and Zulus resembled the British. Here, then, alien peoples were subdued by bloody and sustained assault by organised imperial forces and afterwards run, on colonial lines, from St Petersburg.

When war broke out in 1914, the Russian Empire, a solid landmass, extended from Vladivostok to Warsaw, from Petsamo and Murmansk to the frontiers of India and Persia, from the Baltic to the Amur River. But when, three years later, the Bolsheviks made their Putsch against the new Provisional Government set up after the March Revolution, Lenin denounced the whole concept of Empire and was for the moment ready to concede the independence of all its component parts. But only for the moment. The exigencies of civil war and Western and Japanese intervention made it necessary to carry the Bolshevik Revolution to the uttermost possible limits. Soon the supranational Bolsheviks found themselves fighting to retain the conquests of the detested Czars; and there could be no thought of autonomy until the Whites had been driven out and the Reds were in control.

It should be remembered that in the early years of the Revolution Lenin still had the idea of a genuine federation of equal peoples, not an empire, in which Bolshevik Russia would be linked amicably, fraternally, and equally with a Bolshevik Ukraine, a Bolshevik Georgia, and above all a Bolshevik Germany. For during the critical years he was expecting – more, he was blindly counting on – successful revolutions elsewhere in Europe, especially in Germany, without which, he was convinced, Bolshevism could never survive in Russia. In the end, the collapse of the revolutionary spirit in Europe and the consequent 'capitalist encirclement' of the Soviet Union (the old Russian Empire shorn for the time being of its Baltic and Polish possessions) drove the Russians under Stalin to turn inward once again and to glory in their apartness.

'Socialism in one Country' for Stalin meant building up the Soviet Union in isolation, using what Western help could be obtained without strings, and forcing Russia through her industrial revolution at a breathless and calamitous pace. For a period of eighteen years, from the introduction of Lenin's New Economic Policy in 1921 to the Russo-German non-aggression pact of 1939, the Russians had their hands fully occupied with domestic matters, and, save for an abortive attempt to help the Chinese revolution, removed themselves from the arena of active imperialism – though they were quick to use force and subdue dissident peoples in Turkestan, the Caucasus, and the Ukraine, the remaining assets of the old Czarist imperialism.

In the outside world, apart from China, the only evidence of an aggressive foreign policy was the inconsequent mischief-making of the Comintern, a reversion to the old Czarist habit of trying to sow alarm and despondency with nonexistent threats. Foreign Communists were, to Stalin, as the Christians under Turkish rule had been to the later Czars. Their cause was coldly betrayed, their claims and pretensions ignored, their leaders summoned to Moscow and arrested, just as it suited their master in the Kremlin, who now, like any Czar, had become the leader and slave driver of a reborn Russian state, the Soviet Union. We shall never know what the mature Stalin thought about Communism in the secret corridors of his mind: all we know is that publicly he used it, with perfect cynicism, as an instrument of power – as the Czars had used Christianity; as the early traders had used beads, bright cloth, and firewater.

Then in 1939, there came a change. The gathering weight of the Soviet Union made itself felt in the outside world. And, with war in the offing, Stalin embarked on a deliberate course of strictly limited expansion which had plainly nothing to do with world revolution, but which was concerned with the securing of definite strategic advantages.

It is not the purpose of this essay to debate the cleverness or the clumsiness of Stalin's policies. All we are concerned with here is what he actually did, and why. And what he actually did, after hesitating a good deal, was to seek an accommodation with Hitler which would postpone a German attack and at the same time secure for the Soviet Union some of the territories lost from the old Czarist Empire, with an immediate eye to making things harder for Germany when war finally came. It was to this end that in 1939 Stalin invaded and occupied a part of Poland and launched his Finnish War. It was to this end that in 1940 he infiltrated and then liquidated Estonia, Lithuania, and Latvia (all parts of the old Empire). What was happening here, disguised by a smoke screen of Communist terminology, was a resurrection of the old Russian strategic imperialism of Ivan the Terrible and Peter the Great. It had, as I have said, a strictly limited aim: defence against a predatory Germany, pushing east.

Nobody who has read the story of the negotiations which culminated in the attack on Finland and continued throughout the course of the Winter War can doubt the fundamentally non-ideological motivation of Stalin's actions. Poland was a pushover: Germany had done the hard work and would have occupied the whole of Poland but for the Soviet stipulation. The three Baltic states were in a hopeless position. But Finland, as always, was a tougher nut to crack, and the Russians knew it.

Stalin did not want the whole of Finland. He was not interested at that time in Bolshevising the Finns. He simply wanted certain frontier changes which would give him a cushion in front of Leningrad; and he wanted to be able to close the Gulf of Finland to enemy warships by cross fire from the coasts of Finland and Estonia. He would have liked to obtain all this without war. And there is every reason to suppose that had Finland been able to agree to an exchange of territory in Karelia and the lease of Hanko on the southwest coast there would have been no war and no further attempt by Stalin to reduce the country. Finland, of course, could not meet these demands and, with wonderful heroism, took on mighty Russia singlehanded.

But the Finnish War showed two things. First that Stalin's territorial ambitions in 1939 were not unlimited, but had a strictly utilitarian purpose. Second, that once Stalin had set his mind to such a limited aim, nothing would deter him from achieving it – neither the contempt of world public opinion nor considerations of humanity. These two points were important;

they showed the world what to expect now that the Soviet Union was beginning to feel her oats as a major power.

These points are still important, as we enter the period which everybody thinks he knows about: the period of Stalinist expansion which culminated in the Berlin blockade and the Korean War. I suppose it is generally taken for granted in the West that during all this period, and even earlier, Stalin was pursuing with fanatical concentration of purpose a single aim: world domination. I question whether he ever held this aim in view.

To argue this matter in detail would require an article by itself. I content myself with simply questioning the general assumption, made as a rule from ignorance of Russian history and based as a rule on meaningless analogies with Hitler. That is why I have tried to show how the Czars got their Empire, the spirit behind their expansionism. And I am content to suggest that what happened in Stalinist Russia from 1939, with the conclusion of the non-aggression pact with Germany, until the death of Stalin in 1953 is much better seen as a continuation of the old Russian imperialist dynamic, complicated and reinforced by a distorted Marxism, than as a calculated bid for world dominion or world revolution.

It is generally believed that throughout the war Stalin was plotting to occupy Europe after the war. Anybody who was in Moscow during the two years after the Nazi invasion knows that this is total nonsense. From June 1941, until, at the earliest, the Stalingrad victory in February 1943, Stalin was wholly preoccupied in saving the Soviet Union and his own regime. Even much later, when final victory was in sight, Stalin was far more interested in keeping the anti-Nazi coalition alive than in Communist infiltration and revolution. In China he built up Chiang Kai-shek at the expense of Mao Tse-tung, in Yugoslavia he repeatedly snubbed Tito, telling him that the Great Alliance was a matter of life and death and that he was not going to let it be imperilled by Tito's revolutionary zeal.

Stalin also showed himself ready to negotiate with the West about dividing Eastern Europe into old-fashioned spheres of influence, a departure welcomed by Churchill but frustrated by Roosevelt, who was opposed to imperialism in general (except when restricted to islands in the Pacific) and to British imperialism in particular. Even after the war, Stalin was against helping the Greek Communists, so ardently supported by Tito, and poured cold water on the aspirations of Mao Tse-tung – in both cases for reasons of state.

I am not in the least suggesting that during the last decade of Stalin's life Soviet imperialism was not a menace to the world as a whole. Clearly, it was very much a menace. But it was a strictly limited menace, and we in the West played into Stalin's hands by confusing his old-fashioned strategic and economic imperialism, coloured now, as I have said, by a distorted Marxism, with an apocalyptic drive to universal revolution. It should have been clear by 1948, when Tito was outlawed, that Stalin was interested in revolution only in so far as it could be used as an instrument of Russian power. It should have been clear in 1949 that he was seriously concerned over the establishment of a Communist regime in China. But even today too many people go about wondering half fearfully whether Mao Tse-tung may one day 'do a Tito' – oblivious of the fact that by his very act of seizing power in China he made himself a Tito. He achieved, that is to say, a Communist revolution in China on his own initiative and with his own arms in the teeth of Stalin's disapproval. The only kind of 'revolution' Stalin trusted was one he had 'made himself' with his own agents working under his own detailed and strict direction.

It is time we considered the new complication – what I have called a distorted Marxism – and its effect on the traditional Russian imperialistic drive. Stalin was an adept at using, or abusing, a doctrinaire theory of history as a smoke screen to cover his imperial designs. By this means he gained control of Poland, Czechoslovakia, East Germany, Rumania, Bulgaria, Hungary, half of Austria, Albania, and for a short time Yugoslavia. He was also able to stir up trouble in southeast Asia and elsewhere. But in the end he overreached himself, unifying and re-arming a disarmed and disunited West.

It was no doubt the Marxist tincture that caused him to overreach himself. No matter how much or how little Communist ideas appealed to Stalin, his mind was certainly conditioned by the Marxist-Leninist conception of history. He believed, at least until the last year of his life, that wars between the so-called capitalist powers and the so-called Communist powers were inevitable. He believed that in the end the so-called

73

Communist powers would have things all their own way, being strengthened by every war and its consequent confusion; and he believed that all wars produced in their train revolutionary situations which must be exploited in the interest of the Soviet Union. All that happened after 1945, with Europe in chaos and Asia in revolt, must have confirmed him in these beliefs, with the results we all know.

After him came Malenkov, Khrushchev, and the rest. Malenkov, for a time, behaved like the leader of a great power, almost desperately on the defensive. But with the rise of Khrushchev we began to hear more about the spirit of Leninism, which Khrushchev invoked over the head of his dead master. Stalin was denounced for a variety of sins, but never for imperialism, which would have been in the eyes of Lenin the greatest of all his betrayals. Thus Khrushchev's Leninism has a strong smell of opportunism about it; and my own belief is that for him and his colleagues, Lenin and Leninism serve primarily as a source of authority outside themselves, an authority very necessary at home and otherwise completely lacking.

It seems to me likely that Khrushchev's mind is conditioned pretty thoroughly by what he believes to be Marxism. After all, he was brought up in revolutionary Russia, in the days when the immediate task within the Bolshevik framework was so great that it gave no active man any time to think: born leaders and organisers are not often given to philosophical speculation. It is easy for the present-day youth of Russia to start asking awkward questions; unlike the present Soviet leaders, they have never had to fight a desperate battle against odds and time in Lenin's or Stalin's shadow. I think it likely that Khrushchev takes Leninist theory for granted much as British statesmen of fifty years ago took the parliamentary system for granted, much as American statesmen of today take the American way of life for granted – that is to say, as the best possible way of doing things.

But even Khrushchev at the Twentieth Party Congress in February, 1956, was at pains to amend the Leninist theses of the inevitability of major wars and the inevitability of revolution through violence – a revision made, though he did not say so, in the light of a new fact of life: the H-bomb. It was a revision, moreover, of the very first importance, though its importance has not been widely recognised in the West. Stalin, while seeking to avoid major conflict for reasons of self-interest, believed war was inevitable and that through it Communism, or Russia, would always grow in strength. Khrushchev no longer holds this simple faith. The capitalist countries, he has declared – and this declaration has been written into an official amendment of Leninist theory or dogma – may now achieve socialism without war and by peaceful means.

But Khrushchev knows as well as Stalin knew what happens when countries achieve Communism without the help and guidance of the Soviet Union. To encourage a multiplicity of Yugoslavias is no help to Soviet imperialism. And Poland and Hungary have lately shown what happens to an overgrown and unhomogeneous empire when the pressure of police rule is relaxed – and it has to be relaxed, sooner or later, if the peoples concerned are to be good for anything at all.

Once again, therefore, Russian imperialism is at a dead end. It is not too much to say, I think, that it is now on the retreat. The Russians may believe that by using every device and trick to disrupt the Western powers internally and to incite coloured or backward races against Western domination, a universal chaos will ensue from which they alone will profit. Certainly they are behaving as though they believed this. But their inner councils now must be muddled. For, again on the long-term view, they know they have on their own doorstep a most serious threat to meet from China. There is also Japan.

The Russian leadership are aware of these problems. And, once more, after the post-war advance into Europe, a very small area, they are concerned above all with consolidation at home. I have tried in this essay to treat Soviet imperialism as a natural and understandable phenomenon, which it is. I have tried, all too sketchily, to show that it is not an immediate threat to the outside world; long-range disruption, designed to weaken and destroy hostile coalitions, is the real menace now. And in this connection I should like to conclude with an appeal to the United States, which holds the present power balance vis à vis the Soviet Union. I should like to remind all Americans that even if Moscow retreated to the frontiers of the Soviet Union tomorrow, Russia would still be the greatest imperial power in the world. At a time when other imperial powers are deliberately, and largely for reasons of decency, surrendering their empires, Russia, quite apart from her dominion over Eastern Europe, which may not last, shows no sign at all of surrendering her dominion over her own colonial peoples.

The fact that in exploiting these peoples she has brought them education and machines is neither here nor there: Britain did the same before her. The Caucasus, Transcaucasia, Turkmenistan, Uzbekistan, Kazakhstan, and the rest are no more part of Russia than India was of Britain. The Soviet Union is an empire, not a country. And the fact should be remembered. Roosevelt forgot it and did the Western coalition in particular and the world in general great harm by this lapse. The time may come sooner than we expect when the Soviet Union, presenting herself as a satisfied and 'progressive' land, will make approaches to the United States, as one anti-imperial power to another. What will America answer?

The nineteenth-century dream of the two young giants, Russia and America, coming together in amity to divide and order the world, was shared by Russians as well as Americans. There will always be Russians, under whatever regime, who will believe in the mighty destiny of their country to save the world from itself and sweep away the stale effeteness of Western European culture. There will always be Americans impatient of the endless profitless bickerings of the smaller powers and the tiny nations and eager to help the world to perfect itself in America's image. It is not inconceivable that the nineteenth-century dream might be reborn. Life would be so much simpler if America and Russia could make a firm front against China and run the rest of the world between them. There will always be Americans whose reaction to the inadequacies of smaller powers and tiny countries is to turn their backs on the whole pack of them and let them stew in their own juice. Both arrangements would suit Russia quite well, so long as she remains an unregenerate imperialist. 'Russia's Imperial Design' – I wonder if she has one? But if I were a Russian statesman, imbued with an invincible belief in the peculiar merits of my own tradition, watching other empires crumble; taking no stock in new-fangled ideas about self-determination; filled with a bottomless contempt for the poor dupes calling themselves Communists who act as my agents all over the world; perturbed most deeply by the dreadful apparition of an industrialised China, with its huge population pressing against my vulnerable and sparsely inhabited eastern lands – if I were a Russian statesman, I should see in America the key to the future. America must either retreat into isolation, disgusted with the world, and leave free and open a large field of operations for the Soviet Union, or else, sooner or later, America must be persuaded to join with the government of Russia in a major feat of global organisation. Since Russia cannot hope to conquer America, there is no other way. I wonder how many Americans think of themselves as the potential allies, one way or another, of Russian imperialism? I wonder what they will do to avoid this situation?

The Past Is
Still Too Close
1959

In January of this year, revisiting Leningrad and Moscow, I found myself feeling very much an Outsider.

In Leningrad at the Astoria Hotel there was a band playing better jazz than I had ever heard in Russia: the performers wore bow ties and fawn-coloured tuxedos, and the dancers on the floor were charming, unassuming, rather shy couples, well turned out in their best suits and dresses, very much on their best behaviour, and cloudlessly happy. The music, unlike the music of most Soviet dance-bands, was pleasant and easy to dance to.

And while I was watching this rather touching scene I found myself thinking that in this place only sixteen years earlier more than five hundred thousand human beings had died of starvation during the siege, and before that thousands, and tens of thousands, and hundreds of thousands, had been taken up by the GPU and the NKVD and sent away to die in the labour camps – all so that their children in pretty dresses should dance to the music of the decadent West.

In Moscow the feeling clung. Standing on the steps of the Bolshoi, on the lookout for old friends, I saw instead their ghosts. So many had gone for ever. And here were the survivors, and the young, flocking, and chirruping eagerly as they waited on tiptoe to see Plisetskaya in *The Fountain of Bakschiserai* and Struchkova in *Romeo and Juliet* – to all appearances unaware of those ghosts.

I wondered whether it was any good thinking about the past. Life, very clearly, was going on. Life was better, life was wonderful. The Soviet Union was on top of the world. Its citizens had the Sputniks and enough to eat, with pretty dresses and the Astoria band thrown in.

Was it reasonable to remember the millions of dead? Did one, when one went to the Free Trade Hall for a Hallé concert, have

78

to remember the dark satanic mills and the children pulling coal trucks on their hands and knees?

Was it not perhaps, in the full flood of the Khrushchev era, time to call it a day and forget? You cannot drive down the Mozhaisk highway out of Moscow without rolling over a thousand corpses. But wouldn't it be as true to say this of a journey through South Wales? And so on.

The answer, it seems to me, is that we can decently forget the immediate past of the Soviet Union as soon as the Russians themselves have remembered it and put it on record. The excesses of the English Industrial Revolution, of British imperialism, have been – still are – remembered and put on record. The excesses of Stalinism are not. Until they are, there is no one to remember them but us. In recent months I have written a good deal about the hopefulness of the Russian present. Today I feel inclined to dwell for a moment on the wickedness of the Soviet past, which, until it is publicly exorcised by the Russians themselves, remains part of the present.

Last week Moscow Radio celebrated the fortieth anniversary of the Amritsar Massacre. Moscow Radio is constantly calling for peace and concord and international understanding; but it nevertheless is running an 'anti-colonial' campaign of remarkable virulence, a virulence that reminds one of the late Dr Goebbels, designed to set Asia and Africa alight against us, and to fan the existing flames.

Amritsar was an opportunity to be made much of, and made much of it was. It was presented as characteristic of British rule in India, and not a word was said to indicate that General Dyer, who gave the order to shoot, was censured, that the affair caused a public outcry. Not a word was said – or ever is said by Moscow – to suggest that British imperialism, for better or for worse, is not what it was.

Two days later, on April 15, there was published in London a volume by Professor Merle Fainsod which summarises and analyses the huge mass of material captured by the Germans from the police and Party offices in Smolensk, and later taken from the Germans by us. This material, some two hundred thousand sheets of original documents, is known as the

Smolensk Archive: and for some time past it has been clear from various items already released that the Smolensk Archive provides an invaluable and unique insight into the workings of the Soviet regime from 1917 to 1938.

It is often exclaimed that if only we could read the secret archives of the Soviet Administration, then we should *know*. Well, now we do know. Smolensk was a region, like a hundred other regions, and the secret papers of the Party and the police are now in front of us. Reading Professor Fainsod's analysis, I felt once more an Outsider.

Khrushchev, with his denunciation of Stalin, is not enough. When Khrushchev attacked his late master, he listed a number of crimes, but they were not the crimes against the people; they were the crimes against the Party. Here we have the crimes of the Party and the police against the people, documented with immense elaboration, and with the tears of the people themselves.

Why do officials keep these things? Files and files of letters from harassed, bewildered, terrified, starving peasants during the collectivisation – letters intercepted by the police and once used to ruin their authors, carefully kept, cries from beyond the grave, to serve now as terrible indictments of the men who kept them. Files and files of charges levelled during the great purges of the middle Thirties – each accusation against the individual a deadly accusation against Stalin and the men who helped him. Secret directives regulating the number of arrests to be made. Files and files showing in detail the organisation of terror and repression.

It is too much to hope that many people will read this volume, which, sober and objective to a degree, bears out and documents all we have ever heard from refugees and ex-prisoners. Is it too much to hope that people, who in the past have dismissed the reports of isolated victims as being unreliable, should read, humbly, the reports and secret instructions of their oppressors? I expect it is.

Does it matter? I think it does. The Amritsar Massacre, which took place on April 13, 1919, caused a great outcry in the imperial capital and shook an empire. The Soviet Amritsars, going on month in month out, year in year out, for decades, aroused no public protest, either by Mr Khrushchev or by anybody else. There was no one to speak of these dead. There was no one to try to make amends.

Things are better now. But still no voice in the Soviet Union can be heard to say that the collectivisation, the mass arrests, the deportations and killings were appalling crimes, past now, but never to be forgotten, and this means in effect that for all the remarkable changes since Stalin, the Khrushchev Government is still condoning those crimes.

The Case of
Olga Ivinskaya
1961

According to Mr Alexei Surkov, lately Secretary of the Union of
Soviet Writers, Madame Olga Ivinskaya, the dearest friend of
Boris Pasternak, the model for Larissa Guishar, the heroine of
Dr Zhivago, is not only an 'ordinary adventuress' but also a
whore.

This remarkable allegation is made in a long letter to Mr
David Carver, General Secretary of the International PEN.
Madame Ivinskaya cannot reply to it because she is in prison
serving an eight-year sentence for alleged currency offences and
alleged embezzlement.

Pasternak's friends were not surprised when she was sent to
prison towards the end of last year, together with her nineteen-
year-old daughter, who was given three years. Pasternak had
told them to expect it. He feared for her even while he was alive,
believing that the Soviet authorities might not dare to touch
him but would strike at him through her. In fact nothing
happened until soon after his death, last July.

When at the end of last year the news of her arrest came
through (it has never yet been mentioned in the Soviet Press)
nothing was said about it in the West for some time for fear of
prejudicing her chances while representations were being made
in private. But in due course the story came out and then Mr
David Carver, on behalf of the English PEN and the Society of
Authors, embarked on an unsatisfactory exchange of telegrams
with Mr Surkov in Moscow, first requesting him to plead for
clemency, then to supply a transcript of the trial.

Mr Surkov tried to brush the matter aside. But PEN refused
to be brushed aside; and the letter now made public was a
belated reply, dated April 3 of this year, to Mr Carver's third
request, on January 30, either for a transcript of the trial or for
copies of the reports of it in the Moscow Press. He asked for
these because Mr Surkov had insisted that it was a perfectly

ordinary trial open to anybody; but of course there were no reports in the Press because nobody knew that it was taking place (if, indeed, it ever took place); the transcript has never been produced.

Mr Surkov's letter, which has now been made public only because there have been public references to it elsewhere, makes no attempt to answer Mr Carver's questions. Instead it sets out to vilify Madame Ivinskaya by offering allegations which are frequently irrelevant and always unsupported:

'Who is Ivinskaya?' Mr Surkov asks, and then answers himself (his English is his own, or his secretary's):

Ivinskaya is a forty-eight-year-old woman, who, since 1946, was known as the private secretary of Pasternak and the last mistress of this elderly man who lived until his very last day with his family. In literary circles, Ivinskaya was known as an unscrupulous adventuress who advertised her intimacy with Pasternak. Despite her advanced age she did not stop to have many parallel and frequent relations with other men.

When I was editor of the *Ogonyok* weekly, a group of staff workers was involved in a financial fraud. An investigation showed that Ivinskaya (that was the first time I heard the name) had repeatedly received fees for articles written by somebody else thanks to the fact that she was on intimate terms with Mr Osipov, my deputy editor, who in this way compensated her for intimate relations with him. Konstantin Simonov told me that he had had to discharge Ivinskaya from her job on the staff of *Novy Mir* magazine because she was surprised in an office with a man doing far from official things. It is very unpleasant to write all this about a woman, but those who take her under their protection must know what sort of a person Ivinskaya is.

The interesting thing is that there was no need for Mr Surkov to burden himself with this unpleasant task. PEN had made no inquiry about Madame Ivinskaya's private life. It had asked for information about her alleged criminal trial. About this, although he declared that he had read every document in the three-volume file of her case, Mr Surkov provided no information additional to what had already been publicly stated.

The gist of this was that Madame Ivinskaya had repeatedly received sums of roubles, royalties due to Pasternak from the foreign sales of *Dr Zhivago*, which had been brought into the USSR by illegal means under the aegis of an intermediary, Signor D'Angelo: that she had converted this money to her own use, and that the whole transaction had been kept a secret from Pasternak and his family.

Proof of embezzlement, Mr Surkov said, was that 'in the first place, the lion's share of the money was received by her *after Pasternak's death*. Secondly, Pasternak's wife and his close friends have assured me that Pasternak could not have taken this money because, till the last day of his life, he lived on his legitimate Soviet earnings.' These, Mr Surkov assures us, amounted to at least 496,000 roubles in the last two and a half years of his life.

PEN was not interested in Mr Surkov's assertions. All it was interested in was clemency for Madame Ivinskaya and the true story of the trial. Mr Carver said so once more in a letter dated April 26:

> Whatever may have been the character or behaviour of Madame Ivinskaya, during the years preceding Pasternak's death, there seems to be little doubt that she was for upwards of fourteen years the most important single person in the poet's life, and, in any case, alleged or even proven immoralities on the part of an accused person, should not have any bearing on the court's judgment.
>
> Your letter makes no mention of Madame Ivinskaya's daughter, whose sentence has, perhaps, shocked people in the west almost more profoundly.
>
> I would like to express the hope that nothing you say in your letter should be taken to affect the promise you gave while in England that Madame Ivinskaya would be released within a period of months.

The promise referred to had been made verbally to a close and influential English friend of Pasternak's during the visit of Mr Surkov to England in March of this year. He was then accompanied by Mr Adjubei, editor of *Izvestia* and son-in-law of Mr Khrushchev, who had brought with him what he called documentary proof of Madame Ivinskaya's guilt. I myself met both of these quite exceptionally unpleasant creatures.

The proof consisted of an assortment of articles that might have been throw-outs from an MI5 dossier. The only item of any interest whatsoever was a photostat copy of a short blanket 'confession' signed by Madame Ivinskaya. There was nothing to indicate that this differed in any essential way from other 'confessions' obtained by the Soviet police.

It was when Messrs Adjubei and Surkov discovered, to their surprise, that it was not taken very seriously that Mr Surkov began to spread his stories about Madame Ivinskaya's sexual morals.

There were other points in Mr Surkov's letter. For example, he said that the authorities were ready to organise a legal transfer of moneys due to him, and Pasternak's rejection of this showed that he did not want to touch the money. He said that Ivinskaya had deceived Signor Feltrinelli, the Italian publisher who first gave *Dr Zhivago* to the world, by making 'false assertions' that Pasternak's archives were in her possession.

He expresses surprise that the 'fastidious advocates of morality and justice have completely overlooked the fact that this clamour and fuss about the unscrupulous mistress whom they have elevated to the rank of the prototype of Lara, humiliates the memory of Pasternak and deeply insults his wife and children, in whose arms he died, having forbidden during his last illness to let Ivinskaya to his bedside.' He said that in Signor Feltrinelli's letter to Madame Ivinskaya, written after Pasternak's death, there was an 'elaborate business instruction of how to handle the legacy [sic], how to ship it over, and, in case Pasternak hadn't signed it, how to fake his letter of attorney . . . .'

Direct contradiction of Mr Surkov's charges may be found in Pasternak's letters to his friends abroad, some of which I have seen. Madame Ivinskaya did not 'advertise' her intimacy with Pasternak. It was he who 'advertised' it, especially after her first arrest in 1948 for political reasons. Pasternak in his letters told how she acted, as best she could, as a shield for him during the various campaigns against him. She used to deal with the authorities on his behalf, trying to 'exorcise the demons'. He also wrote to her daily until he died.

As for Pasternak's refusal to co-operate with the authorities in the legal transfer of moneys due to him, he himself explained in his letters that he feared that such action might be used against him later on. In his last years he frequently complained of being in dire financial straits, contradicting directly Mr Surkov's statement that he was well off; and he said he was driven to adopt Signor D'Angelo's plan as the only safe way of getting the money he so badly needed.

It is at this point that we must take up another thread. In the *Sunday Telegraph* of May 6, 1961 Signor D'Angelo had already revealed that these transfers were made with the knowledge of the Soviet security organs, who tolerated them until they decided to use them, Pasternak being dead, to do away with Madame Ivinskaya and her daughter. At a later date Signor D'Angelo was shown a copy of Mr Surkov's letter of April 3 (by whom, it is not known, and to Mr Carver's surprise) which, besides vilifying the 'inborn adventuress', Madame Ivinskaya, slandered him.

In Mr Surkov's own inimitable words: 'The whole batch of letters written by Feltrinelli, and his agent, the international swindler D'Angelo, exposes them, and together with them Ivinskaya, as dirty cynics, profiteers and evil spirits in the life of the outstanding and subjectively profoundly honest poet, Boris Pasternak.'

Signor D'Angelo has now himself written an open letter to Mr Surkov; and it was this which made it necessary for Mr Carver to make the Surkov letter public. He denies categorically that Madame Ivinskaya acted without Pasternak's knowledge, and his denial is supported by Pasternak's own letters, referred to above:

> ... this is utterly false, as was demonstrated last May when I caused to be published ... some letters written in Pasternak's own hand in which the writer, whom you persecuted during his life and pretend to admire after his death, said that he was in a precarious economic state and asked that a part of the income from *Dr Zhivago* should be sent to him directly, that is, in the only way he considered possible.
>
> It follows clearly from these letters ... that the whole responsibility of Ivinskaya (who neither planned nor carried

out any form of smuggling) is reduced to having received sums of money already converted into roubles, for the sole purpose of handing them over intact (as the documents prove) into Pasternak's hands. The disinterested and generous nature of Ivinskaya's actions is not lessened by the fact that she was sent a final sum of money on July 31, 1960, by which time the writer was already dead. The initiative in this was taken by me without my being requested because . . . I preferred to respect Pasternak's explicit wishes rather than appropriate money which did not belong to me.

Signor D'Angelo then goes on to remind Mr Surkov of his leading role in the persecution of Pasternak, which is already familiar to readers of the *Observer*. Mr Surkov indeed led the pack, using the language of the gutter; so that it is strange to hear him now speaking of the man he hounded to death as an 'outstanding and subjectively profoundly honest man'.

He denies categorically that he or Signor Feltrinelli ever suggested that the transactions be concealed 'from Pasternak's family (both in Moscow and in Britain), from Pasternak himself and from his French representative, Mme de Proyart'. He ends by defying Mr Surkov to prove the contrary publicly and again asks for the records of the trial.

All these denials are confirmed by Pasternak himself in his own letters.

Finally Signor D'Angelo points out that the article of the criminal code under which Madame Ivinskaya and her daughter were charged lays down a maximum penalty of ten years, 'but concerns only the case of a professional smuggler who personally carries across the frontier "explosives, drugs, poisons, arms and munitions" '.

What is it all about? Why, in Khrushchev's Russia, does the chief spokesman of the Soviet literary world, himself known as a poet, find it necessary not only to support a brazen injustice but also to confuse the issue by making irrelevant and totally unsubstantiated allegations in a manner reminiscent of the late Mr Vyshinsky, about the sexual morals of the chief victim?

The answer is all too clear. The Russians wish to rehabilitate Pasternak and to claim him as their own now that he is safely dead. But they are embarrassed by the existence of his great novel. The discrediting of the inspiration of that novel is a necessary part of the rehabilitation process: it can then be written off as an aberration of a great man under the influence of an evil woman.

Mr Surkov spoke of having 'closed the futile correspondence about the Ivinskaya affair'. But, to quote Signor D'Angelo again: 'The conscience of all civilised and honest people will not permit it to be "closed" until justice has been done.'

What Khrushchev Meant
1964

Nikita S. Khrushchev is this week celebrating his seventieth birthday in the middle of a vast political crisis affecting the whole future of the Communist world. To imagine what the split with China means to Russia we should have to think of the effect on the United States of the break-up of NATO and of a violent political assault on Washington not only by Western Europe but India, too.

It may well be that Khrushchev will go down in history as the man who presided over the liquidation of the Communist empire and almost of Communism itself. That, no doubt, is how Peking sees him. Others, especially Russians, may remember him most as the man who brought political and economic reform at home and in the East European satellites; who revealed and ended the brutalities of Stalinism; who proclaimed the beginning of the 'Communist construction'; who presided over the launching of the first men into space. Yet others, outside Russia, will never forget or forgive him for Hungary, the execution of Imre Nagy or his assault on Dag Hammarskjöld.

But all these successes or failures shrink into insignificance beside Khrushchev's main role as a world statesman, a role unprecedented in history: his responsibility for dealing with a quite new and deadly situation in which the future of the human race, in the crudest terms of physical survival, has lain in his hands.

The last ten years, in which he has been at or near the apex of power, have also been the first ten years in which the world has lived under the shadow of total disaster from nuclear war. It is a disaster which he – and the President of the US – could personally precipitate, if they chose, by either error or design. How far has he grasped the significance of his situation? What has he done to discharge his greatest historical duty of ensuring that the human race survives and that this survival will no longer be left to chance?

Khrushchev's most celebrated contribution to the theory and practice of war and peace has been the revival of the idea of 'peaceful coexistence between States with different political and social systems' – first attributed to Lenin – and the establishment of the doctrine, as a revision of Lenin, that war is not inevitable and is not a necessary step on the road to Communism. Khrushchev's position can be summed up: Communism is inevitable, but war is not.

However, ruling out nuclear war does not, he believes, necessarily mean stopping 'just wars' of 'national liberation'. Nor does peaceful economic competition between socialist and capitalist countries mean that there should be political and ideological coexistence between them.

What does all this really amount to? Westerners asking themselves this question are sometimes told they attach too much importance to foreign policy in judging Russian affairs. We do, indeed, need constantly to remind ourselves that Khrushchev is engaged not only in dealing with the West but also in governing a huge country of two hundred and twenty million people. It is also true that foreign policy often appears to be a reflection of changes inside Russia. A relaxation of world tension and disarmament may, for example, be sought not so much for themselves as because they are needed if more home resources are to be diverted from defence production to modernising the economy and raising living standards.

Consequently Western diplomacy has been much obsessed with the 'sincerity' of Khrushchev's motives and the nature of his personality. Does he really want peace and friendly relations or is 'peaceful coexistence' merely a tactic imposed by domestic needs and the dangers of Western nuclear strength? Is he trying to lull the West into lowering its guard and splitting its alliances, while he continues the struggle for Communist world domination by every means short of large-scale war? Is he an opportunist with a gambler's temperament or a statesman who takes a steady constructive view of world affairs?

There have been many East-West crises during the last ten years – in Europe, the Middle East, the Far East, even in the

Americas. How Khrushchev has handled his side of these crises can be interpreted to prove any of the above theses.

But for more conclusive evidence of the real priority Khrushchev has given to questions of war and peace, nothing is more important than to look at his struggle with China. For whatever else the quarrel with Peking may be about – and there are many reasons of conflicting state interests, personal rivalries and differing concepts of Communist bloc leadership – its constant theme is the nature of war and peace. One may question the validity of Khrushchev's theories of peaceful coexistence and the extent to which he is able to or willing to put them into practice. But the fact remains that he has preferred to break with his greatest ally rather than give them up.

Harold Macmillan once described Khrushchev approvingly as 'the first Soviet statesman to recognise that Karl Marx was a pre-atomic man'. The phrase was apt, but not strictly accurate. The first Russian statesman to declare publicly that atomic war would ruin the socialist camp as well as the capitalist camp was not Khrushchev but Malenkov. This was in 1953, the year that Stalin died, the year in which Russia exploded the first hydrogen bomb. Malenkov did not spell out the implications of this statement for Leninist dogma. Khrushchev took it personally upon himself to contradict Malenkov, then Prime Minister, and insist that only the capitalist world would be ruined – a position he has since abandoned.

This was the beginning of the great debate which has gradually convulsed the Communist world and which is also of profound importance for the West. The debate has centred on three points:

1. Has the destructive scale of nuclear weapons so changed the nature of war that it would mean ruin for both sides? Or would nuclear war merely mean the end of the capitalist system, making it possible for the survivors to build a new world on Communist lines?

2. Is war, as Lenin argued, an inevitable result of the conflicts within imperialism and the imperialist need to try to crush the Communist world? Is the chaos born of war a necessary step towards Communist revolution?

3. How far should Communist countries risk giving military support to revolutionary insurrections and wars of 'national

liberation' in other countries? Is it possible to reconcile peaceful coexistence with the 'imperialist' powers and support for national liberation movements?

Khrushchev's performance as a world statesman has been closely linked with the zigzag course of this still unsettled debate – some of it, especially the third point, still unsettled not only between Moscow and Peking but even, it seems, within the mind of Khrushchev himself.

But in judging the reality of the debate a number of other factors have to be borne in mind. There is the constant tension between Russia's two roles since the Revolution, as a Great Power with her own national interests and as the leader of the world Communist movement.

There is the constantly changing relationship of Communist doctrine and Communist practice. It can, for example, be shown that, while on each of the three major points in dispute China has taken a more extreme stand, she has in practice been just as cautious as Russia.

In Korea, which began as a mistaken adventure by Stalin, China did not react militarily until the Americans crossed the Yalu river. In Indo-China, she agreed to the 1954 compromise settlement which the US would not sign. In Laos, she did not intervene directly, although it is right on her frontier, but accepted the neutralisation agreement. She has left British Hong Kong and Portuguese Macao alone – as Khrushchev tauntingly pointed out when answering Chinese criticisms of his retreat from Cuba. She signed the five principles of coexistence with India in 1954 and took a leading part in the Bandung Conference the following year, before Khrushchev had really woken up to the importance and the possibilities of co-operation with the non-Communist Afro-Asian states.

Finally, there is the use made of doctrinal authority in the rivalry between the Communist leaders themselves. Throughout the development of his coexistence policies, Khrushchev has had to show not only that they produce profitable results for Russia but also that he is holier than Mao and a truer interpreter of the Lenin scriptures than Molotov and other critics.

On the first point of the debate it was not long before Khrushchev faced the obvious facts of nuclear war as Malenkov had done. More recently, in a speech in Berlin in January last year, he gave his most forceful answer to Mao Tse-tung's claim that a nuclear war might still mean victory for Communism.

Foreign scientists and military experts estimate that the US now has roughly forty thousand hydrogen bombs and warheads. Everyone knows that the Soviet Union, too, has more than enough of this stuff.

What would happen if all these nuclear weapons were brought down on people? Scientists estimate that the first blow alone would take a toll of seven hundred to eight hundred million human lives. All the big cities would be wiped out or destroyed – not only in the two leading nuclear countries, the U.S. and the U.S.S.R., but also in France, Britain, Germany, Italy, China, Japan and many other countries of the world. The effects of a nuclear war would continue to tell throughout the lifetime of many generations causing disease and death and the worst deformities in the development of people.

I am not saying these things to frighten anyone. I am simply citing data at the disposal of science. These data cannot but be reckoned with.

There can be no doubt that a nuclear world war, if started by the imperialist maniacs, would inevitably result in the downfall of the capitalist system, a system breeding wars. But would the Socialist countries and the cause of Socialism all over the world benefit from a world nuclear disaster? Only people who deliberately shut their eyes to the facts can think so. As for Marxist-Leninists, they cannot propose to establish a Communist civilisation in the ruins of centres of world culture, on land laid waste and contaminated by nuclear fall-out. We need hardly add that in the case of many people the question of Socialism would be eliminated altogether, because they would have disappeared bodily from our planet . . . .

Thus there can be no doubt that Khrushchev is fully aware of the facts of nuclear war, facts which were not foreseen by Marx and Lenin. But it was not until the Twentieth Party Congress in February, 1956, with Malenkov still a member of the Party Presidium, that Khrushchev proposed and secured the formal revision of the Leninist canon of the inevitability of war. War, he said, was no longer 'fatally inevitable' because the socialist camp had become so overwhelmingly strong and the voices of the people in capitalist lands so clamant for peace that the imperialists could be prevented from launching war. The same Congress also revised Leninist doctrine to admit that in certain countries, unspecified, Communism might be achieved by non-violent means, and that there were many different roads to socialism which different countries might choose. The Chinese endorsed all these resolutions, although they have since criticised Khrushchev for pushing them through.

During those years when Khrushchev was beginning to preach coexistence, he was also campaigning for a return to the true revolutionary spirit of Leninism. At home he glorified the dominant role of the Communist Party and abroad he did all he could to stimulate and encourage 'liberation' and anti-colonial movements. But there were also the years of 'thaw' at home and abroad: the Austrian treaty, the Indo-China and Korean settlements, the détente with Tito and Khrushchev's visit to Britain with Bulganin.

Khrushchev's foreign policy was both more moderate in tone and more ambitious in scope than Stalin's. Stalin had kept a tight hold on his European empire but had been squeezed out almost everywhere else in the world by the American 'containment' policy based on nuclear superiority. The chief Communist activity internationally was then in Western countries and in the international 'peace' movements intended to undermine Western defence and rearmament.

Stalin's Iron Curtain worked both ways: it kept Russia inviolate but also hampered her relations with possible new friends and allies. Russia was then not truly a world power on the same scale as the US because she had not a comparable military basis, no H-bomb and no long-range rockets, aircraft or effective fleet. Her sphere of influence was limited to her immediate neighbourhood because she could not bring her power to bear in defence of distant allies or directly against the US.

By the time Khrushchev came to full control in the Kremlin, Russia had the H-bomb and was beginning to develop long-range rockets and aircraft. This had two consequences. It enabled Russia for the first time in her history to feel sure that she would not be overrun, that she could not be defeated. At the same time it gave her the possibility of breaking out of American 'containment' to assume a world influence more commensurate with her actual power.

There was no question of direct military conquests, if only because of US nuclear power. But Russia's new power could be used to back up political and economic action and to ward off military intervention from the West. To exploit these possibilities of non-military action it was necessary to make Communism more attractive to other countries and more open to view (rather in the same way, President Kennedy realised later that to restore US influence abroad it was necessary not only to rearm but also to show that the US was herself a dynamic, progressive society). In this foreign and domestic needs worked together. But there was also the middle way of helping 'liberation movements' in countries freeing themselves from colonial or imperial control. Stalin had confined what help he gave to areas where the Red Army was in occupation or near at hand – Persia, Greece, Korea – but had never been very successful outside Eastern Europe.

Khrushchev was more adventurous and found the method of arms supplies and the threat of long-range nuclear intervention useful. By his arms deal with Egypt in 1955 he leapfrogged over the barrier of the Baghdad Pact and began his penetration of the 'third world' of Afro-Asia. This had a double purpose. It was meant to roll back Western military containment in the shape of local military bases which were vulnerable to nationalist hostility. It was also intended to encourage Soviet influence in countries which were shaping their future political systems after breaking away from imperialist or colonial control.

From the beginning, Khrushchev's policy followed a zigzag double line aimed at keeping what territory Communism had gained while seeking opportunities of taking a hand in the dynamic internal evolution of other non-Communist states. It drew a distinction in theory between maintaining state frontiers and preserving the political system inside states – but this difference was not allowed to apply to the Communist bloc.

In practice, this meant that, in Europe, Khrushchev insisted on the status quo, including a divided Germany: if a country

such as East Germany or Hungary had once become Communist, it could not contradict 'the laws of history' by changing back
again. Yet even here it was not clear whether he was really
concerned with preserving Communism or with the military
security interests of the Soviet Union. For within the limits of
the Warsaw Pact he was ready to allow the East European
countries to water down their 'Communism' to an increasing
extent. Khrushchev recognised that in Western Europe it was
not worth his while to try to interfere in internal affairs; for the
Western Communist Parties had obviously no hope of achieving power. But outside Europe there was a free field for
competition even in areas traditionally regarded as Western
spheres of influence. The first Berlin crisis was an obvious
attempt to secure Western recognition of the status quo in
Eastern Germany. But Cuba was an example of the more
flexible revolutionary approach that he has followed outside
Europe.

Hence Khrushchev's doctrine of war and peace drew a
distinction in theory between nuclear and local (limited) wars
and wars of liberation. It declared that Communism would not
export revolution but would not tolerate the export of counter-
revolution – as Khrushchev saw Western policy in the Congo,
in Vietnam, in Laos and in Cuba. In practice, in all these crises,
Khrushchev has shown himself aware of the dangers of local
wars escalating into big ones.

Khrushchev's views on this vital point, his concept of the
'dynamic status quo', were brilliantly analysed by Walter
Lippmann in his account of his first interview with the Soviet
premier in 1958. In Khrushchev's mind, he wrote, 'the social
and economic revolution now in progress in Russia, China and
elsewhere in Asia and Africa *is* the *status quo* and he wants us to
recognise it as such. In his mind, opposition to this revolution is
an attempt to change the *status quo*. Whereas we think of the
status quo as the situation as it exists at the moment, he thinks of
it as the process of revolutionary change which is in progress.
He wants us to recognise the revolution not only as it is, but as it
is going to be.'

This dangerous ambiguity in Khrushchev's coexistence
theory – the attempt to have the best of all worlds by holding a
balance between de-Stalinisation at home and militancy

abroad, between a standstill agreement with the major Western powers and a free hand to encourage revolutionary change outside the Soviet sphere of influence – has been the main cause of his difficulties not only with the West but also with China and other Communist countries.

It contributed to his first big crisis with the West over Hungary and Suez in 1956 which ended the first period of 'thaw', and almost cost Khrushchev his own position. More serious indications of the limitations of the theory came in the Middle East crisis of 1958 when, to China's disgust, Khrushchev refrained from sending troops into Iraq to forestall an American intervention, and, again, in the Cuban crisis four years later. Both cases showed that while Russia could check an American military intervention in support of counter-revolution, she could not herself necessarily intervene actively in support of a revolution in progress. Thus, to the nuclear stalemate was added the concept of strategic 'neutralisation' in the theatre of possible local wars, a concept which was to have its first formal application in the agreement on Laos.

Cuba showed Khrushchev the danger of bringing nuclear weapons, even passively, into a crisis over 'national liberation'. It proved to the US the need to refrain from active military intervention to overthrow a successful Communist-type revolution even in its own sphere of influence. Above all, it taught the fundamental lesson that questions of maintaining world peace are more important than ideology.

The nuclear test-ban treaty was the first sign that Khrushchev had taken at least some of the lesson to heart. Against the background of his deepening conflict with China – from whom he had withheld nuclear knowledge since 1958 – the test-ban treaty was a virtual public declaration that Khrushchev now put the achievement of nuclear stability *before* the demands of world Communist solidarity. Over the Yemen and Cyprus, Khrushchev has since shown a new caution in leaving local crises of 'national liberation' to be handled through the once-suspect United Nations.

But the full implications of the simple lesson of Cuba have not yet been fully digested by either side. For the past year, Khrushchev seems to have been marking time in his movement towards a closer understanding with the US on the control of

97

nuclear weapons. This is partly because America herself has not been ready, and partly because Khrushchev feels he cannot move forward until he has settled his quarrel with China one way or another. But it may also be because it is altogether too difficult for him, an old embattled Communist, to face the full consequences of thinking right through the theory of peaceful coexistence in a nuclear world.

For the preservation of peace now demands a degree of co-operation between the nuclear powers which it must be increasingly difficult to combine with uninhibited struggle and conflict in other fields. But to admit theoretically that this co-operation can be extended to questions of politics, economics and ideology – however much this may be happening in practice – involves no less than a revision of the whole dialectical basis of Marxism.

Khrushchev has already shown great courage in daring to say and do unorthodox things. Within the limits of his own philosophy he has pursued a coherent vision of the world which is constructive and humane. We have all probably been lucky to have him in his place during this period of danger. He has understood the dangers of war. But whether he is capable of moving further to tackle the problems of a permanent peace remains to be seen. Perhaps it may need a Russian of a younger generation to think through the dialectic of peace. But Khrushchev has at least already paved the way, not only by his renunciation of nuclear war but also by putting 'goulash before revolution' and bringing the idea of Communism itself down to earth.

The Polarisation of the Communist World
1964

Once there was one Communist world, based on Moscow. Now there are two, one based on Moscow, the other on Peking. Here, then, at first sight, is the polarisation the title of this paper implies. And the obvious and immediate questions would seem to be: what do these two opposed Romes stand for? What sort of a following can the two Popes, temporarily Khrushchev and Mao Tse-tung, aspire to, and why? Which will win, and why? If neither wins, if we are in for a period of uneasy coexistence between the two rival authorities, what effect will this have on what we think of as the Communist movement and the West's relations with it?

All those questions, and more besides, are fair enough. But they are not perhaps the most important questions. They arise only if we take the Sino-Soviet conflict at its face value as an essentially ideological struggle. But we should not take this conflict at its face value. And the more we contemplate the problem the more we shall find that what we are watching is not the polarisation of the Communist world, but its fragmentation. I shall suggest that far from being two Romes, in fact there is no Rome at all.

There is only one way of organising a world-wide ideological movement, whether secular or spiritual, and that is on the basis of a universally recognised central authority. If this authority is effectively challenged from any quarter, one of two things can happen. Either the original authority falls and is replaced by the challenger, or else the movement splits and, dissipating much of its energies in internecine strife, ceases to be a coherent global force. Peking has not yet superseded Moscow, and shows no signs of doing so. This means that the world Communist movement is split and, axiomatically, is more concerned with its own divisions than with the world outside the Communist party.

This would be true even if the Russians and the Chinese Communists were in fact quarrelling about doctrine, as they insist that they are. Then one would expect an ideological line-up among the fraternal Parties, each individually split, each side passionately convinced that it stood for the truth, and anathemising heresy in the other.

In fact the situation is much more complicated than that. Although the quarrel was first stated in ideological terms and was debated, if that is the word, in those terms by the assembled comrades of the eighty-one Communist Parties at the secret Moscow meeting in December 1960, it was apparent even then to the simplest of the comrades that there was a good deal more behind it than interpretations of Lenin. Many of the delegates on that occasion reproached the Chinese for 'great-power chauvinism' and others criticised Peking sharply for importing questions of state relations (seen as a matter for private negotiation between Moscow and Peking) into what should have been an intra-party ideological discussion. The Chinese reproached the Russians with the same offences. Both were right. Mao and Khrushchev were quarrelling about state power rather than ideology, and both sides knew it. This meant, among other things, that the role of the other Communist Parties of the world was strictly limited. Although both Moscow and Peking demonstratively appealed to them for support in what was presented as a doctrinal quarrel, what was in fact going on, and the Communist leaders knew it, was bidding and counter-bidding for support in an inter-state quarrel.

The implication of this, though it is very doubtful if any of the participants were fully aware of it at the time, was that the fraternal Parties were being invited to vote on a matter from which they were, in effect, excluded. The Moscow Conference of 1960 was not an intra-Party discussion about the Party line: it was a duel between Moscow and Peking, with both sides demanding the unconditional support of the Communist Parties of the world in a quarrel having very little to do with Communism.

Moscow won, hands down. Only a very few southeast Asian Parties, plus, queerly, the New Zealand Party, stood up for Peking. And it seems to me that one of the best ways of enquiring into the nature of what is still flatteringly called the

Communist movement as it is today is to ask why Moscow then won so easily. Because, on the face of it, China had the better case. Practically all the charges flung by Peking at Moscow were true. Practically all the charges flung by Moscow at Peking were untrue. Further, the Chinese argument, taken at its face value (which we may do for a moment) was a good Leninist argument. The Russian argument (again taken at its face value) was not – for its Leninism was perfunctory in the extreme.

But before considering the behaviour of the fraternal Parties, perhaps we should run over the ground which lay between the assumption of power, in 1949, of the Chinese Communist Party and the formal denunciation before the assembled Communist leaders in 1960 of the thought and manners of the Chinese Communist Party.

It is not at all clear to me in what light the accession of China to the Communist camp in 1948 was regarded by the Communist Parties outside the Soviet Union. Had I been a Communist I should have viewed this climacteric with the greatest unease. But I suspect that most Communist officials in most Communist Parties are, to put it politely, no more intelligent than most American officials in most American departments of state. Why should they be? No doubt the fraternal Parties, just as most worthy Americans, and many Englishmen, regarded the Chinese revolution as a tremendous accession of strength to the Communist cause, instead of as a drastic dilution of Muscovite authority. They probably had no clearer idea of what the Communist cause was than, for example, Mr Dulles.

The man who had a clear idea was Stalin, who knew exactly what it was: it was anything in this world that could be turned to the greater glory of Great Russia, or the Soviet Union as he liked to call it. Stalin was alarmed by the Chinese revolution. He knew he could not manage the Chinese.

I hope it will not be thought that in stressing the power aspects of the Sino-Soviet conflict I am ignoring the force of ideology. I am very well aware of the force of ideology. I know a little – though luckily from observation, not from participation – of the overweening dynamic of those happy enough, individually or in groups, to be seized of the conviction that to them has been vouchsafed the vision of ultimate truth. I can guess, a little forlornly, as it were from the outside, something of the intoxication of those among them who, having read some difficult books, feel that they can fortify this vision with rational argument. How can anybody in the world who was born early enough to receive baptism at the hands of British imperialism and who in one short span has felt the impact of Lenin, Mussolini, Hitler, the Spanish Civil War and the American Way of Life *not* believe in the power of ideology? If I speak of the Soviet Union, and now China, more in terms of *Realpolitik* than in terms of Marxist and Leninist ideology it is because I think we have too much ideology. As long as there are ex-Communists (as I hope and believe there always will be), they may be trusted to keep us informed of the ideas which were betrayed. As long as there are government officials in the West who come, generation after generation of them, with minds fresh, open, and ready to be shocked by the duplicities of Lenin (and I hope and am sure there will always be such), we shall be kept fully informed of the intricacies of the great conspiracy. But I feel we should also remember people; and man does not live by ideas alone.

Stalin knew, then, he could not manage the Chinese. Between the wars he had discouraged the Chinese Communists because he needed, or thought he needed, a reasonably coherent China to be used as an ally in face of the Japanese, the Germans, the British or whoever. Kuomintang China seemed more likely to fill this bill than any other China. After the war Stalin indicated to Mao Tse-tung that the time was not ripe for a Communist revolution in China. He may or may not still have had hopes of Chiang Kai-shek. He certainly wanted to have his way in Manchuria in a manner inimical to any Chinese state. And he certainly knew that he had no hope of controlling China in the way in which he was able to control the East European satellites – by his army and police, or by the threat of their intervention. Throughout his lifetime Stalin was always quite clear that the only Communists he wanted in power anywhere were those to whom he could dictate absolutely.

This equivocal, inward-looking Russian attitude cannot have escaped the Chinese, who themselves had no intention of being controlled by anyone. In the early days of the Chinese revolution, with Chinese publicists glorifying Mao's way, there was some speculation as to whether China might one day 'do a Tito' and assert her independence. It escaped the notice of the speculators that by the very act of carrying through her revolution, China had already 'done a Tito'. The Communists had seized power in Stalin's despite, though in the name of Leninism, and without any help from Russia.

The situation being as it was, it was clearly in the interests of the Soviet Union to make the best of a good job by pretending that China was the greatest accession to their cause and a colossal ally vis à vis the West, and of China to embroider on a good job by obtaining as much material help from the Soviet Union as she could get without a sacrifice of sovereignty. The task of each was made so much easier by the conduct of the West, above all the United States, whose main object in life appeared to be to magnify the Communist menace and insist that all peoples calling themselves Communist must be clamped ever more firmly into each other's arms by outside pressure. It took the greatest determination on the part of Marshal Tito to bring Yugoslavia out of the Communist camp in the teeth of Western disapproval – he just managed. The Chinese were content to stay where they were, so long as they could do so with no apparent sacrifice of honour.

The great alliance persisted through the Korean War and until after the death of Stalin. Nobody questioned it. The Chinese Communists, as novices in the game of government, evidently felt they could accept Moscow's supremacy without loss of face in return for a great deal of vital Soviet aid. The language held by Stalin during the worst period of the cold war was the sort of language they liked to hold themselves. Stalin was a great man, a man of exceptional stature, universally recognised as such, and he had decades of practical experience behind him. It was becoming for the proudest Chinese to recognise him as the father-figure and to keep his reservations to himself. It was also expedient.

When Stalin had gone it was another matter. The senior revolutionary figure in the world was now Mao Tse-tung. The Russians could not decide whether they wanted Malenkov or Khrushchev to rule them, and neither of these when it came to prestige and grandeur could hold a candle to Mao. All the same, as far as we can gather, the Chinese for the time being were content to let things ride. No matter how much they may have distrusted Stalin's heirs, as they manoeuvred for position, it was very much in their interests for the Soviet Union to re-establish itself under a strong leadership. The only visible sign of independent thinking on the part of Mao at this stage was the difference of tone he permitted himself when speaking of Stalin. The Russians, though still three years from the Twentieth Party Congress, began to play down Stalin's role immediately after his death: the Chinese did not join in this game and continued to pay homage to the great genius and teacher of mankind.

In 1956 came the Twentieth Party Congress in Moscow, and Khrushchev for the first time emerged as a serious revisionist. His new role was at first concealed from all but the most attentive by the heat and excitement engendered by his notorious secret speech, with its selective denunciation of Stalin's ways. More important in the long run, however, was his amendment of the Leninist canon: war was no longer 'fatally inevitable'; in some countries revolution might be achieved without violence; it was necessary for all Communists to recognise that there were different paths to socialism. This amendment was a climacteric. It brought Moscow Communism into the mid-twentieth century. It recognised by implication the facts of nuclear warfare and was doubtless forced upon Khrushchev by the knowledge that in the atomic age the simple, belligerent certitudes of Lenin (who thought of wars in terms of guns and bullets and mud and slogging death) would no longer do. What was the good of seeking revolution through war, when modern war would destroy the very raw material of a new society?

Later the Chinese were to reproach Khrushchev bitterly both for his disrespectful attitude towards Stalin and for his amendment to the canon. But at the time, as far as we know, they allowed themselves to subscribe to the new doctrine. It was not until the autumn of that same year of 1956 that, for the first time since the 1949 revolution, Peking began to make itself felt as a powerful and independent voice, though still harmonising with Moscow. Then, as we know, under the impact of the de-Stalinisation, the European empire of Muscovy started going up in flames. We knew at the time that Chou En-lai made a flying visit to Warsaw, and other places, to lend, to all appearances, his moral support to Khrushchev, who badly needed it. But it was not until 1960, certainly at Moscow in November, perhaps at Bucharest in July, that the Chinese claimed that it had been they who had persuaded the Russians not to put down the Polish revolt in blood and, a little later, to move troops and tanks into Budapest in order to smash the Hungarian revolt. We do not know the truth of these claims: we only know what the Chinese have said. But there is no essential contradiction in Communist eyes between the policy of restraint in Warsaw and violence in Budapest. Had Russian troops tried to put down Gomulka, the Soviet Union would have found itself with a war on its hands, the whole Polish nation, Communist and non-Communist, united against it under a powerful Communist leader. In Budapest the situation was sadly different. Here was a divided people; here the Party and the people were irreconcilable. Had the revolt triumphed, Communism would have been swept away and Hungary would have been free to turn its back on the Soviet Union and make friends with the West. Unlike the Poles, the Hungarians were not hemmed in by East Germans and Czechs.

Be that as it may, Khrushchev, under heavy domestic fire for the consequences of his policies, was under a deep debt of obligation to the Chinese for sustaining him. He, in his turn, had committed the revolutionary act of bringing China, for the first time in history, into Europe – a most extraordinary performance for a patriotic Russian statesman.

At this stage the Chinese must have begun to feel that the time had come to claim equality with the Soviet Union. But they did not apparently press this claim with arrogance. Their great moment came in the autumn of 1957 at the celebrated Moscow Conference of Communist Parties which culminated in the publication of the first Moscow Declaration, a policy statement setting down the Party line, which was to be binding on all Parties. Although this Moscow Declaration did not deny the thinking of the Twentieth Party Congress it was essentially the outcome of a fence-mending operation, a new assertion of revolutionary vigour, and some of the language used was a great deal more belligerent and uncompromising than anything that had been heard from Moscow for some time. We know now that the Chinese were invited, to their very great joy, to assist in the drafting of the declaration, which was simply put before the other Party leaders for their signature. We know that some of the other Party leaders, above all Gomulka, were reluctant to sign. We know that the Poles relied on Mao Tse-tung personally to act as a moderating influence, as Chou En-lai had acted as a moderating influence in their favour a year before – and that they were deeply shocked and disappointed when Mao showed himself tough and uncompromising. We know now that it was at this meeting that Mao developed his notion of the East Wind prevailing over the West Wind and made his famous observation, which the Russians were later to throw in his teeth, to the effect that nuclear warfare might be a dreadful thing, but that good Communists would not flinch if faced with it, because, even if three hundred million Chinese died in it there would still be three hundred million left to build the earthly paradise in a world from which capitalism had been blasted away in blood and fire.

It seems possible, in the light of subsequent events, that Mao went away from this meeting well content. He had put some stiffening into the Russians, into Khrushchev in particular; he had helped to redefine the objects of the Communist movement in sufficiently dynamic terms; above all he had at last been admitted as an equal on policy-forming occasions by the Soviet leadership. China had arrived. Henceforward Peking and Moscow would march forward in step, consulting each other in all matters requiring fresh initiatives, and, between them, laying down the line for the lesser Parties to follow. Given all this, Mao was perfectly content to concede public recognition of the Soviet Party as the leading Party. He showed himself very keen on the concept of a leading party at a time when some of the more sophisticated Western Parties were trying to get it done away with – substituting a concept of equality between all Parties, best defined by the Italian Togliatti in his thesis on polycentrism. Was this keenness due to the fact that Mao looked forward to the day when the Chinese Party would become the leading Party? We do not know. But by 1960 he was clearly thinking along these lines.

I do not propose to move step by step through the events of the next two years, from the end of 1957 to the end of 1959. But it was during this period that various things happened to show Mao that he had overrated his influence on Khrushchev, and to show Khrushchev that Mao was very much determined to follow a path of his own at home (this was most manifest in the affair of the communes and the Great Leap Forward); to recommend the Chinese path, as opposed to the Soviet, to other unsophisticated peoples seeking to make their own revolutions; and to exploit, and persuade the Russians to exploit, in the interests of the East Wind, the vaunted supremacy of the Soviet Union in the matter of rockets and nuclear bombs. It was during this time that the Russians refused to support Mao in the matter of the offshore islands; refused to exploit their military supremacy at the time of the Iraq crisis – instead of threatening, Khrushchev made a desperate appeal to President Eisenhower to meet and talk ('the guns are almost firing') in order to stave off disaster – while the Chinese were breathing fire. It was during this period that the Russians refused to give the Chinese atomic weapons and nuclear know-how. There was clearly a basic misunderstanding on the part of the Chinese of the realities of armed might. They believed genuinely that the Soviet Union had achieved overwhelming superiority in long-range missiles. They were not alone in this! They were outraged by what they took to be Khrushchev's pusillanimous (or treacherous?) refusal to exploit this superiority.

But appearances were kept up until the autumn of 1959, when Khrushchev achieved his heart's desire, visited the United States, talked as an equal with the American President in Washington, and came back praising the good sense, peace-loving character and statesmanlike wisdom of President Eisenhower. Very soon, first in Bucharest, then in Moscow, the Chinese were to single out this attitude to Eisenhower as the supreme iniquity, the supreme betrayal of the revolutionary cause. At the time, it was only clear that there was a great difference of opinion between Moscow and Peking. Khrushchev's visit to Peking and to Mao after his American trip produced no heart-warming declarations of solidarity and unity. There was no adequate reception of the Soviet leader, and no communiqué was issued when he left. Instead, the

Chinese went on condemning Eisenhower as the arch-fiend, while Khrushchev went on referring to him in amiable terms. From now on, too, Khrushchev used every possible occasion to stress his preoccupation with securing the prosperity and material progress of the Soviet Union, with no more than the most perfunctory reference to assistance to other less happily situated Communist lands, or to the struggling masses still outside the pale. References, implicit or explicit, to the presumption of the Chinese in thinking that they had found a special road to Communism through the communes and the Great Leap Forward became increasingly frequent and contemptuous.

It is clear now that the end of 1959 marked a turning-point. The Chinese were ready to accept the supremacy of the Soviet Communist Party so long as this Party acted as a trustee and a mainstay for the Communist movement everywhere, above all in China, and provided that they had a voice in decisions of high policy. They were not, however, prepared to accept a subordinate position to a Russia interested above all in achieving physical security by unilateral deals with the enemy and material prosperity of an increasingly bourgeois kind at the expense of aid to the faithful – again especially the Chinese. There were other elements in the situation. I have not, for example, mentioned Russia's betrayal of China in the Indian border dispute; I have not mentioned the material cost to China of the immense expenditure the Russians were compelled to make in order to set the European satellites on their feet after the stormy period at the end of 1956; I have not mentioned Russia's equivocal attitude to national liberation movements, which it ought to have been wholeheartedly supporting. It is enough now to say that by the turn of the year 1959 to 1960 the scene was set for a heavy confrontation, and it came.

The Chinese prepared the ground, and they made the decision to challenge the Soviet Union in the field of ideology. This was easy for them. All they had to do was to remind the comrades of the true essence of Lenin's teaching – above all those elements of it which had been jettisoned by Khrushchev at the Twentieth Party Congress – and to denounce those who departed from it in a revisionist sense. They were helped in this in that revisionism, as opposed to dogmatism, had been pinpointed as the main immediate danger at the 1957 Moscow Conference. The Yugoslavs were the arch-revisionists, and all the Chinese had to do was to attack the Yugoslavs and attribute to them Khrushchev's sins as well as their own. They had all the holy texts on their side. When the first broadside was fired in the article 'Long Live Leninism' in April 1960, they could make a cast-iron case for their attitude, based entirely on a conventional reading of Leninist texts.

For the Russians it was harder. They had departed from the texts. Furthermore, they knew very well that this ideological dispute was not the real essence of the quarrel, which was already clearly a power contest. They replied in kind, but their replies were ideologically inferior, and often perfunctory to a degree. In straight doctrinal argument they were the losers – although they could and should have done much better.

Evidently Khrushchev was not particularly interested. He had another card up his sleeve, which he proceeded to play for all he was worth. He played it for the first time at the Bucharest Conference, before a limited audience of Communist leaders, in July 1960, after the Paris Summit fiasco, when he decided to expose the iniquity of Peking in simple terms. He did not reply to Chinese ideological arguments. He had observed that the Chinese had been talking very recklessly about atomic war and its consequences, that their preaching about national liberation struggles and the need for Moscow and Peking to support them, could only end logically in local wars which might escalate into a major war. He knew that Communists all over the world, no less than non-Communists, shared his own healthy distaste for the prospect of incineration in a nuclear holocaust. So, playing on these deep elemental fears, he charged the Chinese with warmongering tendencies – and kept at it thereafter. He may or may not have believed that the Chinese might run the world into war; but it was easy for him to show that their thinking appeared to invite this conclusion. He poured scorn on the Chinese for their chatter about paper tigers, for underrating the continuing strength of the imperialist powers, for their total failure to understand modern warfare. He did not argue with the Chinese; he was content to accuse Mao of spinning theories in a void. And he had another trick. The Chinese had been seeking actively to propagate their heretical views by underhand means: instead of putting them forward in proper comradely conclave, they had been agitating against the Soviet leadership behind its back. They were thus guilty of the sin of all sins, of defying Party discipline and lapsing into fractionalism.

This charge, of course, was carried on into the Moscow Conference four months later, until the Chinese spokesman, appalled and shocked by the strength of the line-up behind Moscow, was stung to declare in effect: 'Very well. Call us fractionalists. If trying to influence comrades in the correct sense is fractionalism, then we are fractionalists and proud of it. In this matter we follow Lenin. What was Lenin but a fractionalist when he split the Social Democratic Party into the Bolshevik and Menshevik wings? We shall continue in our ways, and time will show which of us is right!'

This, in November 1960, was the real split. The Chinese Communist Party had thrown down the gauntlet to the Soviet Communist Party and declared its own infallibility. The Russians replied with the most pressurising kind of lobbying, with abuse, with charges of warmongering, with charges of uncomradely behaviour amounting to treachery. The assembled comrades, many of whom had not the faintest idea of the bitterness of the dispute, were left to make what they could of it. They were confirmed in their natural inclination to back Khrushchev by the extraordinary performance of the leader of the tiniest and most vulnerable Communist country in the world, Enver Hoxha of Albania, who stood up in the Kremlin hall and hurled Billingsgate at Khrushchev personally, denouncing him as the betrayer of Lenin and Stalin, above all Stalin, and for trying to starve the brave Albanian Party into toeing his abominable line.

The comrades have been trying to make up their minds ever since. And ever since, all that has happened between China and Russia (the most decisive act was the withdrawal of Soviet technicians from China, together with their blueprints – an act of cold war which threw Chinese planning into confusion) has been a long-drawn-out campaign of manoeuvre. By November 1960 the leaders of all the Parties knew what was going on. But it was not until the winter of 1962 to 1963 that the realities of the quarrel were more or less openly published and presented to the Communist rank and file, as well as to the outside world. Since then each side has been striving to put the other decisively in the wrong as part of a sustained effort to win the faithful to its banner.

No doubt a great many Communists of a lesser degree do in fact still think of this quarrel primarily in ideological terms. There are individuals and groups in all Parties, sometimes large groups, who must feel deeply troubled by Khrushchev's bourgeois preoccupations and his evident determination to build up the Soviet Union as a super-power, with the strongest emphasis on local material prosperity, regardless of what goes on outside. They must feel troubled by his opportunism, by his Russianness; and no matter how much they tell themselves that Lenin was the supreme opportunist, reading themselves to sleep over the relevant passages in 'Left-wing Communism: an Infantile Disorder' and elsewhere, they must ask themselves where it is all going to end – at what point, if any, is the Soviet leadership going to feel that its own country is sufficiently invulnerable, its own people sufficiently prosperous, to permit it to pay more attention to the needs of the global revolution? At what stage will it feel ready to give more full and active assistance to despairing revolutionaries all over the world instead of using its resources to bribe the uncommitted and the bourgeois neutralists into staying neutral? And so on.

There is little doubt that had the Chinese shown less arrogance and more sense and flexibility in presenting their case, they would have won more adherents. If their speeches had been less warlike and provocative; if they had attacked the Russians more in sorrow than in anger; if they had not made it so clear that it was Khrushchev's head they were after; if, later, they had limited themselves to preaching the pure doctrine of Leninism, instead of injecting matters closely connected with inter-state rivalry, having nothing to do with ideology – border claims, betrayal of military pacts, charges of racialism, etc. – if they had conducted themselves in this way and confirmed the popular, but apparently erroneous, image of the Chinese as a people worldly wise, tolerant, subtle, flexible and gentle, whiter than white and wiser than wise, they could have made a better effect.

III

But they did not so conduct themselves. Instead, they went on attacking all along the line, until a new climax was reached with the Cuban crisis of October 1962. This gave the Chinese a first-class opportunity to develop a personal attack on Khrushchev. By retreating before President Kennedy, they said, he had not saved the peace, as he claimed, he had only made war more likely. But the edge of their attack was blunted by their own conduct in staging at this moment a massive invasion of Indian territory. Nevertheless, some of the things they had to say about Khrushchev were near enough to the truth to be awkward, and there were many earnest comrades all over the world who were inclined to agree with the Chinese when they likened Cuba to Munich and charged Khrushchev with 'irresponsible adventurism' followed by 'capitulationism'.

It was against this background that the Russians decided that the time had come to drop all camouflage and pursue their quarrel with Peking openly. The first man to come out into the open, to say 'When we mean China we have no need to say Albania', was Signor Pajetta, speaking at the Rome Congress of the Italian Communist Party in December 1962. He was soon echoed by others. But still the hard political facts behind the quarrel were largely concealed: it was not generally known, for example, that the trade between Russia and China had dwindled to practically nothing, and that Moscow had made no move at all to help the Chinese in their fight against famine arising from fearful agricultural disasters.

On March 1, 1963, Peking made what seems to have been its last bid to keep the quarrel on a high ideological level. *People's Daily* published a long and definitive article which was a direct challenge to the ideological leadership of Moscow. It contrasted the revolutionary purity of the Chinese with the opportunist manoeuvring of the Russians. In a most striking passage attacking Khrushchev directly (though still not by name), it paraphrased the opening words of the *Communist Manifesto* in terms calculated to send a shiver of appalled recognition down the spine of every devout Communist: 'A spectre is haunting the world – the spectre of true Marxist-Leninism, and it threatens you. You have no faith in the people, and the people have no faith in you. You are divorced from the masses. That is why you fear the truth.'

In an attempt to draw the Russians, the Chinese printed in its own Press the translations of a number of Soviet attacks on China, and dared Moscow to reciprocate. But Moscow was unmoved. After a good deal of manoeuvring for position a Chinese delegation arrived in Moscow in June 1963, supposedly to discuss differences in a calm and friendly atmosphere. But the atmosphere was neither calm nor friendly, nor was there any discussion. The talks took place only because, despite intensive mutual provocation, neither side was prepared to take the blame for cancelling them.

Then, in August 1963, came the nuclear test-ban treaty. At this point the Chinese seem to have decided that there was no longer any point in pretending that the great quarrel was ideological in origin. By signing the treaty, they said, the Russians had not only betrayed the revolutionary cause, but had also entered into what was nothing less than an alliance with the imperialists, directed against China. Then grievance after grievance came tumbling out. On August 14 Peking announced to the whole world that in the summer of 1959 the Russians had refused to give them technical know-how in the matter of nuclear arms and to let them have samples of atom bombs. This, they said, amounted to the unilateral denunciation of a treaty of mutual technological assistance signed in October 1957, i.e. just before the Moscow Conference, which represented the high peak of Sino-Soviet co-operation. To make matters worse, they said, the Russians had confided the terms of this treaty to the Americans. Finally, and in a way which showed how mutual suspicion and rival ambitions as between two neighbouring sovereign powers completely dominated the quarrel, in September 1963 Peking accused the Soviet Union of 'provoking frontier incidents' in general as far back as 1960, and in particular, of engaging in 'large-scale subversive activities' in Sinkiang.

As time went by it became increasingly apparent to all interested observers that there was a very marked discrepancy between Chinese revolutionary theory, as propagated in the great debate with Moscow, and Chinese political practice. This discrepancy was particularly marked in the matter of support for national liberation movements in the backward areas and for oppressed Communist Parties in bourgeois states. While reproving the Russians for inactivity in these matters, China in fact showed very little activity herself. And when she did show activity, as in the matter of the Indian border dispute, what had this to do with Communism? Again, with all their talk of paper tigers, the Chinese seemed no more anxious to invite an armed collision with the West, with America, than Khrushchev himself. They, too, for reasons of *Realpolitik*, could engage in agreements with a hostile state, Pakistan, of a kind which they would have denounced with righteous indignation had they been entered into by the Russians.

In a word, China, with all her talk about the sacred trust of Leninism, seemed to be behaving in the international field scarcely less obviously as a great power as such, with an eye to her own state interests, than the Soviet Union. Even in Indonesia she seemed more anxious to lend comfort and support to the Chinese entrepreneurs, Communist or not, than to the strong indigenous Communist Party.

Finally, by her arrogant, exclusive and excluding, touch-me-not aspect, she has reminded many Communists all over the world that, throughout her history, China has not shown the faintest comprehension of what it means to play a part in an alliance – or even of what is meant by diplomacy.

It is because of all this that, at the beginning of this chapter, I queried the conception of polarisation. Where are the poles? We can discover no clear-cut ideological division. On examination, the great schism presents itself as a conflict between two powerful and unfriendly neighbour states, each trying to exploit the once apparently monolithic Communist movement in its own material and territorial interests.

One of these states, moreover, belongs to Europe, the other to Asia (some of us may like to think of the Russians as a quasi-oriental people, closer to Asia than to Europe, but this view is shared by extremely few Russians and by no Chinese: certainly the Soviet Union comprehends a number of Asian peoples, but these are clearly seen as such by the dominant Russians, and they play no effective part in the evolution of Soviet Government attitudes towards the outside world). Already, as we have lately seen, attempts have been made by each side to present the other in the most damaging light imaginable – as seeking to divide the world on racial lines and to organise conflict between East and West – or, more accurately nowadays, North and South. The less developed peoples of Asia, Africa and Latin America are supposed to be rallying round China, in opposition to the more fortunate 'have' peoples of North America and Europe, including the Soviet Union from Minsk to Vladivostock.

In fact there are no clear demarcation lines. Far from representing a polarisation of the Communist world, the Sino-Soviet conflict seems to be well on the way to releasing movements and forces which cut across all the familiar groupings which, since shortly after the last war, we have accepted, foolishly I think, as virtually immutable. Thus, already General de Gaulle is profiting by the conflict in order to further what he takes to be, perhaps rightly, perhaps not, the interests of France, putting new strains on the Western alliance. There will be other strains arising from the different attitudes, different approaches, different expedients assumed and resorted to by individual Western Governments vis à vis individual Communist states or Parties seeking to profit from the breakdown of Moscow's absolute control of their destinies, or thrown into confusion by the terrible necessity of making a choice: the whole point of becoming a Communist is that by making one choice one is liberated from the responsibility of ever choosing again – how fearful, how calamitous to be expelled into the rough light of day from the dark and cavernous certitudes of a universal womb – and just because a Chinese had to quarrel with a Russian.

The Communists of Eastern Europe see a new freedom of manoeuvre. The challenge to the West is to meet them half way – and the West will quarrel about it. The West is already quarrelling about Cuba, about British Guiana: Castro, owing so much to Mr Khrushchev, flirts with China, assumes Chinese attitudes, makes it up to Russia, buys omnibuses from the British, whose willingness to sell is an affront to the United States. Canada sells wheat to Russia and China, America only to Russia – to deplete her gold reserves, according to Washington. America puts pressure on the British to stay in British Guiana to keep it from going Communist, but wants British troops out of Borneo, cost what it may to Malaysia (small) in order to appease Indonesia (large) because Indonesia has a powerful Communist Party. Pakistan makes deals with China: India makes deals with Russia. Nearer home the new mood among the great European Communist Parties will soon lead to startling changes in the domestic political arrangements of a number of countries, above all Italy, where, by the look of things, the flexibility of Togliatti and other Communist leaders will shortly make it hard for the Italians to reconcile domestic harmony and perfect loyalty to NATO.

Behind it all lies the very long-term threat of ultimate physical conflict between the Soviet Union and China, which could embrace us all.

Revisionism and Reform in the Soviet Union Since 1953
1966

In discussing change and reform in the Soviet Union we must first make a bow to those who insist that there have been no real changes at all, only tactical retreats and concessions which may be reversed at any time. But retreats and concessions from and to what?

Reluctance to admit that there has been any fundamental change since the death of Stalin appears to be due not to deep-rooted ideas about original sin, but to certain professions of Lenin, Stalin, Khrushchev, about the unchanging aims of Bolshevism and the permissibility, the desirability, the imperative necessity indeed, of dissembling those aims on occasion in order to effect temporary alliances with individuals, groups, parties – by implication governments too – opposed to Bolshevism and marked for ultimate destruction on the way to world revolution. It is odd to find historians, diplomatists, and politicians, who, of all people, should be conscious of the everlasting gulf between the expressed aspirations of statesmen, even left-wing statesmen, and their actions, being taken in by this sort of thing.

A classic text occurs in Lenin's pamphlet, 'Left-wing Communism: an Infantile Disorder', dedicated, appropriately enough in more ways than one, to David Lloyd George:

It is possible to conquer a powerful enemy only by exerting the most intensive effort, by taking thorough, attentive, meticulous and skilful advantage of each and every split among the bourgeois of the various countries, and by taking advantage of every opportunity, even the most trivial, to gain a mass ally, though this ally may be temporary and unstable, vacillating, conditional and unreliable.

These are the words of a man intoxicated with his own cleverness and ruthlessness. Apart from the invocation of the masses, there is not a word in that exordium which has not been thought and put into practice by every statesman since the world began. Lenin shared Bismarck's weakness, a compulsion to spell out, with the air of a man making a great discovery, truisms known to and acted on by others in their sleep.

Bolsheviks profess to think that there is no morality except class-morality, therefore what is moral is what advances the interests of Bolshevism, seen, with a high element of fantasy, as the voice of the working class. Duplicity is in order provided it serves the ends of the working class. 'Who tells a lie as for Thy laws . . . .' And so on. There is nothing new about this, just as there was nothing new about Stalin's homicide, except in the matter of scale. The one has been practised in the name of patriotism or religion for a great many centuries; the other was adequately summed up in Machiavelli's anecdote about Castruccio Castracani of Lucca: asked how he could bring himself to murder his old friends, Castruccio replied: 'I do not kill old friends; I kill new enemies.'

Perhaps, more than anything, it has been the unhappy example of *Mein Kampf*, which still fascinates in a hypnotic manner so many who did not take Hitler seriously when they should have done. Indeed, it is a common thing to find Hitler's programme and the open statement of it equated with the Bolshevik programme and the open statement of that. We discounted the one, the argument runs; we must on no account discount the other. Nobody wants to discount the Bolsheviks. How is this possible? They have created the climate of our existence. *Mein Kampf* (without at all going into scholastic details about Hitler's intentions) was offered as a straight account of a plan of action, of what one man intended to do, and, more or less, how. There was no theory about this: it read like an operation order. At no stage, at no time, have our Russian comrades ever issued an analogous manifesto. All they have done is to state that a certain interpretation of history works, therefore it must be true; a projection of this interpretation into the future shows that such and such events will occur, involving the Communisation of the globe; the Soviet Union, being the first country to conduct a Marxist (sic) revolution, has the right and the duty to assist, by whatever means, other countries to achieve their own revolutions; only when all the world has achieved Marxist revolutions will universal peace be guaranteed and justice and equity be established on earth.

I have put this statement in simple words because it is high time that it was put in simple words. The first point to be made is that the spirit behind this statement, which sums up fairly accurately the position of Lenin, is wholly different from the spirit behind *Mein Kampf*: the first is a declaration of faith, the second a declaration of will.

We know what happened to the will: after a promising start it was frustrated. This is what usually happens to a declaration of will. What has happened to the statement of faith?

In the first place we may, perhaps, agree that to take Lenin's statement of faith at its face value is to admit the validity of that faith. Most of us do not make this admission: what then are we worrying about? What we are worrying about is a perversion of the faith. When a faith is perverted it loses its virtue and immediately dissipates itself into a collection of expedients cloaked by holy words and calculated to serve an ulterior purpose. But we, to magnify the deadliness of the Bolshevik purpose, assist in maintaining the camouflage. Thus when Mr Khrushchev, paying lip-service to a faith long abandoned, declares 'we shall bury you', we hasten to take him at his word.

In discussing change, there is no need to go back to Marx. The man we are first concerned with is Lenin, who owed his inspiration to Marx and Engels but, to justify his own conduct in carrying through a *coup d'état* disguised as a proletarian revolution without a proletariat, had to do some quick *ad hoc* thinking, including the brilliant mental switch which transposed, in effect, the proletarian revolution outside Russia into an anti-colonial revolution. What we are dealing with today is not Marxist-Leninism but the heritage of Leninism, which owed a great deal to Marx as a 'starter' and then abandoned him to the Mensheviks.

At no stage did Lenin or any of his successors declare that they intended to conquer the world in the name of the Revolution. When at one stage, it looked very much as though Stalin had in mind to conquer at least a good deal of the world, he was acting not in the name of the Revolution but in the name of Great Russia, which happened to be the headquarters of the Revolution. By the time Khrushchev arrived on the scene this process had shot its bolt, and when he announced 'we shall bury you' – in the name of Lenin – the phrase was already absurd. Who was 'we' and who was 'you'? Did 'we' include Yugoslavia? Did it include China?

Marx was a great one for lies, but he did not believe in the unlimited lie: Lenin did. Marx was not above using force to overthrow the enemy, but he did not believe in the continuing use of force by a self-perpetuating group of rulers to terrorise workers and peasants into obeying their commands for half a century. Lenin did not believe in this either, but he created the conditions in which it became possible, even likely. The Soviet Union has been ruled since 1918 in the workers' despite, and since 1929 by precisely such a self-perpetuating group interested first in preserving its own power, then, in varying degrees, in using that power to build up a strong Soviet Union and extend its dominion or influence by whatever means, from military occupation to long-range political subversion. Stalin, most cautious in extending his power, savage and irresponsible in the exercise of it once it was won, was careful to ensure that there was no revolution anywhere which he could not physically control, except in the case of the Chinese revolution, which was not his fault: Yugoslavia was a simple error of judgement; Stalin had reckoned without the Southern Slavs. Khrushchev, more of a gambler, tried to cash in on Cuba, seen not as an outpost of revolution but as a military base in the Russo-American conflict: he forgot about sea-power, and he soon lost interest in Castro when Cuba ceased to be a rocket-carrier.

What people mean when they say that nothing has changed in the Soviet Union is roughly the following: Lenin's revolutionary aims still dominate the minds of his successors; the domestic Terror may have been relaxed, but it can be restored at any time; the Soviet system and all its institutions, perfected by Stalin for the convenience of his personal dictatorship, have been preserved intact by his successors in order to maintain theirs; this system and these institutions, so long as they survive, preclude any possibility of fundamental reform. There are two lines of argument here, and they cancel each other out. How can men concerned above all with their own power be regarded as dedicated crusaders for universal brotherhood?

Obviously a great deal has changed in the Soviet Union since Lenin's day: some of the changes may appear to fall under the head of what the Chinese call revisionism; some do not. Some may be regarded as permanent in an evolutionary sense; others may only be provisional and impermanent.

It is worth considering this matter of revisionism. Revisionism is one of those loaded words which can be used to mean whatever you want it to mean – or nothing. The Chinese use it in just this way, so that, at first glance, it tells us no more about Soviet or Yugoslav, or Italian CP policies than any other word of simple abuse. The Russians until a few years ago were no better than the Chinese: in the Moscow Declaration of December 1957, drafted by Russians and Chinese and signed by all the Communist Parties of the world (by some reluctantly), revisionism, as opposed to dogmatism, was singled out as the chief evil of the moment. This was a demonstration against Marshal Tito, who had been irritating the Russians and scandalising the Chinese, and against all those fraternal Parties, above all the Polish Party inside the bloc and the Italian Party outside, which had shown signs of taking too literally the promise of the Twentieth Congress of the Soviet Communist Party about differing paths to socialism. It also stood for a closing of the ranks in face of certain disruptive consequences of the de-Stalinisation campaign.

But the word still has a technical meaning, and both the Russians and the Chinese know what it means. It was first applied to the reformist ideas of the distinguished German socialist Edward Bernstein, when he broke away from Marxism and insisted that social democracy should 'find the courage to emancipate itself from a philosophy which has, in fact, been long outmoded, and be willing to show itself for what it really is – a democratic socialist party of reform'. What Bernstein had in mind about the Marxist philosophy being outmoded was what was later to become a general criticism of Marxism – namely that in his insistence that capital would come to be concentrated in ever fewer hands, and that the misery of the workers would increase throughout this process, Marx had been proved wrong by events. Seventy years ago this in fact was not a watertight argument. Marx himself had allowed that under capitalism there could be false dawns, and the only thing that could be said for certain at the turn of the century was that the inevitable process was moving more slowly and erratically than Marx had predicted. Bernstein was a good prophet, but for the wrong reasons.

Nobody wants to accuse the Russians of Bernsteinism. On the other hand, for some time past they have been revising their attitudes fairly drastically. To find out what this amounts to and the extent to which Marxism, or Marxism-Leninism, has been changed or undermined by Kremlin policies the best thing to do is to stop using Marxist-Leninist terms and try to discover in plain English what has been going on. What has been revised, and how?

Lenin had already distorted Marxism out of all recognition when he decided to go for a proletarian revolution without waiting for the bourgeois one. The Chinese have never criticised him for this, nor have they criticised themselves for carrying out a peasant revolution – in Lenin's name. The reason for this is that the term revisionism in the pejorative sense is applied only to those shifts in doctrine which are calculated to lead to a slowing down or cancellation of revolution, never to those shifts which are calculated to hasten revolution.

Thus, although the Chinese are now using the term revisionist as a generalised term of abuse, when they argue seriously they attach the revisionist label above all, and on the face of it correctly, to certain Soviet actions, leading to doctrinal changes, carried out in response to historical developments not foreseen by Marx or Lenin and calculated to postpone world revolution, or even to substitute for violent revolution reformist methods of achieving socialism throughout the world as once advocated by Bernstein.

The main Soviet offence is discovered in certain important departures from the Leninist canon made at the Twentieth Party Congress: specifically, the adoption of the thesis that war is no longer inevitable and that in some countries socialism, then Communism, may be achieved without violent revolution, e.g. by parliamentary means. The Chinese also see in coexistence a retreat from the proper business of undermining and destruction in the interests of revolution. The Chinese accepted these departures at the time, early in 1956. Perhaps they felt compelled to do this, so great was their need for Soviet aid at that time. Perhaps, like many in the West, they imagined that Khrushchev was merely indulging in Leninist trickery, pending Soviet supremacy in long-range ballistic missiles, and only later discovered that he meant what he said and was shaping his policies accordingly; if so they displayed deep ignorance of Soviet ways. Perhaps, inwardly, they already despised post-Stalin Russia so profoundly that they already regarded a Soviet Party Congress as a local affair, not binding outside the Soviet Union.

Be that as it may, the cry of coexistence (which, in Russian eyes, means only physical coexistence: the ideological war, for what it is worth, is still on) was not a confidence trick, and the resolutions about the non-inevitability of war and socialism without violence were not part of a calculated attempt to lull the West in to a sense of false security. There is all the difference in the world between the formal resolutions of a Soviet Party Congress concerning doctrinal modifications and the innumerable deceptions, blessed in principle by Lenin, practised both by Stalin and Khrushchev, in their efforts to augment the security and influence of the Soviet Union, to weaken the unity and resolution of the 'enemy camp' and to seduce the non-aligned.

Khrushchev and his successors can no longer believe in the simple certitudes of Lenin, who, at the time when he was most actively theorising, was an internationalist, expecting that revolutionaries in Germany and elsewhere would soon triumph and come to the aid of the Soviet Union. They know very well, as Lenin never foresaw, that if every country in the world were to carry out its own revolution of whatever kind, in the name of Marx, or Lenin, or Mao Tse-tung, the world would still be fragmented and divided into mutually hostile groupings: in the last decade they have seen that the Communist world cannot even hold together in face of what it calls the threat of war from the strongest power on earth. In a word, there is no future in world revolution for the Soviet Union as a power. And the prime interest of the current successors to Lenin must be the preservation and further development of the Soviet Union as a power: it is the only base of their own power.

Knowledge, however, does not invariably condition behaviour, which may be affected by irrational dreams originally projected from premises long seen to be false, nostalgia for lost certitudes, and simple habits of thought. In a word, we all do things which are not good for us, and which are bound to lead to the very consequences we most seek to avoid. There is no doubt at all that the imagination of many highly placed Russians is still sustained by antique dreams of global revolution which will not bear looking into for one moment. In the first place their own state is itself a contradiction of those dreams: should it ever succeed in imposing its pattern on every other state, it would show itself as the antithesis of everything Lenin desired. In the second place – but need we go on? This is not necessarily an expression of total cynicism: an Anglican bishop proclaiming the virtues of meekness, humility, poverty, and enlarging on the camel and the needle's eye, is not, as a rule, perpetrating a conscious fraud.

We all have to rationalise our behaviour or go mad. The current Programme of the Communist Party of the Soviet Union is the rationalisation of the behaviour of men who cannot pretend to derive their authority from a supernatural source e.g. God, or from the people over whom they rule. Owing their power to nothing but trickery and force and the favour of a discredited dictator, they have to pretend to some authority outside themselves. Lenin is the answer. The Lenin mystique still holds throughout the Soviet Union, and there is no doubt that it also affects in some degree the present incumbents of the Central Committee and its organs as well as the Council of Ministers. Everything they do has to be justified in terms of Lenin's teaching, which is also intermittently a useful guide to policy and conduct: at any rate, they have no other guide, and men cling to what they know, even when it is clearly leading them up the garden path.

Every departure from Lenin's teaching also has to be justified in terms of Leninism. Lenin believed, for example, that the path to revolution led through war: war created the conditions most favourable to revolution, therefore long live war! The comrades bore this doctrine like a millstone round their necks long after the atom bomb had made it absurd: it had always been obscene. Stalin tried to escape from it shortly before he died when he put forward the view in his celebrated thesis for the Nineteenth Party Congress that although there must be wars, as Lenin had taught, the balance of power was now such that with good luck and good management the Soviet Union could hold aloof from them, leaving the capitalist powers to tear each other to pieces. Stalin never got the credit for his essay in revisionism because it was soon forgotten in the excitement over the doctors' plot, then over his death. Malenkov during his brief premiership announced that another war would mean the ruin of the Communist as well as the capitalist world; but this was not put forward as Party doctrine. It was left to Khrushchev, who had attacked the Malenkov view, to formulate this truism as new doctrine, to embody it in a resolution of the Twentieth Party Congress, and to justify it in quasi-Leninist terms.

It is now part of the canon, and will remain part of it. The same applies to the possibility of some countries achieving Communism without violent revolution. There was no question of Khrushchev monkeying about with the Leninist canon in order to deceive the enemy. This is not done: deception is practised by other, so to say secular, means: peace fronts, popular fronts, lying propaganda of a thousand kinds. There is in intention a difference in kind between the principles which, as it were, legitimise the progress towards Communism and the expedients resorted to for the fulfilment of those principles. A resolution formally passed at a Party Congress lays down the law to the Party. It cannot be changed except by another formal resolution. On the other hand specific actions within the framework of the general principles, whether proposals for a summit conference or for co-operation with social democratic parties in Europe, or offers of increased trade or cultural exchanges, or whether, at home, toleration of unorthodox writers, concordats with churches, concessions to peasants, and so on – specific actions of this kind must, on Lenin's own showing (Trotsky's too), be regarded as tactical expedients designed to strengthen the Soviet Union vis à vis the outside world and the power of the leadership at home. Nevertheless, what may begin as a tactical expedient may imperceptibly be transformed into an enduring custom, may, indeed, become institutionalised. A number of Russia's most abominable institutions had their genesis not in action taken from conviction but in a tactical expedient introduced in an *ad hoc* manner with no thought of permanency: the development of Lenin's Cheka is a case in point.

Domestic reform in the Soviet Union has, in fact, nothing to do with revisionism, because the customs and institutions which need to be reformed have nothing to do with Marxist or Leninist theory. The persecution of minorities, religious and racial, the suppression of free speech, the prohibition of contact with the outside world, the disciplining of artists of all kinds, the eccentricities of Soviet law – these, together with the situations which have developed as a result of the collectivisation of agriculture and the over-stressing of heavy industry, owe little to ideology and everything to the Party's determination to retain power for itself and to strengthen Russia against the outside world. What happens, of course, is that the leadership strives to lend to such expedients what can only be called a moral justification by attaching to them a quasi-ideological value. In so doing they end by deceiving themselves and make necessary change that much harder to effect. Modification, indeed, is accomplished only with extreme reluctance and much half-heartedness only when the ruling circle finds modification immediately necessary for its own survival. As everybody knows, however, such modifications are in fact arrived at, and some are bound to stay. If a harsh expedient resorted to by the Soviet leadership to solve an immediate specific problem can harden into a custom or become institutionalised, there is no reason at all why an ameliorating expedient should not enjoy the same transformation. As for motives, it by no means follows that the man who falls back to jump the better will be given time to execute the manoeuvre as planned.

Khrushchev gave as his reason for abandoning the thesis about the inevitability of war the vastly increased strength of the socialist camp (which then included China), which, he said, was now (1956) sufficient to deter the imperialists from starting a war. Lenin, he said in effect, could not have foreseen this situation. What he really meant was that the advent of nuclear weapons and intercontinental rocketry made war unthinkable.

And a few years later, in his polemic against China, he was in fact admitting just this. Then he went further: even local wars must be avoided for fear that one of these might escalate into a major war, ending in universal destruction, Russia not excepted. By implication local wars included any war of liberation, any civil war, indeed, which might give cause for intervention by major powers. Similarly, the new concept of different ways to socialism and the possibility of achieving socialism without violent revolution quite clearly arose from Khrushchev's realisation that it was beyond the power of the Soviet Union to impose itself and its system on at least a large part of the world.

Once these tremendous leaps of the imagination had been made, it followed that, for its own good, the Soviet Union had better come to some sort of an accommodation with the enemy, specifically, the United States. Logic is one thing, action in obedience to it quite another. To abandon Lenin was unthinkable (so unthinkable that it was never even contemplated). Under sheer irresistible pressure of events, e.g. the development of nuclear weapons, it was possible to jettison some of Lenin's teaching with only a perfunctory attempt to justify this action in Leninist terms. But where events were not so pressing it was inevitable that refuge should be sought in odd corners of the dear old doctrine. And when China started making her bid for Lenin's mantle at the very moment when the Russians were disentangling themselves from its folds, while urgently pretending to be doing something quite different, it was too much. Leninism might be in some particulars outworn, but the Soviet Union knew no other authority: if it were to be seized by another power before the Soviet Union had time to grow a new skin the results would be too terrible to contemplate. Hence these tears.

Hence, also, the profound misunderstanding on the part of so many in the West of the processes which are now under way in the Soviet Union. The Russian leadership is being forced by China to justify in ideological terms attitudes and actions which have nothing to do with ideology. China accuses the Kremlin of revisionism, and the Kremlin feels inevitably constrained, though not consistently, to fight back in these terms. The force of the old magic of the Leninist ideology is thus in a measure revived. It inhibits the Soviet leadership from straight thinking and it alarms the West.

The West should not be alarmed. No matter what the Russians may say they are long past revisionism. Revisionism is the move from conviction about one way of achieving universal socialism to another e.g. from violent revolution to gradual reform. Socialism is the aim. Lenin, like Marx, thought that it had to be achieved through violent revolution; Bernstein, taking another look at the world, decided that reformism was the better way. But socialism on a global scale, international brotherhood between equal peoples, was the aim, never the greater glory of a single power. Who would dare say that the international brotherhood of workers was Stalin's aim, or Khrushchev's, or Kosygin's?

When Khrushchev introduced his amendments to the Leninist canon in 1956, he dressed them up in ideological camouflage. But, in fact, far from revising Leninism he was abandoning Leninism. He was concerned wholly and solely with the security and prosperity of the Soviet Union – as Stalin had been before him. His act, if not his intention, was on the level of all these internal reforms, usually half-hearted and incomplete, often half withdrawn when made, carried out by his Government first to loosen the strait-jacket imposed by Stalin on the Soviet people, then to satisfy, however reluctantly and incompletely, the great hidden pressure of popular demand which followed, as night follows day, the first loosening of the bonds. In partially freeing the Soviet people so that they could hold up their heads and work better, Khrushchev was responding to the pressure of reality in precisely the same way as he responded to the pressure of reality when he announced that war was no longer inevitable, and in precisely the same way as Kosygin is responding to the pressure of reality when he experiments with the profit motive in industry or scientific inquiry into the way people live and work in the Soviet Union. Conversely, in resisting popular demand – for more personal freedom, for more butter before guns, etc, the Soviet leadership is responding to reality in precisely the same way as the Czarist Governments responded to reality – attempting to contain popular demand by police action, lest it should gather sufficient momentum to sweep them away.

All these actions, whether liberal or reactionary, still have to be justified in Leninist terms – because the leadership knows no other terms. But the Russian people are not deceived (though they may be muddled, because Lenin was a saint), and we should not be deceived.

The day may come when a government in Moscow will apply itself to some hard thinking about socialism, using elements of Marx, perhaps of Lenin too, as well as lessons from Russia's own experience, to develop a blue-print for society which will capture the imagination of the world. That would be revisionism indeed! But that day is not yet. The Soviet Union now is a great power struggling to escape from its own past, hampered by fears which are no longer relevant, ambitions which are outmoded, dreams which it has confused with reality and a sense of mission without a goal.

The Russians in Prague
1968

The higher leadership of the Soviet Union has closed its ranks for the kill. The KGB has been turned loose among the Czechoslovaks in the wake of Soviet tanks, as the Gestapo was once turned loose in the wake of German tanks.

With Mr Dubcek by all acounts a broken man, with the Russians, like Hitler before them, preparing to divide Czech from Slovak while at the same time making threatening noises and gestures against the Romanians and the Yugoslavs – with all this nothing would appear to be more irrelevant than continued speculation about the strains and stresses inside the Soviet Union.

But it is not irrelevant, because the whole hideous situation, the return to darkness at noon, is the direct outcome of those strains and stresses as they have been building up in general since the death of Stalin and in particular under the ignorant, mediocre and indecisive leadership which took over from Khrushchev.

Khrushchev, for all his shortcomings, made things happen. For just on four years the present leadership has made nothing happen at all. It has been dragged along by circumstances. (The most spectacular example was the way they allowed the Arabs to involve them in the Six-Day War resulting in damage to their prestige.)

The rape of Czechoslovakia was the first decisive action of a group of men who have shown themselves unfit to govern. That they are not the only present-day Government unfit to govern is neither here nor there. So far, for example, the peoples of Britain and America have shown themselves able to survive and hold together without strong government. It is very different in the Soviet Union.

The senior leaders in Moscow are all in this together. Obviously there have been sharp differences among them over what to do about the Czechs – differences going back at least six months. But now they have acted as a body, and they must be judged as a body until one or more of them gets up and publicly denounces the others – and more totally than Khrushchev ever allowed himself to denounce Stalin.

Some, we know, are in many ways a cut above the others – Podgorny, for example, who has frequently shown an awareness that we are living in the twentieth century, not in the seventeenth; Polyansky, the brightest specimen of a younger generation of Party bosses; perhaps, in his morosely groping way, Kosygin himself. But they have all put their seal to this act. They have all connived at the bullying of Mr Dubcek. They all remain colleagues of Mr Shelest who, taking time off from terrorising the Ukraine, was most vocal in his threats to smash the Czechs. And they all continue to sit at the same table with Comrade Andropov, whose secret police, once again happy in their work, are preparing for a field day.

It is a Russian decision. There is no reason to believe the widespread story that the Russians were pushed into it by the East German jackal, Ulbricht. These stories seem to originate from Moscow itself.

There is another story going round that Mr Brezhnev agreed reluctantly to commissioning this crime and was pushed into it, if not by Mr Ulbricht, then by his own Marshal Grechko. In the sense that Mr Brezhnev views with reluctance the necessity of taking any decision of any kind not directly connected with the advancement of his position and the retention of his power, this is no doubt true: he is the brainless wonder of our age. You have to look to Alabama or California to find his equal. But he is the chosen figurehead of the entrenched Party apparatus and, as such is very strong.

Do people realise what they are saying when they suggest that he was pushed into this action by a soldier?

It would mean nothing less than a major revolution in the Soviet power machine. It would mean the abdication of the Communist Party of the USSR.

Whether Marshal Grechko was a prime mover in this crime we do not know. As a chief military adviser he has to be listened to; as a member of the Central Committee, he has some sort of a voice in the Party apparatus. But neither Stalin nor Khrushchev (nor Malenkov, Kaganovich, Molotov and all) would for one moment have allowed any soldier, however distinguished, to have influenced their decisions – which would have been tantamount to inviting the military to take over.

Until we see the Marshal taking over in fact, we had better assume that the decision-makers are the men who say they are, the same men who, in person, not even by proxy, bullied and maltreated Mr Dubcek and his friends before turning them loose – either because, at that moment, they were afraid to murder them and did not know what else to do, or, more likely, because they hoped they would persuade their people to keep quiet until they could be neutralised without too much public shooting.

So the question remains, why did they do it? And the answer is always the same: out of fear. It was fear mainly of the consequences of the victory of the Czechoslovak cause to their own positions inside the Soviet Union and, only in a lesser degree, of the consequences in other satellites.

Even if, as I believed and still believe, some of them saw, and see, the necessity of change inside the Soviet Union and think they could preside over it, they have for the time being, perhaps for ever, lost their chance. We have not heard much yet about open criticism of the Kremlin's action inside Russia. We soon shall. It took some weeks for the Moscow students to demonstrate against the Hungarian action in 1956, and then they were put down quickly and sharply by Khrushchev in person.

Two things have happened in the intervening twelve years. On the broad time-scale, the younger generation, aided and abetted by quite a number of the more cautious middle-aged, have grown used to expressing dissent on specific issues – and there are whole generations which never experienced the Stalin terror and therefore cannot imagine what it did to their fathers and grandfathers, those who survived.

On the shorter time-scale, during the past three years, the security police have been allowed to flex their muscles, flabby from comparative disuse, and to brush up their old techniques, which had grown a little rusty.

Since the last big round of public protest after the trial and sentencing of the dissident Ginsburg and his friends, the dissenters have kept very quiet, avoiding head-on collision, but perfecting subtler tactics, perhaps even a strategy, of the kind which has prevented the KGB from making a quick and final end to a number of distinguished protesters who in an earlier age would have been thrown down the cellar steps and shot before the outside world knew of their existence.

The Kremlin leaders know all about this. They also know that not only the Moscow intelligentsia, but, more dangerously, their many minority nationalities ranged round the periphery of the Union have been forced, against the will of many of them, to turn to nationalism as the only solution. And we, of all people, know all about the tenacious power of nationalism – not the most hopeful aspect of human endeavour, but sometimes the only way of breaking a tyranny.

Mr Brezhnev and his friends are aware of this. Mr Shelest in the Ukraine, who has been behaving for some time like one of Stalin's Gauleiters, is personally up against it.

We need look no further. The Russian leadership, as a body, has decided that the only way to keep its position is to sit firmly on all manifestations of change, whether in the form of nationalism or of mild questioning of their own infallibility.

For the security of the Soviet Union as a whole, they cling with some desperation to the idea of a nuclear understanding with America – as between the two main imperialist powers, neither aspiring to world domination.

They will not lose that understanding. They will lose everything else – but not before they have ruined the Czechs. They cannot reimpose Stalinism on Czechoslovakia without trying to impose it on Russia – and here they will fail. In spite of many appearances to the contrary, the Soviet Union of today is not the Soviet Union of Stalin and cannot be run in the Stalin manner without a check to economic development which would lead to breakdown or explosion. It is to be doubted whether Mr Brezhnev has the brains to appreciate this, but some of his colleagues have. They must be more frightened today than they were when they took their panic decision. The dinosaur is stuck in the swamp and dying. This is small comfort for the Czechs who are flattened beneath the monster's bulk.

The Elastic Détente
1973

If Russia's activity in the latest Middle East war has done nothing else, it has shown that for Moscow the concept of détente is, to say the least, elastic. Not that any such demonstration should have been necessary: a Government that uses the term 'coexistence' to connote an unremitting struggle for mastery, with no holds barred, stopping short only of major war, will obviously have its own special meanings for other innocent-looking words. Détente is one of these. To judge by recent events, what the Kremlin means by détente is a state of coexistence modified to allow for temporary accommodations with the enemy in order to receive advantages and concessions which only he can give.

Once this is accepted, there is no need to waste time and energy wondering whether Brezhnev really means what he says when he declares his passion for détente. Of course he means it. He wants trade, credits, technology, etc. from the West; and he wants them very badly indeed.

Nor is it necessary to attribute every fluctuation in the apparent Soviet line to the machinations of an anti-Brezhnev faction in the Kremlin. Mr Brezhnev is there because his colleagues in the Politburo think he is the best General Secretary they have. Some of them no doubt dislike him; some will have their reservations (echoed widely through the country, in Party offices, in army messes, in the KGB) about this or that aspect of his policies, which are nevertheless consensus policies. But just as Mr Edward Heath, and Mr Harold Wilson in Britain, kicking and laying back their ears, are indissolubly bound together and limited in their actions (not their words, of course) by the intractable facts of social and economic life, so Mr Brezhnev and his senior colleagues are compelled to the same conclusions and policies.

Apparent fluctuations in a general line are far more likely to be the result of miscalculation or irresistible temptation than to policy conflicts inside the Kremlin – as, for example, when Mr Brezhnev recently interrupted his love affair with President Nixon to urge the Arabs on. For the Russians are human too.

Being human means, among other things, that one cannot see round every corner. We know this about ourselves and our sainted political masters; but we find it very hard to believe it about the Russians. We know, that is to say, that the Soviet leadership has a long-term goal, an asset (liability?) conspicuously absent on our side: world revolution.

At least, this is what they themselves are for ever going on about – though why they imagine a Communist USA should be more amenable than Communist China is past understanding. Be that as it may, so long as they insist that it is their duty and their privilege to provide us with new chains we have to do them the honour of believing them.

But – a large but – a long-term aim is not the same as a master plan. For example, it is the long-term aim of many of us individually to achieve goodness: all too few of us, however, can lay claim to the patenting of a master plan to this end. Here is a very potent source of confusion. When considering Russian intentions we fail to separate the near from the far, the immediate from the contingent, the reality from the holy aspiration. This is natural enough, though undesirable; and it comes all the more easily to us because the Russians are equally confused.

Thus it must be the hardest' thing in the world for Mr Brezhnev and his friends today to decide on the correct course of action almost anywhere. And it is not made any easier (though they may not yet have cottoned on to this themselves) by the inherent idiocy of the long-term aim of world revolution, as understood by them, to which all their shorter-term policies are supposed to be adapted. The world as viewed from the Kremlin must present an unsettling spectacle; not immediately dangerous, perhaps, but in many ways alarming. And perplexing enough, one would think, to make Mr Brezhnev sigh for the vanished certitudes of the cold war at its most chilly; a world in upheaval torn to ribbons with contradictions, its points of reference constantly in flux, so that sometimes it must seem that the only fixed point in the whole global landscape is the indomitable smile of Dr Kissinger lingering in space while the magician passes on.

By all the old familiar standards the Russians should be well pleased by what they see of the general Western mess. For so long it was an accepted aim of Soviet policy to break up the Atlantic alliance and undermine the stability of its component nations. Now that the West has achieved so much in this direction by its own efforts – admittedly with some Soviet help from time to time – there should surely be cause for rejoicing in Moscow. And, furthermore, three cheers for the Arabs for taking the plunge and doing what Russia has for so long urged them to do: use their oil as a weapon. But far from proclaiming with glad cries the imminent demise of capitalism, with appropriate descants on the vileness of the political leaders of the West, the Soviet orators are silent.

The silence may not last. It probably will not. But its quality so far is a tribute to the intensity of cerebration now furrowing those not very lofty brows in the Kremlin. Their conclusion so far has amounted to little more than wait and see.

It is not an easy situation. Mr Brezhnev did not pursue his celebrated policy of détente for fun but, in its various aspects, for definite purposes – ranging from the acquisition of American technology to consumer goods and food; from a more precise ordering of expensive armaments to the fixing of the status quo in Europe.

These and other objects were rendered desirable by the need to lift a dragging Soviet economy from relative stagnation and to face China without having to worry too much about potential threats from the West. It depended on the continuance of a stable West for an indefinite period of time.

It is one thing to look forward in a benevolent sort of way to the ultimate ruin and disruption of the more prosperous parts of the world so that their inhabitants may emerge, those who are not liquidated, purified and purged, happy soldiers of Lenin. It is quite another thing to hurry on this process at the very moment when you wish to call on the fruits of their technology.

Obviously the Russians must view the present state of the West with a certain *Schadenfreude*. But what appalling problems would be presented by the need to police the whole of Europe as well as the satellites. And what opportunities for China to make mischief. Is it a good thing, anyway, for Japan, so close to China (and to the Soviet Union), to be driven desperate by the oil threat? Is it really a good thing on any medium-term view for the Arabs to have a strong independent voice in the ordering of a world which suits Russia pretty well as it is?

There are many other problems to be considered by Mr Brezhnev before he decides on his next move. The Russians are very good at chess, but the world offers more than sixty-four squares.

What I have been suggesting is that faced with problems of the complexity only suggested in this article it is improbable that the Russians will strike out on the clear-cut apocalyptic line which would have appealed to the good Lenin. They will go on wavering between service to a long-term aim which regarded coolly is absurd (but they will not, cannot yet, regard it coolly) and the need of the moment, which is the conservation of the status quo.

Why the Prophet
Was Wrong
1976

*(A reply to the somewhat wholesale nature of Solzhenitsyn's
indictment of the West)*

I hesitate to take issue with one of the outstandingly great men
of the age, a writer of genius, tremendous in vision, heroic in
spirit, unimaginably enduring. It is impossible to be in his
company without being all but overwhelmed by a sense of his
superiority, to use a term now (to our loss) out of fashion. This
does not make him infallible.

Very well, Solzhenitsyn is superior. Besides being a hero and
a genius, he is also a prophet. Prophets, when they bring the
sort of credentials Solzhenitsyn carries with him, must be
listened to. They are too often right, in the spirit if not in the
letter. But they are not necessarily the best people to go to for a
cure. The improvement of society calls, as we all rather drearily
know, for the arts of the possible, and it is the very soul of a
prophet to have no truck with the possible, and to fix himself on
the ideal.

Of course, Solzhenitsyn is right about many things. He is
right about the present demoralisation of the West, above all of
this country and America, in their different ways. He is right
about the military might and the malign hostility of Russia. But
I think the conclusions he draws from both perceptions are, in
important particulars, wrong.

There is no need for me to go on about the West. At the
moment we find ourselves in a fairly comprehensive mess. I
could fill this page with a catalogue of last week's public
ineptitudes, sillinesses, hypocrisies, funks, muddles, greedi-
nesses and betrayals. *So, now, could almost everybody else.* And this
it seems to me is critical. More and more of us are feeling
ashamed and resolving to do better. For the West changes. It
changes constantly. Time and time again in this country, or all

together, we seem to be on the edge of final ruin, and time and time again we pull back. This present moral collapse is so radical and universal that it surely must presage some very great change, unless the whole development of Western history has broken off. We shall emerge, battered, but at least partly purged, on the approaches to a new sort of society. I think the change is taking place even as Solzhenitsyn speaks. And parts of his speech will accelerate the process by making us look more closely at ourselves.

Change of this kind is alien to a Russian. Russia, when it is not engaged in blowing itself up, changes with such glacial deliberation that it is hard for any Russian to grasp our chronic condition of instability and flux. Nor does Solzhenitsyn really like the West. He thinks he is disliking the shabbier, tawdrier aspects of it – drug-culture, porn shops, a Parliament (guardian of our liberties) that listens with respect to Mr Michael Foot. He thinks that what most of us regard as a passing phase of unusual squalor is permanent and irreversible decline.

But I believe that, with so many of his countrymen now and in the past, he does not like our basic ways. He says he used to worship the West, and seems to think it has only recently betrayed itself. But he would have felt the same, coming from Russia, at any time in centuries past. Alexander Herzen in the 1830s also worshipped the West, and was sustained in adversity by his faith. When he came here he was filled with immediate revulsion and spat in our faces. What he had worshipped was not the West, but his image of it. So it is, I believe, with Solzhenitsyn.

Deeply imbued with the quasi-religious, quasi-mystical tradition of Russian patriotism, he is not democratic by nature and cannot really understand how any society can allow the inferior to obstruct the improving activities of the superior. The way we go on seems to him anarchy, not freedom. Contrast him with his friend and admirer, that other hero, Andrei Sakharov, the great physicist and father of the H-bomb, who is so remarkably free from Russian preconceptions. He could write from the pit: 'Only in democratic conditions can a people develop a character fitted for sensible existence in an ever more complicated world.'

This may prove to be impossible even in democratic conditions, but certainly character of the kind required cannot be developed in any other way – only corrupt servility. So many excellent nineteenth-century Russians steadfastly opposed the very idea of a representative assembly because, they said, the people were not ready to participate in government. How were they supposed ever to learn without practice? They were given no practice – and we know what happened.

It was ironic that on the day when Solzhenitsyn in London was urging us to contemplate the invincible might of Russia, the terrible power of the official ideology and the growing hold of the Government over the people, Messrs Brezhnev and Kosygin and the assembled high and mighty of the Soviet Union were beating their chests and droning on about the very same thing, in what turned out to be a very changeless way indeed, on the occasion of the twenty-fifth Party Congress in Moscow.

I do not believe in the Soviet Union as a dynamic power. Anyone who has had the patience to read my far too copious writings over the last thirty-six years will know that I have never believed in it, and why. Certainly Angola has not made me change my mind. Anybody reading the total output of speeches at this Party Congress (or any preceding one) would, I am sure, feel the same. They are the speeches of men without vision or real drive, even the drive or vision of conquest. They are frightened men, greedy for power, desperate for security.

They preside over a deliberately crippled country, vaster and richer in resources than any other in the world, which still cannot feed itself after sixty years of the new régime, which still finds itself unable to maintain what it considers to be an appropriate military establishment as well as a decent standard of living, a country in which initiative and independence of mind, though not erased at sight as under Stalin, are still officially discouraged and kept down by a monstrous police force. Men without an idea in their heads, other than parrot cries from Lenin and deep cunning in ways and means of clinging to power, they hang like a blight over a richly gifted people who are not allowed to think.

Solzhenitsyn, it seems to me (and in this sense Sakharov has also spoken very commandingly), thinks far too much in terms of Marxist ideology as the key to Russian actions, far too little in terms of conventional but extremely cautious imperialism. He also says that the Soviet military establishment is now such that the Politburo cannot avoid war even if it wants to. He says that the nuclear deterrent of the West is unimportant. Why should Soviet Russia need nuclear war to conquer you? he asks. It can take you with its bare hands.

I wonder . . . . Why then does the Soviet Union spend all its riches to the point of exhausting its people, on 'the nuclear deterrent'? Why, if it wants to, doesn't Russia take us with its bare hands instead of spending the substance of its people on making expensive trouble in the Middle East and elsewhere? What does Solzhenitsyn's statement mean? That Russia will overrun first Europe, then America, and colonise us? How? What for? Russia can do very little with its bare hands when it cannot tell for certain that America will not counter intolerable aggression with the atom bomb. Russia can never be sure that this won't happen. And if it comes to bare hand against bare hand, where does Russia stand against China? A little reflection indicates that the last thing Russia can want at the moment is the collapse of the West, for obvious reasons. This remains true even if we deserve to collapse.

Angola has come at a critical moment in African history. Russia, after centuries of trying, has at last, a hundred years too late, broken out into the Mediterranean and the Indian Ocean and is feeling its oats. After the shock and humiliation of its Cuban defeat (far deeper than most of us here realise) Russia is getting its own delicious revenge in Africa – though doubtless rather wryly asking (the more sensible ones among the Politburo) how much this luxury is going to cost.

We have to remember that Mr Brezhnev is in fact what he looks – three-quarters of a century behind the times. It will take some years for the intoxication of free naval movement to wear off. In Russian eyes this stands for that long-deserved, long-denied parity with the Great Powers of the West. Of course there are voices in Moscow urging adventurism: there were always such voices under the Czars. Traditionally, the voices of caution, pulling the other way, usually won. It is possible that the adventurists will overreach themselves and go a little too far. But unlikely. Provided the West does not continue to appear too naked and too uncertain for too long.

Meanwhile, if Solzhenitsyn helps the Americans to get over their Vietnam guilt and come to life again, that will be good. If he could, improbably, persuade Britain to make at least a show of the will to defend itself, that would be good. If he can make us all stop chattering about détente, that will be excellent. But already, even as he was speaking, President Ford was announcing the burial of that idiotic and deceptive word. (This is an example of what I mean by change.) But it will not be good if he encourages the adventurists and the panic-mongers on our side to embark on further Vietnams.

With intermittent lunacies, we have managed to keep our heads for the thirty years since the war. We have lost them lately. But it is about time that we came back to our senses. This sort of thing happens quite often. Meanwhile, Russia appears always the same, but it is indeed slowly changing. We should forego quick profits for businessmen, or even our own treasuries, if this is necessary to keep up the pressure for change. Change must come, however slowly. It is impossible even for Russians to continue for ever under the sort of leadership exhibited at this last Congress. Sooner or later younger men will come up who are sufficiently detached from the past to modify present rigidities.

It is possible, indeed, that among the new names now coming forward there may be some of these. May Solzhenitsyn live to see the beginning of this change. I hope and believe that this splendid figure will have the satisfaction of seeing himself proved as wrong in his political diagnosis as he is unerring in matters of the spirit.

The Lie That
Cripples Russia
1977

All governments are in some degree prisoners of their own pasts, like all individual men and women. But no regime in the history of Europe has been for so long so absolutely imprisoned in its past as the Government of Russia, of the Soviet Union, which claims to be the most forward-looking state ever known. And what a past . . . .

One of the things that distinguishes modern man from, say, the ancient Egyptians, is the never-ceasing attempt to escape from the past, to atone for past errors, to turn bitter experience to good account. Admittedly we do not get very far most of the time, but at least we try – and go on trying. Only the Government of Russia remains stickily fixed in total immobility. It is as though, born in upheaval and coming of age in terror, it never dare move again. The whole extraordinary set-up reminds one of those agrarian theocracies of antiquity, standing still for ever, bowed before brazen idols, until swept away by flood, pestilence or barbaric invasion. And Russia is indeed ruled in the name of a God-King, V. I. Lenin, who supplanted an earlier God-King, the Czar.

It is a voluntary subjection to the past. Mr Brezhnev and his comrades evidently do not want to escape from it. They would not know what to do if they tried. There was a moment in the 1950s when it looked as though, with Stalin dead, Russia would come to life (I say Russia because the Soviet Union is still under the thumb of the Great Russians, who set the tone and rule over the many other peoples, in aggregate almost as numerous as they); but when Khrushchev started knocking down the walls, his colleagues got rid of him and built the walls up again.

So there they are today. And there they were last weekend celebrating a myth, urging us all into the future by pointing resolutely at the past, an anachronism to end all anachronisms, this handful of very elderly heralds of the new dawn standing in a row on top of the God-King's tomb and watching a breath-taking display of lethal hardware that is the supreme achievement to date of the convulsion that was once the dream and hope of millions.

What were they celebrating?

Ten years ago, when the jubilee of the October Revolution was being staged with such overwhelming pomp, I was still writing regularly about Russia, as I had been for twenty years before then. I gave up soon after because with Khrushchev gone, Soviet affairs became so excruciatingly dull – but offensively, brutally dull, not cosily dull – that there seemed nothing new to say. What Mr Brezhnev and his friends were celebrating then, in 1967, was not the Revolution but the emergence of the Soviet Union as a Great Power, equipped with a ruling class in the shape of a formidable bureaucracy, a subservient and profoundly cynical intelligentsia, and an unfathomable proletariat. There has been no change in the last ten years.

Except that this year Mr Brezhnev personally celebrates his apotheosis, his assumption of the Presidency as well as the General Secretaryship of the Communist Party, and the new Brezhnev constitution, which is about as bogus as the Stalin one of 1937, except for one important item: the Communist Party of the Soviet Union is now formally recognised as the seat of power, with the Supreme Soviet as its rubber stamp. And, of course, there was the giveaway vileness of the crushing of the Czechs and Slovaks.

So perhaps it is wrong to say that Mr Brezhnev is immobile: he has regressed a little . . . . And more than a little if one considers his attitude to matters not mentioned at anniversary celebrations, such as the treatment of individuals who are brave enough to query some of the nastier workings of the system.

Russia of course has survived another ten years. It has not collapsed. It has not had a new revolution. It is still a land in which gigantic portraits of Mr Brezhnev can be plastered like grotesquely swollen ikons all over the townscape without anyone ever throwing as much as a rotten egg at one of them. The Kremlin has had its triumphs. For example, by patient and unremitting dedication to the business of building up colossal armaments it has managed to frighten people who should know better.

It still has strange, sometimes comic, effects, the strong Soviet magic. So that, for instance, at the very moment when so many European Communists are turning away from the Muscovite example, up pops a visiting politician, one of the gentlemen who apparently run the British Labour Party, a Mr Kitson, to proclaim to his Russian audience how pleasant he finds it to be in a land that is not run by the British Labour Party . . . .

But the Soviet leaders, to justify all the horror and the wickedness of the Stalin years, to say nothing of the brutal clumsiness of the present, stand in need of greater triumphs than these. They need movement. And they dare not move: for the real cause of Mr Brezhnev's immobilism is not flat feet; it is that he cannot move without letting in a little of the truth.

Soviet power is real, but it has nothing to do with ideology, only with industrial technology; and Russia was making first-class artillery before the Revolution was ever heard of. The power is real, but the Revolution is a myth.

The myth can be kept alive, and the sacred memory of Lenin with it, only by the rigorous concealment of certain truths: the truth, for example, about pre-revolutionary Russia, in 1914 well into its industrial revolution despite feeble government, and culturally bursting out all over, despite an imbecile censorship – that and the terrible truth, never to be whispered, that it was not Lenin who made the Revolution: he was not there.

The Revolution made by others in February 1917 was betrayed in October by Lenin, who then went on to destroy those who had made it – as Stalin, following in his master's footsteps, later went on to destroy nearly all of those who had aided Lenin.

The trouble about myths, or lies, is that those who foster them are stuck with them. Without these myths of the Revolution to sustain him Mr Brezhnev would possess not a shadow of legitimacy or authority. Yet by sedulously maintaining the myths, he makes it impossible for Russia to look truth in the face and wake up and start behaving like a grown-up power instead of a great clumsy idiot child with nasty domestic habits for whom we are for ever having to make allowances.

Heaven knows, I yield to none in my distaste for many aspects of Western life and most Western politicians. But aspects change and politicians do not rule for ever. All govern-ments lie about their records; but in countries where govern-ments are changed every few years, the lies do not have long to stick. All ruling classes lie about themselves, but in relatively free societies there is no way they can close the mouths of those who point to the lies. The Russian Government is never changed and its lies are never challenged except by recklessly courageous individuals, who know that the very people they are fighting for will think them crazy.

All Western peoples have done vile things in the past sixty years, some of them have done appalling things. But there is not one among them that has not seen its misdeeds publicly acknowledged in genuine efforts to escape from its own past. Only Russia has refused to break with its past, pretending that the crimes of two men, Stalin and Beria, are all that has ever been wrong.

How can the future ever be squarely faced, the Soviet peoples salvaged from corruption, the problems of today and tomorrow tackled honestly, if the appalling past, upon which the present Soviet leaders take their stand, is not rejected instead of being absorbed with all its poison into the living present?

And this prostration before the myth, the lie, affects not only the Soviet peoples, it affects us all. For so long as the rulers of Russia go on pretending (or convincing themselves, it does not matter which) that their country has anything to celebrate but the size of its armed forces and the scale of its armaments, so long as they pretend to believe, or convince themselves that they believe, in the nonsense they talk about world revolution, so they condemn themselves to perpetual struggle with the West, a struggle that cripples their own people even more than it cripples us.

The Price Brezhnev Should Be Asked to Pay
1977

The Helsinki story is much older than most people imagine, or remember. It goes back to the closing years of the Khrushchev time when the idea of a European summit conference, a peace conference in effect, to bring about a new understanding based on recognition of the status quo, was being quietly and informally floated in a number of European capitals.

Khrushchev fell in October 1964, but less than a year later came the first formal call for the conference that finally materialised at Helsinki. The ideal was now Mr Brezhnev's own baby, and he pressed it very hard upon a reluctant West – until, in 1968, the crime against Czechoslovakia made a mockery of Russian overtures. But quite surprisingly soon, the West showed itself eager to let bygones be bygones and to forget the savage bullying of a people no less European than any member of the EEC.

The game was on again, and for year after year Moscow plugged away, gradually overcoming Western resistance to a vast conference that many saw as being at best meaningless and at worst setting the seal of approval on the Soviet presence in the middle of Europe.

The Final Act, signed by thirty-five nations at Helsinki, after three years of stubborn wrangling, turned out to be a long way from what the Russians desired. On the one hand, for example, the countries of Eastern and Central Europe were not formally delivered into their hands; on the other, they themselves had to agree to all sorts of stipulations to do with human rights, freedom of movement, free dissemination of information, etc., which they regarded with extreme distaste. This was the price Mr Brezhnev had to pay for presenting himself as the architect of détente.

The fact remained, nevertheless, that the conference did throw a cloak of respectability, rather desperately needed, over the Brezhnev Government; and the main thing to set against this was the (from Moscow's point of view) subversive potential of the human rights, etc., stipulations. The question was, would Moscow carry out her pledges and, if not, would the West turn a blind eye?

I stress this past history because, to hear some people talk, one would think that détente was a tender plant jealously nurtured by the West and liable to be blighted for ever by a Brezhnev reacting sharply against any Western criticisms. It is nothing of the kind. The pursuit of détente has been a consistent and sturdy element in Soviet policy for at least a decade and a half – no less real and no less sturdy and in Soviet eyes, necessary, than the arms race.

Indeed, it is not too much to say that it is one aspect of the arms race. For it is through détente that the Russians have hoped to increase the availability of Western credits, know-how and material to support the heavy burden of their armaments – and at the same time to take the heat out of superior American technology.

This does not mean that détente is necessarily disadvantageous to us, unless we wretchedly deceive ourselves into believing that it is no longer desirable to make ourselves strong enough to stand up to the Soviet army and navy. For a century and a half Western statesmen and soldiers, in most matters sane and clear-headed, have allowed themselves to be hypnotised into a state of chronic jitters by the spectacle of Russia's apparently overwhelming armed might, which has invariably, when put to the test, proved inadequate.

So it is today. I am not suggesting that the weapons now in Russian hands are not infinitely more terrible or lethal than anything dreamt of before; but I do believe that the minds behind the hands are no more decisive than the minds of their Czarist predecessors – infinitely dogged in defence, aggressive in short bursts.

It is reasonable enough to ask what on earth the Kremlin wants with so formidable an accumulation of armies and military hardware if no aggression is planned.

But do the Americans plan aggression? No, it is fear that drives them to prodigies of invention and technology. The Russians are also driven by fear, and their fear is none the less real because it is misguided. Further, to the traditional Russian paranoia, augmented by the consequences of 1917, is now added a resurgence of pride. Obviously the Party leaders and the generals and the admirals want to be ready for war; but they are also, I am sure, intoxicated (perhaps even dangerously so) by the consciousness that they, children of the very common people, have succeeded where the Czars forever failed: they have won the freedom of the seas, access to all parts of the globe, to which their aristocratic predecessors aspired in vain and to which they believe they have as much right as the British, or the French, or the Americans – as, indeed, they have.

What they will do with this freedom remains to be seen. No doubt they are pleased to feel that they can, if it seems profitable, show the flag in a threatening manner all over the place, lend moral or physical support to far-flung disciples if this seems desirable, cope with the NATO navies and cut the supply lines of the West in the event of war. But I find it hard to believe in any clear belligerent intention on their part. In so far as Russia is in a mood to expand it is likely that her forward movement will be in the old Czarist and Stalinist tradition, not leaping forward, but cautiously feeling out and absorbing what comes close to hand, a mud-slide rather than a *Blitzkrieg*.

Détente in itself does not mean disarmament, still less an end to the ideological offensive. To the Kremlin it means conceding as little as need be to ensure such controlled intercourse between East and West as seems imperative – that and an insurance against China. The first part of this formula would seem to be reasonable from our point of view as well. The matter for discussion among ourselves is how far we should go in helping Mr Brezhnev to develop the Soviet economy (for the Soviet Union is still an underdeveloped one) when he continues to be openly hostile. This, of course, depends on a sensible estimate of the depth and force of the hostility – which is where the Belgrade preparatory conference comes in.

As for the immediate question that worries so many people, whether President Carter's proclaimed determination to stand up for human rights will wreck détente, the short answer is that it will not. It exasperates the Russians and sharpens their suspicion of American intentions: they simply don't know what to make of Jimmy Carter (are we ourselves so sure?). They will make threatening noises and commit a few *bêtises* to indicate their displeasure. It is also understandable that some people with special interests to safeguard may feel that Carter is rocking the boat a little recklessly, e.g. Chancellor Schmidt with his special arrangement for the purchase of souls from East Germany.

But it should be obvious to us that to allow our leaders to be blackmailed by Brezhnev into keeping official silence about his outstandingly nasty actions would be the ultimate betrayal of decency. This would be so even if the chief violator of the decencies had not put his signature to a document celebrating the rights he violates, and even if he himself were less free with criticism of those he attacks for presuming to criticise him.

Mr Brezhnev is evidently an extremely vain man. For some time he has shown himself as determined to figure in the history books as the fountainhead of peace as well as the master of land and sea forces on a gigantic scale. Now he has gone one better. He has given his unfortunate country a new constitution (the fact that it means no more than its ludicrous predecessor, the Stalin constitution, is neither here nor there), and on top of that he and his colleagues have agreed (no doubt with the exception of the incontinently dismissed Podgorny) that the Soviet Union cannot exist without a supreme chieftain, thus combining leadership of the Communist Party with the formal office of Head of State for the first time in its history.

This has nothing to do with Belgrade. What does matter there, as the delegates try to hammer out the procedure and the pattern for the full-dress conference later this year, is that the Western spokesman should continue to exact a price from Brezhnev in return for his claim to be a peacemaker and a champion of the people – this time by exposing as often as necessary and in proper detail the breaking of so many of his Helsinki promises, and asking again and again why in the Soviet Union and elsewhere men and women are being actively persecuted for trying to hold their masters to their pledges. If this means that we must pay more attention to the motes in our own eyes, so much the better.

The Old Men in
the Kremlin
1980

Too often and too easily, hypnotised by sheer quantity, we
think of Russia as an unfettered giant; her Government's
freedom to move in any direction it likes inhibited only by fear
of nuclear incineration.

In fact, like every other country in the world, she is the
prisoner of her own history, traditions, preconceptions, immemorial fears. Perhaps *more* than any other country, because
Russia's history has been so special to her, her traditions so
ingrown, her preconceptions so deliberately exalted into articles of faith, her fears so ancient and frequently well founded.

Certainly the Government of Russia, more than any other,
shivers at even the most distant prospect of any departure from
the status quo, sitting on the lid so heavily that it takes an
explosion on the scale of the 1917 Revolution to bring about any
effective change. Even then, when the dust has settled, it is
soon discovered (thankfully?) that ancient customs have not
died.

One of the troubles with Russia is that almost any useful
change in the status quo is bound to be giving something up: so
often her ingrown habit of taking hold of more than she can
comfortably manage, simply because if she does not somebody
else may, produces a situation in which the slightest change of
grip means that something escapes. This is not to be borne! So
the grip is not changed, even when it hurts.

At the same time the age-old principle of over-insurance,
which drives her eternally to push absurdly extended frontiers
ever farther outwards, continues to operate in an unco-
ordinated and opportunist manner (which she invariably seeks
to rationalise as some sort of a crusade), making that grip still
more convulsive.

There is some excuse for this. The vast bulk of Russia, the
Soviet Empire, on the map so frightening to Western eyes, looks

very different when you are sitting in the middle of it. Then you are conscious not of protective bulk but only of an extravagant and terrible length of highly vulnerable frontier.

To be in Moscow, as I was, when Hitler had sliced through that frontier and watch on the map the sinister black arrows marking the armoured spearheads of the German advance snaking ever closer, with no natural obstacles in their way, until they were actually beginning to curl round the city itself, was to understand something of the depth of the compulsion to push that frontier away, even if this made the land still harder to defend.

In the light of Russia's past the only thing new or revolutionary about the march into Afghanistan was that we allowed it to happen. Ever since the days of the wretched Czar Paul, there have been Russians in high places who have hankered after control of that wild country, the gateway to India – and there have been others, more influential, who have said enough was enough. Until lately, Britain put up a warning notice on that gateway; but this has been taken down, and it was only to be expected that sooner or later Moscow would be moved to gild the lily by 'making sure' of Kabul – whether as a vaguely defensive move against nameless dangers from Iran or Pakistan, or as a potentially useful jumping-off ground for further adventures, I imagine Mr Brezhnev himself would be hard put to say.

In the light of Russia's past, also, it is clear that as the old, old men in the Kremlin contemplate the goings-on in Poland and wonder what on earth to do, they must be visited by a sad sense of *déja vu*. The great Lenin himself burnt his fingers over Poland in the early days of the Workers' Paradise, while Stalin, never an optimist, seems really to have believed that he had destroyed Polish independence once and for all when he murdered practically the entire Officers' Corps in Katyn Forest and elsewhere – and then invited the Germans to massacre the Home Army, the Resistance Army, in Warsaw.

But in 1956 the Poles bobbed up again, and Khrushchev (or his advisers) knew enough about history to realise that Soviet tanks could not smash the Poles as quickly as they could smash the Hungarians, or quietly subdue them, as they were later to subdue the Czechs. Brezhnev and his advisers still know that.

This does not mean that they might not decide that a destructive combination of civil and national war is the lesser of two evils. It does mean that they are having to think very hard indeed – not theoretically and irresponsibly in a void, which comes naturally to them, but practically and with reference to an immediate issue – the sort of thing which goes against the grain of these incorrigible doctrinaires.

So although there is nothing to stop them crushing Poland, as Hitler crushed her forty-one years ago, and Czar Alexander II before that in 1863, and Nicholas I before that in 1830, and Catherine the Great before that in the eighteenth century, they know that they would be facing a nation in arms, that the fighting would be bitter and perhaps protracted, costly, *and very close to home* – that to invite the East Germans to fight Poles would (there is no other way of putting it) bring the house down: the house being the Warsaw Pact.

Even without East Germany, Russian intervention would bring the house down anyway. The bogus fabric of the Warsaw Pact would be in tatters. I say bogus because the Warsaw Pact exists only, as it were, by courtesy of ourselves. We imagine it. What on earth are all these peoples, held together by the Soviet Army, supposed to have in common except mutual hatred? And the mutual hatred of the Russians and the Poles is something special: even that free and liberal spirit, the great poet Pushkin, was tainted by it.

Of course the Soviet Army is all lined up and ready to move at a signal from Moscow: it is no good thinking about using force if you are not in a position to apply it when needed (a lesson we have still to learn). But, the more fire-eating marshals notwithstanding, I don't think the signal will be given unless and until Brezhnev sees the very foundations of the Communist order, the security police, being seriously threatened. If that happens it will.

The trouble is that Russia cannot take Poland without reducing it to the condition it was in after the agonies of 1863, and Brezhnev knows it. He may be compelled to do this if the Poles can't stop in time. His tougher and sillier advisers even now may urge him, hoping that the West will undertake the feeding of the Poles (Moscow certainly cannot) once the Soviet marshals have had their fun and the country is in ruins. I doubt it. Russia would be left a moral leper, with a ruined 'grand alliance' and a crippling economic liability.

This is the sort of thing I mean by Russian vulnerability. The Soviet Union is in such a pickle with a limping economy (one of the differences between Russia and us is that we can sometimes publicly recognise our failures; the Russians cannot), shortages of the most elementary foodstuffs, a dead hand of a political system, and the appalling burden of armaments, apparently considered necessary to show how up to date they are, and to stare America, Western Europe and China in the face. To what purpose? Even Mr Brezhnev must sometimes ask that question.

Yury Andropov: Prisoner of His Country's Lies
1983

What could be more beguiling, what more in tune with the spirit of the age, than the plea from Moscow, contained in Mr Alexander Bovin's article in last Sunday's *Observer*, for a new mood of tolerance and compromise between East and West and an easing of ideological, or 'theological', conflict? Live and let live . . . .

No doubt in the eyes of the Lord we are all sinners. If Mr Andropov has been converted to this view, then let us give thanks. He will have a great deal of highly instructive confessing to do. But there have been no confessions yet, and a Soviet Attenborough would have a pretty rough time of it today. So we have to assume that Mr Bovin's article is part of a new and cleverer propaganda offensive: this should help to keep us on our toes, and we shall be none the worse for that.

Nobody, I imagine, could be more critical than the present writer of the crude imbecilities, and the sins, of so many Western leaders in the handling of the Russian problem. The fact remains that the Reagans and the Thatchers and the Foots, etc., are, and have to be, responsive to ordinary men and women of good will who want to make the world a better place and expect (which is not the same as getting) certain standards from their champions. Mr Andropov is not responsive in this way. He is, in the deepest sense, irresponsible.

Failure to recognise this simple little fact is one of the things that make all talk about the sort of man he is (intelligent? flexible? cultured?) largely irrelevant and vain. He is *Kremlin Man*. And *Kremlin Man* is different in kind from all other politicians, speaking his own language and basing his conduct on assumptions radically different from those of the rest of mankind.

The Soviet leadership does not accept, and has never accepted, the principle of 'live and let live' in its relations with the outer world. In the person of Lenin it declared war on bourgeois society everywhere, and for some time thought it might win quickly. It is very much to be doubted whether Mr Andropov today really and actively believes that the entire world will one day be Sovietised, happy to look prayerfully towards Moscow for leadership and light, but he *talks* in these terms and his talk is reflected in his behaviour – or vice versa.

If Andropov wants to change things all he has to say, in suitable arcane phrases, is that once upon a time, and for what then seemed to be quite good historical reasons, the Bolsheviks believed that they were destined to revolutionise and re-order the world, and that anything or anybody standing in the way of this manifest destiny must be destroyed – or helped to destroy itself. But, he might go on, the world no longer looks quite so simple and the Soviet Union, having achieved Great Power status, understands that other societies must be allowed to go to hell in their own way: it will devote its future energies to the promotion of its national interests in so far as this activity is compatible with maintaining a balance of peace – in other words, to behave like any other country, and, no doubt, with at least the same proneness to expensive error.

He has not said this, or anything like it, nor is he likely to do so. Why not?

The Kremlin is the prisoner of its own lies. I don't mean the sort of shabby lies of expediency that all politicians and most of the rest of us fall into. All societies depend very much on hypocrisy and self-deception, and the active compulsive liar (who would not know the truth if he saw it) often supplies that little extra *zing* that keeps things moving. From time to time an entire people, or the greater part of it, goes mad (Dreyfus, McCarthy, Suez, Vietnam). Sooner or later these failings, offences, crimes are publicly exposed and we hope to do better next time, and sometimes do. To go no farther from home, look at Germany . . . . Like the preacher, we are all against sin.

But not Kremlin Man. In Russia there is no sin except against the state – which, at the moment, is Yury Andropov. In the Soviet Union the lie is institutionalised, not a cheap expedient, brazen or furtive, but an instrument of policy, cherished, burnished. The sanctification of the lie by Lenin, who declared in effect that the only moral criterion was whether a given action helped the Revolution or hindered it, and the basing not only of the Soviet system of government but also of Soviet foreign policy on systematic deception, sets Kremlin Man apart.

Mr Andropov is caught up in the lie. The Soviet Union is the only country in the Old World which has not begun to escape from its past by admitting its past crimes. This is surely a most prohibitively heavy burden: not only crushing morale, initiative and human decency, but also distorting and crippling an economy based on doctrinally inspired agricultural and industrial systems which have only faint connections with reality and have to be subverted before anything at all can be produced.

Clearly it needs something like a genius to break out of this situation, which would be ludicrous if it were not tragic. Brezhnev did not even try. It suited him down to the ground, just as it suited, and suits, the horde of official functionaries (not just the upper crust, the *gratin*, the famous *nomenklatura*, but the Party activists all down the line from Red Square to the remotest provinces) over whom Mr Andropov has now assumed formal control – for how long, nobody can guess.

Khrushchev, erratically and often dottily, tried very hard, somehow hanging on to full membership of the human race through all. But Andropov?

Even if he has perceived the lie, or some of it, and would like to break out of it, has he the power? Think for a moment of the almost insuperable difficulty facing any reforming minister in any Western democracy when he tries to get rid of the duds in his own department and cut out red tape, overmanning, waste. Then reflect that *every single aspect of life* in the Soviet Union is in fact a part of the state apparatus and that the tempo and quality of life are regulated by literally millions of Party officials and state functionaries, largely duds (this being a law of life) possessing almost infinite powers of obstruction and a vested interest in the status quo.

But does he want to try? Andropov on the face of it is Kremlin Man *in excelcis*. It would be quite wrong to think of him as one of those rather jolly and intelligent KGB careerists who know that almost everything is wrong but have decided that if you can't beat the system you had better join it and avail yourself of its fruits. There are not as many of these as is romantically believed, but they exist, sharing the uniforms and the privileges of the vilest of the vile.

Andropov is made of sterner stuff. He is not a KGB man at all. He was put in above the KGB to clean out the stables. And he was put in by the Party, which is his only home.

After some years as a dedicated and quietly rising functionary in Stalin's Party, which brought him into the power house of the machine, he was shunted off to Budapest and there, first as Counsellor, then as Ambassador, made good. Somehow he persuaded Hungarians to trust him, and when the time came to put down the 1956 uprising he kept his head when all around him were losing theirs. His crowning achievement was to make the Hungarians believe that the Soviet tanks were going away for good. He was able to persuade General Maleter, commander of the 'rebel' Hungarian forces, to visit him under safe conduct at the Soviet Embassy to discuss the situation. There Maleter was seized, taken away, and in due course shot. The tanks, of course, came back.

This display of firm and decisive treachery made him the obvious man to take charge of Moscow's relations with Communist Parties inside the Soviet bloc. And it was from this eminence that in 1967, in good time to preside over the re-Sovietisation of Czechoslovakia, he was moved to run the KGB, reorganise it and make sense of it.

Certainly he improved its image, which needed a bit of polishing. But what he will be remembered for has been the systematic elimination of dissidents wherever they showed their heads, while at the same time clearly perceiving the necessity of permitting, encouraging even, some degree of intellectual activity if the Soviet Union was not to die of cerebral inanition.

Compared with Beria, Andropov has been gentleness itself; but it is a gentleness that shows itself in peculiar ways: for example, the practice of consigning awkward citizens to lunatic asylums (particularly those who base their position on the Soviet Constitution and/or the Helsinki agreement) became under Andropov a growth industry.

Of course he is an improvement on Stalin, more intelligent than Brezhnev (therefore more worth watching). But it is hard to see how he can be expected to inaugurate a new era. The main hope for Russia now, it seems to me, is that Andropov will be intelligent enough to sack the Party duds in droves and bring in new talent born into the post-Stalin era, new talent which might indeed, freed from antique institutions, see the way to change.

Stalin himself was forced to do this sort of thing as an emergency wartime measure in 1941 and 1942 when the old guard of dug-out commanders had to give way to a new wave of younger generals who went on to win the war. But Stalin remained Stalin, and it is hard to believe that Andropov will suddenly transform himself.

It might be a good thing if the West made the most of this slow change to develop an intelligent and coherent policy of its own, based on unshakeable strength but also actively seeking ways and means of reducing the grounds for Russian distrust – perhaps by trying to behave at least as well as we should like the Russians to behave.

No Tears . . .
and Not Much Hope
1984

No tears for Yuri Andropov . . . (who and what induced Mrs Thatcher to express 'regret' at the demise of this wretched man? Surely the Foreign Office can do better than that.)

All his life he was a party careerist in the direct Stalin tradition. Wholesale slaughter of his betters in the 1930s gave him his big chance. He moved into the Western consciousness in 1956 when, as Soviet Ambassador to Hungary, he exhibited a talent for elaborate treachery and deception and ruthlessness in execution (from persuading the Hungarians to believe that the Russian tanks were moving away for good to handing over Imre Nagy to his death) which must have stimulated the reluctant admiration of his rivals.

Putting a proper value on these talents, Brezhnev after a short interval made him head of the KGB in time to preside over the final crushing of Czechoslovak independence in 1968. He occupied his office in the Lubyanka for 15 years, being transferred back into the ruling party apparatus in time to make a successful bid for the Brezhnev succession.

During those 15 years he showed more interest in intrigue, misinformation, subversion of every kind, than in killing; but he devoted a special corner of his attention to the dispersal and destruction of any dissident movement that showed above the surface. Above all, those simple individuals who took the Helsinki Agreement seriously and set out to monitor its terms.

Solzhenitsyn was thrown out, Sakharov exiled to Gorki; many to this day languish in his camps. Above all, he created a growth industry in the imprisonment of perfectly sane people as lunatics in psychiatric hospitals in order to avoid open trials. Many of these victims languish as he lies dead in state. Will the survivors find new hope in his departure? I doubt it.

How he might have developed as Führer, we shall never know. He was at least an activist in a nasty sort of way, which is more than can be said of Brezhnev, who was content for years to rest on his faded laurels. He saw the need for waking up Soviet industry, shaking up the entrenched bureaucracy and making some sort of show of stamping out not merely corruption but endemic and professional idleness. But he never really began to face the basic causes of these troubles.

His succession was not effortless: there was quite a struggle with the entrenched beneficiaries of Brezhnev's stagnant regime, and he never had time to complete the rout of the opposition. If the Politburo can think of nothing better to do than put the dreariest of them all, Chernenko, in as at least a caretaker the lookout prospect for any immediate change is thin.

In foreign affairs he had no time (even the inclination) to make any serious impact. Soviet relations with the outer world quietly seized up. After all this nonsense about a cold, how on earth can we take the country seriously that makes non-excuses of that kind and cannot admit that its chief is seriously ill over a matter of a year? All Gromyko could do, assuming this aged champion wished to do anything at all, was to find every excuse for bringing as much foreign activity as possible to a standstill, while restraining the more reckless elements in the Armed Services from unnecessary adventures.

Andropov never showed the slightest awareness of the need to re-think East-West relations – any more than Mrs Thatcher or President Reagan seemed to have done until a week ago.

How he would have developed we have not the faintest idea. He started off the notion of a domestic spring-cleaning with a bang, distributed a few exemplary punishments, got rid of a number of dead-heads, replacing them when possible with professional policemen. He began to stir up a stagnant condition of trade and industry – and then effectively died.

He was hampered by Chernenko's men, a vast satrapy of bureaucrats and provincial party bosses and their followers, whose sole interest was the preservation of their own interests and the status quo. Most of these are still there.

There have been hopes that the 52-year-old Gorbachev might be groomed for the succession, but even Gorbachev would be hemmed in by his seniors, and so would the rather older Romanov – the suspect but able Leningrad chieftain who lived it up a little too obviously (has he been forgiven some of his extravagances, such as illegally using one of Catherine the Great's dinner services in the Hermitage for a private junket, and being careless enough to break some of the pieces?).

But Andropov could not have achieved the succession without the support of the 75-year-old ageless wonder, Andrei Gromyko, and the 76-year-old Dmitri Ustinov (now looking very ill himself) who must be the most able manager in the whole of the Soviet Union, though few had heard of him until he emerged as Minister of Defence, his chest covered with medals, a few years ago. He had kept himself until then, for reasons quite unclear, very much in the background. His calibre is best shown by the fact that he controlled the whole of the armaments industry throughout the war, an unknown figure presiding over miracles. But both these men must be very set in their ways.

What we do not know, and may not know for some time to come, is the way the Gorbachevs are thinking – they and what must be a host of their contemporaries in fairly high and responsible positions. Are they so coloured by their lifelong environment and corrupted by their rivalries that they are incapable of launching any radical attempt to make the Soviet Union work and bring it back into the brotherhood of nations?

Or have they minds of their own? Meanwhile, the least we can do is exhibit an immediate readiness to bring Russia back into the global fold if she shows the least sign of wishing to do so. This will involve some radical thinking on the part of an American administration which has shown very little sign of thought or global consciousness, or the least idea of any sort of action, except lobbing 15-inch shells into the Lebanese hillside. It will involve, for instance, understanding that Russia, if she is to be brought back into the world, will have to be a party to any agreement in the Middle East: she simply cannot be frozen out. Can Reagan, can Thatcher, think more clearly about that than their new opposite numbers? It would be nice to think so.

PART II

The Germans in Russia
Review of *Dance of Death* by Erich Kern
1951

It is just ten years since the German armies, killing and burning as they went, swept across the Russian frontier through the fields of high summer. Life in those days had a beautiful simplicity. There was only one problem: how to kill Germans. The Russians looked like killing a great number, and so the Government which until the day before had been quietly assisting in our own destruction, became overnight our ally. Caught up in this colossal process, very soon I myself was in Russia, as part of a military mission; and almost at once we were being treated to a private preview of the Kremlin's way with foreigners which has since nearly driven the world to despair. It made us pretty desperate at the time. But the Russians were killing Germans: and, the Kremlin notwithstanding, we in Moscow were filled with a profound sense of community with the Russian people then suffering intolerably at the hands of a nation which seemed to think that trampling down other people's corn, burning their houses, killing and torturing anyone who resisted, was the proper way to solve the more complex human problems.

Later in the year, I remember, when dusk fell early to begin the deadly nights of the most terrible winter for a century, I would sometimes watch the endless busloads of Russian wounded, still filthy, unshaven, and with first field-dressings soaked in blood, being unloaded in the snow at the steps of a Moscow hospital; and I would comfort myself with the thought of the Germans at that very moment miserably freezing on the bare and windswept plain which stretched away from the city. Among them was the author of this book.

This is what he felt like that summer, ten years ago, when he moved with his division into Russia:

But soon our nostrils were filled with the stench of burning villages. The air trembled with the distant rumble of guns.

Our hearts beat faster, seasoned though we were to war. Tomorrow's battle never fails to put a clamp round the heart. We wrote our first postcards home.

This sort of thing had to be stopped, and so, at unimaginable cost, it was.

Life, alas, is less simple today. Russia has become the enemy, and we see that in a sense she always was the enemy. We tend to overlook the distinctions between one enemy and another. Instead, we find ourselves sighing for the lost certainties of war – some of us so deeply that to save the pain of thinking we would plunge tomorrow into the cooling oblivion of the great illusion, moving more than half way to self-destruction. I can think of no better antidote to this sort of mood than this book by a soldier, intelligent, likeable and serious, who is so perfectly identified with a race which has sought again and again for cut-and-dried solutions to the insoluble, for short cuts to impossible ends. This, told with extreme vividness and considerable narrative power, is the story of one of the short cuts. Its author, chastened but still uncomprehending, is now looking for another.

He was a young sergeant of the Waffen SS, a peacetime journalist, a convinced Nazi, serving in the crack division, Leibstandarte Adolf Hitler; and although he was always being sent off on special missions to do with SS affairs, he saw a great deal of heavy fighting in various parts of Russia. He could think for himself, and he differed violently from his superiors in a number of ways, even to jeopardising his whole future by protesting about the Rosenberg policy of subjugation, exploitation and atrocity. This was not because it seemed wicked to him, but because it was inexpedient. He believed, probably correctly, that if the Germans had treated the Ukrainians as human beings they would have won the war. He would not have regretted this. He saw the whole Russian campaign not as an act of wickedness but simply as a mistake. It would be a tenable point of view were it not spoilt by the fact that it is not extended to the other side. For example, Sergeant Kern considered the Kremlin very wicked to condemn Leningrad to the horrors of its long drawn-out siege. And he can describe with bitterness the shooting of six German prisoners by the Russians and with no emotion at all but a sense of strangeness and incomprehension the bearing of the four thousand Soviet prisoners who were lined up and shot in reprisal for that action. He remains, proudly, a Nazi betrayed by his leaders.

But if this book is invaluable for its unconscious revelation of certain aspects of the German mentality, it will be read mainly as a first-hand account of the fighting on the Eastern front as seen from the German side, and for what it has to tell about the Russian people and their army under the stress of war. The swift narrative of the apocalyptic strike against the background of forest and steppe is moving and enthralling; some of the set scenes, like the tremendous withdrawal to the non-existent Dnieper line, are superbly done and stamp the memory; the evocation of the disintegration of the whole German army before Malinowski's final drive on Budapest and Vienna has a quite extraordinary power. But even more fascinating than the record of the fighting is the picture of the Russians as seen from the other side. All the ingredients are here for an understanding which the author himself comes nowhere near achieving. In a thousand glimpses from real life, recorded with vividness and fidelity to fact, we enter into the endless paradoxes of Russian behaviour, and are given the raw material to construct an image of the whole for ourselves: the mindless automata, products of the Stalin regime, who suddenly reveal in each and every individual the human spirit shining at its brightest; the surrounded company fighting with desperate stubbornness to the last round, and then surrendering with total submissiveness and a sort of naïve delight in their captors; the prisoner who, lined up for execution, seizes a shovel to split the skull of the hated commissar standing next to him – and then, when offered release, proudly steps back into the ranks to be shot with his comrades; the mass desertions and the heroic stands; the loathing of countless individuals for the regime which goes side by side with acceptance of it as the cross the beloved country has to bear.

German character, Russian reality, the war in the East: this book may be read for its light on all these things. It is also, in a sense, a parable.

Spectator

165

Introduction to *Child of the Revolution*
by Wolfgang Leonhard
1957 [1967]

Here is a book which floods some very dark places with light. It is the story of a gifted and highly intelligent young man, a German, not a Russian, who was brought up in the Soviet Union and in the bosom of the Soviet Communist Party. At twenty-seven, in 1949, he broke away, sacrificing a most promising career as a privileged Party functionary in Ulbricht's East Germany. He took this courageous step not because he hungered for the flesh pots of the West, nor because he had become infected with bourgeois ideas, but, as he saw it, for Lenin's sake. And he made his escape from East Berlin, carrying his life in his hands, not to the bright lights of the Kurfürstendamm but to the then dreary rigours of Tito's Yugoslavia, in those days hungry, cold, and dangerous.

It is this aspect of his story which makes his testimony unique: he writes not as a lapsed Communist, or a man turning against his God, or a refugee from the harshness of the Soviet system, but as a convinced Marxist who thought he was a better socialist than his Soviet foster-parents. These had reared him in unimaginable seclusion, cut off from all reality, with the ruling idea of fashioning him in their own image; readers of this book will see how nearly they succeeded in this aim. And just as a very good way of grasping the true nature and structure of a foreign language is to listen attentively to a foreigner talking broken English, so an excellent way of understanding the Soviet Communist mentality is to listen, no less attentively, to Mr Leonhard telling his experiences. It took him some time to learn the language of the West at all, and even now he is far from word perfect and thus gives us invaluable insights into the idiom he has forsaken. Further, he refuses all truck with wisdom after the event, which seems to me admirable and refreshing. How easy it would have been for him to put a distance between himself and his long years in Russia, to write of his Russian life in the light of knowledge lately acquired, to slant his narrative at an angle designed to appeal to Western sentiment, to smother the absorbing actuality of his early life in hindsight, all done with mirrors. Instead, apologising for nothing, he has given us an exact image of that life as he lived it and a recension of his blinkered thoughts as he thought them.

I don't know at all precisely what Leonhard's politics are now. He has promised to tell us in a later book. But it is clear that he remains certainly a Marxist and probably a Leninist of sorts. He was certainly an ardent and uncritical Leninist when he broke with Russia. But he has learnt a great deal since then. It was soon after he had burst through the Iron Curtain that I had the privilege of meeting him in Belgrade; and he was rather like one of those legendary young men who, we are told, from time to time emerge from the jungle emitting strange sounds, having spent their childhood and adolescence in the exclusive company of wolves – or bears. Communication was, to put it mildly, incomplete. He had broken with Stalin, but he still could not face the bourgeois world in its starkness. Although his instinct and his reason had told him that there was something badly wrong with the Soviet system he was still very much of the opinion that his quarrel was with Stalin only – an opinion then shared by Marshal Tito, on whose mercy he had thrown himself. At that time (it was 1949), when Yugoslavia was being made to suffer bitterly for Tito's defiance of Stalin, Djilas was publishing articles to justify the Yugoslav heresy. And I remember arguing with Leonhard that if Djilas went on developing his ideas he would soon find himself in direct opposition not only to Stalin but also to Lenin and the whole concept of the dictatorship of the proletariat. This turned out to be an accurate prophesy, but Leonhard contested it hotly. Nevertheless, although communication was incomplete, he was the first believing Leninist with whom I found it possible to talk politics in a sensible and coherent way.

I am sure Leonhard will not mind this somewhat clinical approach to himself and his very human narrative. After all, his story is gripping and enthralling by any standards, but its first value is essentially clinical. It is the story of a slow awakening, unconscious, like all awakenings. We may wake up in the small hours to the noise of a motor car revving up in first gear: we say this was the noise that woke us up. But in fact there have been many preceding noises, the slamming of doors, shrieks of unaccountable laughter, boisterous farewells, futile attempts to start the engine before the ignition is switched on . . . . These noises have been going on for a long time, and all the time they have been dragging us from sleep, slowly nearer to the surface of consciousness, perhaps weaving the inane racket into a waking dream. The noise we first consciously hear, the engine at last starting, marks only the moment of return to perfect consciousness. This was the moment of Leonhard's life represented by the expulsion of Yugoslavia from the Cominform. This, he thinks, is what woke him up. But in fact, it is clear from his narrative, he had been waking up long before then.

As a child he was fast asleep. His mother was one of those foreigners, a German, who went to Moscow to work for Lenin's Revolution and found themselves sent to Siberia by Stalin. We are all by now familiar with the mood in the Soviet Union during the great purge years of the middle Thirties, when Leonhard was at school in Moscow. Many know a great deal more than Leonhard knew – either then, as a schoolboy, or later, when he made his escape. A few may even be a little irritated by Leonhard's conscientious and far from complete recapitulation of matters so familiar to them. I ask them to lay irritation aside. For what they are being told is not the history of the purges but what the purge years looked like to a youngster brought up in the seclusion of a Party school. We have not had this before. We see a consciousness already, in childhood, three-quarters paralysed by careful conditioning, so that this child could accept the sudden and unexplained disappearance of his mother, the impact of the purges on teachers and the parents of his school companions, and still not ask questions. After that, Leonhard had no other parent than the Soviet Communist Party, which treated him well.

From my own observation, I should say that Soviet conditioning reaches its peak of completeness at about this period, twelve to fifteen. Then, on the surface, it may appear to be perfect. But soon afterwards, except in the case of those chosen in advance for total dedication to the Party apparatus (a mere handful of the Party membership) the effects of the conditioning begin to wear off, until they fall away under pressure from the irresistible drive of human nature – that human nature which reformers refer to in tones of contempt and contumely, but which, developing, is in fact the sole and glorious asset of mankind – though always lingering in odd corners of the mind. For the ordinary Russian, brought up in the Pioneers and the Komsomol, but not going on to full Party membership, is, I should say, rather less thoroughly conditioned that the average product of a British public school, for reasons which we need not go into here – and a great deal less thoroughly conditioned than the average American high school product. Leonhard was not a Russian, but a German, thus, perhaps, more malleable than most Russians; he was a foreigner, thus, perhaps, tending to try harder in the desired sense; he was an intellectual, thus easy prey for the practical men of action who now rule Russia in the name of Communism; and he was chosen and dedicated from his childhood. His conditioning was thus unusually complete. But in the end it failed – as in fact it fails with everyone; and in Leonhard's case the failure was acknowledged and proclaimed because he was a man of unusual integrity who was prepared to sacrifice his career and put his life at hazard for the sake of principle.

It was a big sacrifice. He had gone so far that at the age of twenty-three he was selected to return to East Berlin in the train of Ulbricht to build up a Communist regime in East Germany. And he was so far gone that he enjoyed it. Even so, he had been turning uneasily in his sleep for a long time past. He had, indeed, under the shock of a certain stimulus, almost awakened in the summer of 1941. So artificial and cloistered had been his existence until then, that he is still able to say in good faith that the German invasion immediately gave the Soviet people a sense of identity with their leadership. In fact, at the moment of which he speaks, whole units and formations of the Red Army were surrendering with relief, others, still fighting, were cursing the leadership which had exposed them unprepared, undeployed, inadequately led and insufficiently equipped, to Hitler's tanks and aircraft. The civilian population of White Russia and the Ukraine were welcoming the invaders with bread and salt and flowers. Moscow was on the edge of an explosion. Leonhard knew nothing of this because, as a Party protégé, he was cut off from all reality. But he too, now, was to have his first glimpse of that reality, and it nearly broke him. Pitched out of his privileged shelter, one among a million evacuees, he found himself in Kazakhstan, living the life of the ordinary Russian refugee, half-starved, hounded by the back-area police, and meeting, as in a nightmare, honest peasants who not only hated the Government but were also ready to say so. A few more weeks of this, and Leonhard would have woken up in 1941 instead of 1948. But on the very edge of waking he was put to sleep again. The nightmare vanished when he was suddenly picked up to continue his political indoctrination on a higher plane, this time in the Comintern School, with young men and women from all over Europe. The disaffected masses, angry, humiliated, abased, and dying of hunger, were left far behind, and young Leonhard went back to the womb.

It is his picture of this school which, for me, is the highlight of the book. Everything that leads up to it combines to give a unique picture of the Soviet Union seen from the point of view of the Communist élite (not always a comfortable picture, as the millions of Party members who were condemned by Stalin at one time and another could testify; but a picture very different from that of the ordinary Russian). Everything that follows, including the inside story of the remarkably haphazard way in which the so-called German Democratic Republic was built up by a handful of Moscow agents, sustains the interest of the earlier part. But the account of the Comintern School stands by itself. To my knowledge it has never been publicly described, and to read Leonhard's description is to understand why. Here the children of revolutionaries from all over the world were admitted for training as the Kremlin's agents on condition that they renounced utterly and for ever their previous identities. To arrive at the school they were passed from hand to hand, from cell to cell, shedding more of their identities at every stage, through an elaborate and obsessionally secret one-way channel, for all the world like one of the escape routes organised by the resistance movements of Europe during the last war – but leading the individual to prison not to freedom. They arrived inside with new names and elaborate cover stories. These were the shining hopes of the young generation of Communist management; they were the most trusted of Moscow's agents: yet they were not trusted even among themselves, even inside the concentric circles of moral – and physical –

fortifications which cut them off utterly from the outside world. They were forbidden under pain of the more dire punishment to communicate their real identities with each other or to exchange a word about their past lives to their closest companions and associates. The system of communal confession in case of the least transgression, or suspected transgression, was carried to its logical and appalling conclusion. Here is the complete apparatus of 1984 – but without the spirit of 1984; because, as Orwell would have known had he ever lived in Russia, the apparatus does not work.

I have dwelt on the deeper implications of this remarkable book because they seem to me supremely important, and they go very deep indeed. But I should like to finish by stressing the interest and excitement of the book as the narrative of an extraordinary life story and a marvellously absorbing picture of the Soviet scene.

Child of the Revolution was published in the United States in 1967.

The Rebirth of the Great Russian Novel
Review of *Dr Zhivago*
1958

'Expansion. That is the idea the novelist must cling to. Not completion. Not rounding off, but opening out.' Mr Forster, surely, was right; and what is wrong with all but a handful of novelists is that they are concerned above all with completion, with fixing and de-limiting and rounding off their own little section of experience.

If this happens in the West, where the speculative mind is still allowed a small corner, how much more must it happen in the Soviet Union, where it is not? There completion is all. The Soviet novelist, urged to celebrate the Revolution, the catastrophic bursting of millennial bonds, is first told just what happened, and how, and why; is presented with a finished, unaltered edifice, the ark of the received truth, and expected to embellish it with a static frieze showing scenes from real life.

What is required is not an artist but a monumental mason. So no wonder the great novel about the Revolution did not appear; and no wonder now when, looming high in splendour, dazzlingly armoured in its imperfections, it unmistakably has appeared (against all probability, for cataclysmic events do not usually inspire great art, and artists prefer not to be imposed upon by them) – no wonder the Soviet panjandrums are perplexed and put out.

In Boris Pasternak they have a genius on their hands; and they know it. They have sighed for a genius for many years, and they are not such fools as to believe that genius can be submitted to the rough and ready carpentry which will turn earnest plodders after self-expression into propagandists for the Cause. They need time to think. Thus, as the result of a transaction now familiar to those interested, this greatest achievement of the Russian spirit for half a century reaches us before it reaches the Russians themselves.

What worries Authority is not that Pasternak has unpleasant things to say about Lenin or Stalin; they are not mentioned: they might never have existed. How much finer and purer *War and Peace* would have been without Napoleon: What worries Authority is not that Pasternak disparages Marxism and exalts Christianity: he does, here and there, but there are ways of coping with that. The really worrying thing is that his attitude through and through is subversive of all political action, as all considerable Western art since the Renaissance has been, and must be, subversive, because it can only illuminate the human condition which it is the task (and the duty?) of Authority to falsify.

Zhivago's story begins with his mother's funeral in 1905 and ends with his own funeral in 1930. During the earlier period Authority was breaking down; and, for a few years, during the civil war, it ceased to exist, so that there could be no consistent falsification: people were on their own.

The story, of course, is not about the Revolution. How could it be? The great point about the Russian Revolution is that, like all other so-called historical events, except in the minds of a few very specialised people it had no beginning and no end. Where does a whirlpool begin? Where does it end? Can it even be said to exist? Here, at any rate, is a nation caught up in a whirlpool.

Many are sucked down and lost forever. Many more are drawn deep into the depths, paralysed with fright, and thrown out again, white-haired. Still more are swept dizzily round somewhere near the periphery and then, surprisingly, begin to drift away, never having seen the depths. Who devised and controlled this vortex?

All we can know about it is what happened to people caught up in it – living, thus, under the stress of the atomisation of their society. They have no idea when disintegration set in or when the atoms started once more to cohere. Now, looking back, we can see that one falsification has (when did it happen?) taken the place of the old one. The only thing the Russians themselves are certain about is that at some time, for a few years, they lived alone with the truth about humanity, undisguised. And although, as if to blot out the memory of this experience, they have acquiesced in a new and brazen set of lies, the best of them *do* remember, and feel that this glimpse of the truth not only confers upon Russia a spiritual advantage over people like ourselves (whose manipulation of half-truths, a tightrope act across the centuries, is the finest achievement of human society to date), but also a special responsibility which has to be met.

Doctor Zhivago, among many other things, is an attempt to meet that responsibility. It is concerned with truth and nothing else at all; and to pay for this all attitudes have to be sacrificed. For a hero Pasternak has to make do with a man who makes no showing, a special variation of that special Russian manifestation, the superfluous man, the contractor out, for once taken to the logical end of this condition: he clings until death to his integrity, but everything he honours is destroyed or degraded; he himself, a man of gifts, ends his life uselessly after drifting through the bloodstained years over the length and breadth of Russia, through scenes of medieval savagery and horror, powerless to save those whom he loves, and for whom he dies a hundred deaths:

> In me are people without names
> Children, stay-at-homes, trees.
> I am conquered by them all
> And in this is my only victory.

Only his poems remain.

There is nothing in the least high falutin about Pasternak's method. His story begins at the beginning and ends at the end. Zhivago is a man, not a symbol. In his attitude towards spiritual corruption he does not compromise at all; but his relations with people, with women, are one long compromise. We are given his childhood, with an evocation of pre-Revolutionary Russia, with flashes of lyricism, with fore-bodings of darkness; and, at the same time, we are taken into the lives of many other people, whose persons, ideas and attitudes are to support the narrative. Yury Zhivago, although in the end he becomes nothing but an idea, is firmly rooted in reality as we know it, and surrounded by it.

And then we have the childhood of Lara Guishar, rootless, born of foreign parents into the darker and more violent world of corruption and acquisitiveness, but the embodiment of life. More characters; sharper action. Two worlds, soon intermingled, open out before us, and are then swept up by chaos – chaos so complete that the only way in which Pasternak, as creator, can impose a pattern is by the transformation of contrived coincidence into destiny itself. This is all right because the whole kaleidoscope of action is grouped, as though by magnetic force, round the axis of attraction between Zhivago and Lara.

On the face of it, what we have is an episodic novel, which takes in the sweep of a continent, the episodes severally having the clarity and directness of certain Flemish painters; but in fact each sentence, each character, each mood is doing the work of many, charged with symbolism, barely understood as we read, but always apprehended – so that, in the words of Mr Forster writing still about *War and Peace*, a masterpiece as far away in spirit from *Doctor Zhivago* as it is possible to conceive, 'great chords begin to sound, and we do not know what struck them.'

The 'difficult' impressionist poet, whose genius once seemed to lie in verbal associations, who exalted sensibility sometimes to the point of perversity, has broken through the barrier of words. His prose can be as simple, as direct – and as subtle – as Pushkin's, and it has been well served by his translators, Max Hayward and Manya Harari, who have tackled, and largely conquered, an unimaginably difficult task.

Introduction to *Safe Conduct:*
An Autobiography and Other Writings
by Boris Pasternak
1959

In 1954 there was a plan to publish in Moscow a collection of Pasternak's poems. This was during the first 'thaw', which followed Stalin's death in March 1953. During the summer and autumn of that year there was a deep stirring among the writers, the painters, the musicians of the Soviet Union.

Writers, long dead, were at least partly rehabilitated and their works brought out in new editions. Still living writers, long silent, were encouraged to speak again. Chief among these was Pasternak. In April 1954 ten of the poems written for his novel, *Doctor Zhivago*, were printed in *Novi Mir*, the literary monthly which was, two years later, to make new history by publishing Dudintsev's controversial but pedestrian novel, *Not by Bread Alone*.

Doctor Zhivago itself was not submitted for publication until the summer of 1956. In September the typescript was returned with a very long and reasoned letter, which was not published until the great row about the Nobel Prize in the autumn of 1958, two years later. There was no violence in that letter of rejection, at any rate in the form in which it has been given to the world, and although quite clearly it was prompted, at least in part, by individuals hostile to Pasternak and perhaps jealous of the special position he occupied in the hearts of Russian readers and in the estimation of his foreign colleagues, the spirit of the rejection as a whole was closer to sorrow than to anger. At any rate, until well into 1957 it was still hoped that *Doctor Zhivago* might be published in the Soviet Union if Pasternak would agree to make certain alterations. Even as late as that, *Novy Mir* published more of his poems. And when, in the same year, the Italian publisher Feltrinelli brought out the first translation of the novel against the express wishes of Alexei Surkov, Secretary of the Soviet Writers' Union, Pasternak was not made to suffer. These facts should be borne in mind by all those, and they are many, who speak as though there had been a total reversion to Zhdanovism in the cultural life of the Soviet Union.

It was not until the Swedish Academy fatefully decided to award the Nobel Prize to Pasternak that the storm broke loose. Then he was solemnly expelled from the Writers' Union and a number of the most undesirable characters in the land started using the language of the gutter. At this moment there seems to have been a determined effort to drive Pasternak into exile. 'He is free to leave when he likes. Let him receive his contemptible prize. He need not come back!'

But Pasternak, sixty-eight years old, who had endured a lifetime of suffering of an intensity inconceivable to us, refused to meet his persecutors half way. Already once, in 1937, he had defied Stalin's fury by refusing to put his signature to a document approving the execution of Marshal Tukhachevsky and others. There are plenty of other examples of his obstinate, undemonstrative courage. Now, nearly twenty years later, he had finally declared himself in a book which had swept the world. He was evidently in a mood to stand by it, though it killed him; and if killing was not the order of the day in Khrushchev's Russia (as, indeed, it is not), then he, Pasternak, was not going to allow himself, so long as he could help it, to be conveniently shipped abroad and then held up as a traitor to his country. So, as we know, he renounced the Nobel Prize and addressed a personal letter to Mr Khrushchev asking to be allowed to stay. No reply to that letter was ever published; but the outcry was dropped overnight.

This, no doubt, is an over-simplification. There were other and more personal reasons for Pasternak's desire to live as long as he was allowed, and die, in his own land – cost what it might in suffering and privation. But it is important to grasp the real point. It is important because he has since been accused in the West, either through stupidity or malice, of cowardice in his clinging to Russia, in his refusal, so long as refusal lies in his power, to follow so many of his contemporaries from his own and other lands into the bitterness of exile. No charge was ever shabbier or wider of the mark. *Doctor Zhivago* is more than a book; it is an expression of life. In his terrible and self-imposed isolation, with hands outstretched towards him from all over the world, Pasternak goes on living that life.

I have spoken of this because Pasternak in his *Essay in Autobiography* has nothing to say about it, or about the collapse of the plan to publish his collected poems. This essay was written as an introduction to the collection. So it must be seen as a fragment of a book. The poems must wait. The fragment, however, stands by itself. It is autobiographical only in the spiritual sense. It tells us next to nothing about the physical circumstances of Pasternak's life and very little – though enough for the attentive ear – about his anguish of mind. It does, however, tell us a great deal about the sort of man Pasternak is and the influences which culminated in the novel which he himself regards as his life's fulfilment.

Pasternak is sixty-nine. His first poems were published in the autumn of 1914, when he was twenty-four. Because of an injury to his leg in a riding accident he was not called up when war broke out, and he continued to publish until 1932. There was no more original work then, but many translations, until 1943, when he broke his silence with some war poems. In 1946, with Zhdanov's savage attack on 'cosmopolitanism', he fell silent again and did not speak until after Stalin's death, in 1954. But during these long periods of silence, which were self-imposed, one of eleven years, one of eight years, he was a venerated figure, seen as being above the battle, discovered by generation after generation of Soviet youth and passed on to the next, like a torch.

He was not above the battle. He was active and fighting all the time. But the battle he was fighting was his own. While others were fighting with more or less integrity the battle for survival, the battle to be heard and yet to preserve a remnant of their private vision (as though vision were divisible), Pasternak was fighting the battle for truth. When he could speak the truth as he saw it, he spoke; when it was physically impossible for him to speak the truth he was silent.

He was not alone in this battle for the truth; but he is alone among living Soviet writers in having fought it unremittingly and without compromise to the wonderful, the miraculous end, when his Truth suddenly and shatteringly broke through every barrier to flood the world. It does not matter what happens to Boris Pasternak after that, and he must know it, thankfully. He has achieved the impossible. He has spoken from the bottom of a deep pit and his words have been clearly heard. He is the first effective martyr of modern times, in a world which seemed to have made an end of martyrdom by the simple process of drowning it in darkness.

The fact of Pasternak's life-long battle for truth, and his recognition since the late Twenties as a man set apart, is important today because there is a strong movement to conceal it. Innocent visitors to the Soviet Union will be told with disarming plausibility that until the fuss about *Zhivago* very few people had ever heard of his poetry, which appealed only to lovers of the perverse and esoteric. This is categorically untrue. Even at the first Writers' Congress in 1934, when Pasternak, silent for two years, was sharply assailed for his wrong-headed attitude towards the Sovietisation of art, he was publicly acclaimed as a master, and his poetry was in fact quite astonishingly popular. It seems fairly clear that even those who thought of him as being above the battle must have known in their hearts that in fact he was fighting his own battle, which was also really theirs, and what it was about. Because of the language difficulty his public outside Russia was naturally more limited. I suppose the majority of English-speaking readers owe their discovery of his poetry to Sir Maurice Bowra, who made many beautiful translations of individual poems and who introduced him as a major figure in his book, *The Creative Experience*, published just eleven years ago. This volume contains an introductory chapter and six separate essays on Cavafy, Apollinaire, Mayakovsky, Pasternak, Eliot, Lorca and Alberti. It is indispensable for every reader who wishes to know what lies behind *Doctor Zhivago*. It is all the more remarkable in its prophetic insight since it is confined to those poems written before 1923, when Pasternak was thirty-three.

Listen to the closing passage:

Pasternak responds to the special character of his calling with a special sense of the responsibilities which it puts upon him. He believes, above all, that everything he writes must be a work of art, complete and independent with its own life, the final vehicle by which experience is selected and organised and transformed into a permanent shape. He also believes that no work of art has any value unless it is true in a rigorous and exacting sense, true not merely to fact but to experience, to all that the poet sees in it and feels about it. This double ideal is perhaps responsible for his complexities and roughnesses, but it is no less responsible for his final success and for his special importance. In a revolutionary age Pasternak has seen beyond the disturbed surface of things to the powers behind it and found there an explanation of what really matters in the world. Through his unerring sense of poetry he has reached to the wide issues and shown that the creative calling, with its efforts and its frustrations and its unanticipated triumphs, is, after all, something profoundly natural and closely related to the sources of life.

Those words, written long before we had any reason to suppose that Pasternak would ever write a novel, and based on the poetry of his earliest years, could serve well as a comment on *Doctor Zhivago*. Rereading them now, in the light of what has happened since Sir Maurice Bowra wrote them down, it seems to me that not the least of the services Sir Maurice has done is to demonstrate, when it is most needed, that, to adapt his own phrases, 'the critical calling, with its efforts and frustrations and its unanticipated triumphs, is, after all, something profoundly natural and closely related to the sources of art.' Sir Maurice Bowra, too, has had his own triumph and his vindication – which is also a triumph and a vindication for his calling.

This is not irrelevant. Listen to Pasternak himself:

I dislike my style up to 1940, just as I quarrel with half of Mayakovsky's writings and with some of Yesenin's. I dislike the disintegrating forms, the impoverished thought and the littered and uneven language of those days.

And again:

I would not lift a finger to rescue more than a quarter of my writings from oblivion.

And again:

The poems scattered over the past years of my life . . . are steps preparatory to the novel.

Yet to one critic the essence of the novel was implicit in the preparatory steps; and to thousands of readers it was sensed in them. This tells us something about creative writers, too, and about Pasternak in particular. It is worth holding on to this fact as we read Pasternak on himself.

He had written an 'experiment in autobiography' as far back as the Twenties, *Safe Conduct*, long out of print in Russia. This new essay was intended to supersede *Safe Conduct*, which, Pasternak insists, 'was spoiled by its affected manner, the besetting sin of those days'. He seems to have spent thirty years atoning for the 'affectations' of the first part of his life, driven unresistingly by the demand for total directness and truth, a directness and truth which had yet been detected in his earliest work, through all the surface imperfections, by countless readers. The fruit of those years, which have purged away so many imperfections and all traces of the egocentric, is a great novel, some poems and this short essay.

About this *Essay in Autobiography* I have nothing direct to say. It is here between these covers, wonderfully slight and unbelievably strong, with each sentence built to carry the weight of a lifetime's experience. Here, distilled, is the essence of a great writer and a great man, solid, and yet so volatile that it evades analysis and vanishes into thin air, like a butterfly cupped in the hands, like the elusiveness of life itself. For a Russian the whole thing is crystal clear, but because so many of the names which appear in it, because the whole background of Pasternak's life, are unfamiliar to most English readers, it is perhaps justifiable to dwell for a moment on that background.

The young Pasternak was cradled in the arts. His father, Leonid, was a painter of considerable gifts and reputation, the friend of countless painters and writers and musicians; his mother was Rosa Kaufman, a concert pianist, who had been a child prodigy. When Boris was thirteen his parents became summer neighbours of the composer Scriabin, who was also the uncle of the man who was to become Stalin's right hand, Molotov, born Scriabin. In childhood Pasternak's sensitivity to music had been acute, and Scriabin's music swept him on a swift upcurrent into the higher atmosphere: music was to be his life. It is permissible to believe that Scriabin was very much in his mind when Pasternak was creating the character of Uncle

Kolya in *Doctor Zhivago*. And it is worth remembering in this context that Scriabin is one of those composers who do not export well. To most musical Russians he means a very great deal. Scriabin touches in them a dominant chord which, vibrating intolerably, overwhelms the defects of his music – perhaps as Bruckner does for the Austrians.

The young Pasternak was going to be a great composer, relying on inspiration and perfect spontaneity. Everyone was pleased. He had no struggle to get his destiny as an artist accepted by his family: they expected nothing else. His struggle began only when, a little later, he began to understand the seriousness of art. Then, he tells us, from one moment to the next, he threw overboard his pretensions as a musician. The poet, the battler for truth, for the first time stirred within him.

It occurs to me that through the arrangement of these pages I may have given too much emphasis to that aspect of Pasternak's life-long conflict which may be summed up as the battle between the individual and overweening Authority. If so, this can be immediately corrected. Pasternak's first and last battle was with himself and with his artistic environment: it was only in 1932, with the subordination of literature in the Soviet Union to the ideals and disciplines of RAPP, the Russian Association of Proletarian Writers, forerunner of the notorious Writers' Union, that he embarked on his battle with Authority. He was then forty-two.

The second decade of the century in Russia was not an easy time for learning self-discipline. After the Russian collapse in the war with Japan and the striking, rioting and killing of 1905, the sense of impending disintegration was overwhelmingly strong, and among the Russian intelligentsia, battering their heads against the last convulsive stonewalling of the autocracy, it found expression in violently individualistic self-assertion. The mood was common to all Europe in those last years before the 1914 war blew the old culture finally to bits: the Futurists in Italy, the Vorticists in England, the Cubists in France, all formed separate expressions of a universal mood. All were tumbling over themselves to get rid of a past which still tenaciously hung on, and find new words, new images, for a new experience which, without their understanding it, was all too palpably lying in wait for them on the Somme, at Verdun, in the Dolomites, in the Masurian marshes, on the Field of Blackbirds – and in the streets and squares of Petersburg.

In Russia there were many different groups, each regarding itself as the unique repository of the truth, each more concerned with combating the pretensions of the others than with spontaneous creation. These occupied the ground which fell vacant after the collapse of Symbolism. For Alexander Blok, the leader of the Symbolists, the idol of pre-revolutionary youth, outlived the movement he stood for, and his last great revolutionary poems of 1918, 'The Twelve' and 'The Scythians', with their apocalyptic glitter, were very far removed from his early preoccupation with mystical love. All sought clarity and definition, as opposed to vague yearnings. Few found either.

By the time of the Revolution the Futurists, with their absolute denial of the past and their urgent violence, were dominant. Their most gifted exponent was Mayakovsky, who was to kill himself in despair at the turn the Revolution was taking in 1930, not without going half way to meet its demands, so that his bitter posthumous destiny was to see his later and cruder work seized upon by the men he could not live with and made part of the Stalinist canon – or, in the words of Pasternak: 'Mayakovsky began to be introduced forcibly, like potatoes under Catherine the Great. This was his second death. He had no hand in it.'

The two other most powerful movements were the Acmeists and the Imagists. The main feature of the Imagist outlook was its stress on words and word associations and its contempt for matter and content. In its extreme form, and influenced indirectly by Ezra Pound, Imagism abandoned sense altogether. They would have meant very little, but for the fact that a natural genius, Sergey Yesenin, allied himself with them and gave lustre to their company. Yesenin killed himself in 1925. The best of the Acmeists were its founder, Nikolai Gumilev, and the imperishable Anna Akhmatova. Politically they were out of step with the times, and their emphasis was on clarity of expression and the reflection of real experience. Gumilev was shot in 1921. Akhmatova, his widow, survived, with long silences, to be one of the main targets of Zhdanov's savagery in 1946. She survived even that and is now being published once more.

It was against this background – there were countless other

ceaselessly shifting groups – that the young Pasternak, full of confidence, first projected himself. And almost at once, without knowing quite why, he seemed to have realised that there was no place for him in any of these fiercely warring factions. To quote Sir Maurice Bowra again:

Each school suffered from exaggerating its claims. The Futurists' love of violence excluded many legitimate effects, the Acmeists were too traditional for a revolutionary age, and the Imagists spoiled their work by turning a means of poetry into its chief end. What was needed was a poet who could pick up the different threads and turn the modern movements to meet modern needs without giving too much emphasis to this or that claim of the competing antagonists. The man appeared in Boris Pasternak.

After an early spell as a member of a small group called 'Centrifuga' he began to walk by himself; and by 1927 he was the man we know today, standing apart equally from the excesses of so many of his colleagues and from the excesses of the state.

It is against this background that we read what he has to say about colleagues long dead. And it is against the background of Stalin's sustained effort to subordinate the arts to Party purposes that we must understand his long silences. From time to time a new and wonderful figure appears, only to die. The great majority of Soviet artists gave up the struggle in the early Thirties. Some, like Leonid Leonov, tried for a time, and then retired, beaten. Mikhail Sholokhov, whose original version of *Quiet Flows the Don* (published in 1928, but long since expurgated) was the only great novel to be published in Soviet Russia until *Doctor Zhivago*, managed to keep going by not writing much and by compromising a good deal. Others threw themselves apparently heart and soul into the business of building Stalinism. Most took life as it came, with secret reservations. But Marina Tsvetayeva, Pasternak's idol, an original genius, who returned to the Soviet Union in 1939, was dead by her own hand in 1941. And Pasternak's two wonderful Georgians, Yashvili and Tabidze, both died in the Thirties – Tabidze in one of the great purges, Yashvili by his own hand.

183

In 1956 it was the turn of the man who had so long been a pillar of Stalin's and Zhdanov's literary world, to kill himself: Alexander Fadeyev. So the wheel had turned full circle.

It is still turning. A few years ago it was thought a good idea to glorify Pasternak. Now he is in disgrace. But his voice has been heard, and will go on being heard, in a way which six years ago would have been inconceivable. And although he is silent, and although the Party is putting the screw on the arts once again, it seems in the highest degree improbable that the Soviet Union will have to suffer a return to pre-*Zhivago* days. All over Russia young poets and novelists are scribbling away, often in provincial towns which for decades have been neglected and suffered to rot; and what they are writing, though often crude, as often bears no discernible reference to the terms of art as laid down in Moscow. It is almost as if they had not heard the official summons. They will not be shot; most, we may hope, will not kill themselves in despair. And some at least will keep their souls. It looks better than it did in 1932 when Pasternak first stopped writing.

Stalin in Close-up
Review of *Conversations with Stalin*
by Milovan Djilas
1960

Here are the most revealing passages ever written not only about Stalin but also about the Soviet political arena in which Mr Khrushchev received his education.

When Marshal Tito, shrugging off once more the burden of civilised leadership, which he seems to find too much for him, sent his old fighting comrade, Djilas, to prison for the second time, people who had seen his latest book (the presumed cause of the trouble) professed themselves at a loss to know what the fuss was about: there was nothing in it offensive to Stalin which had not already been said many times by official Yugoslavia; no secrets had been given away. Perhaps they were trying to help Djilas.

In fact this disturbing, brilliant book is new in spirit from beginning to end; and it is all one great secret given recklessly away. Because here, for the first time, a man who was a senior Communist politician, who has talked as a Communist with Stalin and his creatures, relaxed, behind drawn blinds, writes of what he saw and heard as a human being writing about human beings. All the abuse of Stalin so far, from Trotsky through Tito to Khrushchev, has been doctrinal, has thus carefully concealed the human secret.

Djilas does not abuse Stalin. He has done a much more dangerous thing. He has helped us to understand him. The one thing forbidden all good Communists is any attempt to understand Stalin, because this cannot be done without letting in the light, as this short book blindingly does, into the hidden areas of the Soviet Union, of the Khrushchev Government, of the Communist system and its policies – including the Yugoslav wing. Stalin is to be rejected, not understood. Mr Khrushchev and the Communist system (but who will call it a system after reading this book?) are to be accepted, not understood.

Djilas's way of seeking to understand is the artist's way, not the politician's way. He has long ceased to be a Communist, though still an impassioned Socialist; now at last he has stripped the veils of scholasticism from a beautiful mind and become what he always wanted to be – a writer.

Everything is concrete. The story of the disenchantment of this flaming revolutionary is told in action, unwinding in a glittering chain of anecdotes, told not for their own sake but to carry the weight of argument and to illuminate the history of an epoch. Not even a poor and shabby translation can dull its edge.

Three times Djilas made the pilgrimage to Moscow: once in 1944 as the lean and hungry partisan leader, straight from his mountain fortress, almost faint with awe; once in 1945, in disgrace, as the man who had dared make what the Russians chose to regard as insulting remarks about the Soviet Army; once in 1948, just before Tito's final break, when Stalin was trying with extreme subtlety to charm and flatter him away from Tito – while with one hand destroying Tito's most bitter enemy, the Bulgarian Dimitrov and with the other spinning a web round Tito himself.

During those three meetings we see the young fanatic and idealist, who was once prepared to believe that all the tales of Stalin's terror were Trotskyite propaganda, who was so suspicious of the West that a mild conventional courtesy from a British officer made him plunge wildly looking for a trap, progressing reluctantly and with fearful questioning to rejection of all that Stalin stood for – and, what was even worse, to doubts about important aspects of Yugoslav policy: his own policy, that is to say, for he was then Tito's right hand.

It is an immense canvas, covered with wonderful economy. And, paradoxically, it is the fallen idol who is the hero of the book – the only person in the Soviet Union who meant anything.

An ungainly dwarf of a man passed through gilded and marbled imperial halls, and a path opened before him; radiant, admiring glances followed him, while the ears of courtiers strained to catch his every word. And he, sure of himself and his works, obviously paid no attention to all this. His country was in ruins, hungry, exhausted. But his armies and marshals, heavy with fat and medals and drunk with vodka and victory, had already trampled half Europe underfoot, and he was convinced that they would trample over the other half in the next round. He knew that he was one of the cruellest, most despotic figures in history. But this did not worry him a bit, for he was convinced that he was carrying out the will of history.

But this ungainly dwarf dominated absolutely by sheer weight of personality, compulsive magnetism, and *brilliance*.

Here in this portrait, or series of portraits, conversation pieces in more than one sense of the phrase, is the missing clue to Stalin: the clue is irresponsibility. He did not care a bit.

We have grown used to seeing him through Trotsky's eyes: the mediocre, doltish, sly Georgian with the 'sickly smile' who had the effrontery to dig a bottomless pit under the feet of the most gifted man in Europe. But what Trotsky really saw was a tenacious adventurer, disguised as a colourless bureaucrat, without a word to say for himself in face of all that rhetoric, steadily, surely, ridiculously, but in the end terrifyingly, preparing his ground for manoeuvre.

We have seen him through Churchill's eyes: the great warlord with nerves of steel, properly serious, infinitely shrewd and steeped in cunning, who understood only the facts of power, who weighed every word – but who could break *gravitas* to eat and drink like a medieval monarch and play the malicious clown. We have seen him, dimly, through his visible actions and the eyes of countless victims, cruelly, passionlessly, implacably killing and torturing all who crossed his path.

Now at last we see him at the height of his power, no longer compelled to intrigue except for fun, or on that global scale at which intrigue becomes statesmanship, no longer seeking to impress a dangerous or a gullible ally, but holding court, without a care in the world, among his own people. And the image is the image of an overpowering Renaissance tyrant, moody and capricious, operating on a continental scale and with all the apparatus of the industrial age.

Djilas saw him always when he was feeling on top of the world, and the aspect that strikes hardest is the irrepressible emotionalism which drove this man who was supposed to have no emotions. Here is a play-actor of appalling proportions who could make a moment's fantasy come true, who, far from weighing his words, was as often as not carried away by them.

Here, among his creatures, Beria drooling drunk; Koniev the soldier, coolly rendering Caesar's due, but no more; Mikoyan running the economy more or less single-handed – here he expanded into a figure of manic vitality, now bullying, now hectoring, infinitely destructive – now for fun, now for convenience – cursing, pleading, sometimes weeping with real tears, acting now with breathtaking subtlety, now shamelessly hamming, always carried away by the mood and the role of the moment. So that the Machiavellian quality in him, which normally seems to have operated with deep, unconscious, instinctive certainty, could be momentarily booted out by sheer emotional exuberance. But never for long. Because there was Molotov, invariably and inseparably, the *alter ego*, detached, inscrutable, passionlessly scheming, and always at hand to bring his master down to earth.

This is not the complete picture, obviously. To set against the manic flights, or the dazzling, almost Italianate volatility, there were clearly periods of black depression (Djilas never experienced more than a flicker of these). And then the gay, impulsive killer, who allowed himself to be adulated because it was convenient to be adulated and sometimes amusing, who killed because he was a natural killer, out of anger, out of sadism, malice, convenience, megalomania, or boredom, all according to the mood – then this extraordinary creature became morbid and paranoic, with what results we know.

Stalin was clearly far more of an original than we have ever guessed. His emergence in these pages as a hysteric for the first time makes sense of the man and the spell he cast – a human being more dangerous, if possible, than we realised, but as a portent far less frightening.

Introduction to *A Hidden World* by Raphael Rupert 1960

The first thing to be said is that this is a true story. I had the privilege of meeting Mr Rupert when he finally escaped from Hungary in the autumn of 1956 and was still too dazed to talk much about his Russian experiences. But it was then at once clear that he was a man of exceptional honesty and that anything he cared later to say about his life in Soviet labour camps would be of especial value because of this. And so, I think, it turns out to be.

In writing of what he lived through in the hands of the Soviet political police he has not been tempted, as a more imaginative, more self-conscious individual would have been tempted, to strive for effect or to generalise from his personal experience, or even by meditating aloud on causes and effects to blur the particular image of what happened to him. Although he had already had glimpses of Soviet reality under Stalin he had no clear picture of what he would have to suffer and when he was finally sentenced to twenty-five years' forced labour, on a trumped-up charge of espionage for the British, he went off on that appalling prison train as on a voyage of discovery. Indeed, one of the most fascinating aspects of his story is the Man-from-Mars view of the dark side of a continent.

It should not be thought that Mr Rupert had no standpoint of his own. On the contrary, his standpoint was so firm that he took it completely for granted. It was that of the convinced, instinctive liberal individualist. His father was a distinguished Liberal politician, and he himself had hoped to follow the family tradition. But the war came and, in lieu of politics, Mr Rupert turned his hand to helping allied airmen and Jews to escape from the Germans. This seemed to him the most natural thing in the world. It was the 'liberal' thing. Thus, when he told his Russian captors that he was a Liberal, and suffered terribly for it, what he really meant by Liberalism was simply the principle of freedom to be oneself. It is plain that even now he has not realised the massiveness of the forces working against this simple principle, and not only in Communist countries.

But even if I had never met Mr Rupert I should have recognised at once the truth of his story. I should have had no doubt at all that everything happened to Mr Rupert precisely as he has set it down, and it seemed to me that the value of the picture he builds up is all the greater because of the matter of fact limitations of his approach. It is this which gives a particular value too to Mr Rupert's account of the last phase of his imprisonment and his final release some time after Stalin's death. We are here taken into the world of prison camps in the process of breaking up and receive remarkable insights into the Soviet way of doing things when good, not evil, is the aim. More than this, in the extraordinary, interesting record of Mr Rupert's final interrogations in the Lubianka prison (now no longer as an accused, but as a witness for the prosecution of Beria's accomplices) we are given a glimpse from behind the scenes, which I think is unique, of the agonised process of de-Stalinisation as it affected the apparatus of police terror.

For the rest, Mr Rupert has simply told from day to day over a period of eight years what happened when an ordinary, unassuming Central European found himself caught up in the insane ferocity of ideological warfare. It began when he was arrested in Budapest in 1947, and the reader will note with interest that he received more malignant personal violence at the hands of his fellow-countrymen, acting as Rakosi's police-men, than during all his enforced stay in Russia. It continued when he was removed to Baden, the enchanting Habsburg spa in the wooded hills just outside Vienna, which the Russians chose as their Austrian Potsdam. And for me his descriptions of what went on during his imprisonment and interrogation, which ended in a false confession and a twenty-five years' sentence in this cosy little holiday town, almost within visual signalling distance of the Allied occupation forces in Vienna itself, a morsel of the old Europe if ever there was one, has a special fascination which is not surpassed by any of the experi-ences, horrifying and macabre, which were to follow on the long train journey to Russia and in the labour camps themselves. No doubt this is because I knew more about the labour camps than I knew about the interior of Marshal Malinovski's idyllic Austrian headquarters!

Others will, I expect, be more interested by the insights offered by Mr Rupert into aspects of the Soviet way of life.

It is these that I can vouch for. I have never been inside a Soviet labour camp, but a number of my friends, chiefly Russian, have shared the sort of life described by Mr Rupert and some have lived to talk about it. Farther, at one time and another, I myself have had close-up views of forced labour in action. There was a time, during and soon after the war, when life was at such a low ebb throughout the Soviet Union that in the remote areas – and in some areas not so remote – it was often impossible to tell a free citizen from a prisoner. Certain north-ern landscapes seemed to be nothing but a Paul Nash night-mare of geometrically arranged fences of barbed wire – fences punctuated by watchtowers on stilts, with machine-guns and searchlights, the guards heavily, stiffly cocooned in goatskin *shubas* nearly down to the ground so that they looked like wigwams; there were the prisoners, being marched about, or doing fatigues, or man-handling heavy timber, or trying to break up frozen soil and sub-soil to sink foundations. And next to them came free labourers, with nothing in their appearance or the work they were doing to show the difference. Nobody cared: they were all half dead of hunger anyway. I have seen – I have told this elsewhere – gangs of prisoners from a camp in North Russia laying strategic railways, building new wharves, breaking up the ice laboriously with broken tools at forty degrees below zero centigrade – and alongside them there have been gangs of free citizens, 'volunteers', doing the same work, and marching back at the end of their shift to communal barracks. Many of these were girls. I have seen the sort of swift public copulations described by Mr Rupert. And I have had fall dead at my feet a prisoner shot by a guard for falling out of line to pick up a crust of bread thrown from the galley of an iced-up merchant ship – and seen how the corpse was left lying like a dead cat in a slum street, until after a few days there was nothing to be seen but a faint hummock under sifted snow.

This sort of action was not cruelty, but the outcome of total callousness and stupidity, itself produced by the policies of Stalin, coming on top of Lenin and centuries of Czarist brutality. You cannot, agreed, make an omelette without breaking eggs, as Lenin with his ineffable brightness once remarked. But it took Lenin to produce a situation in which, with manic hopefulness, men break eggs by the bucketful – and then find that there is no frying pan, no match to light the fire and nobody around who knows how to make an omelette . . . .

This is the kind of mood which has to be realised before Mr Rupert's story can be understood. Then think back. Think back to Dostoyevsky's *House of the Dead*, to Chekhov's *Sakhalin Island*, to Gogol's *Dead Souls*. All the violence, venality, squalor, degradation and sheer *waste* of human resources exist in these books from before the Revolution. The privileged murderers and thieves who terrorised the camps under Stalin, Mr Rupert's 'bandits', were at it in Dostoyevsky's time, encouraged by Authority, which regarded political offenders as being far more wicked and dangerous than the most brutal criminals. The mindless brutality of the professional camp guards, the corruption and sycophancy of the camp authorities – all these go back to long before 1917. So, even, do the prison vans which made up Mr Rupert's terrible trainloads of deportees: they were the proud invention of a Czarist prime minister, Stolypin, who was himself assassinated while attending a gala performance of opera in Kiev. Although Mr Rupert did not know this, the vans are still called after him.

Having dwelt on the worst, let us look at the other side of the picture. One of the few encouraging developments at an extremely discouraging moment of history has been the improvement during the past few years of living conditions, material and moral, in the Soviet Union. This has been in certain ways so marked that there are already many people who think that we should forget the past and dwell only on the present and the future. I do not refer here to Communists and fellow-travellers who refused to recognise the evils of Stalinism until they were instructed to do so by Stalin's successor. These are past salvation. I refer, rather, to all sorts of well-meaning men and women who, while freely admitting that evil once reigned throughout that vast, unhappy land, nevertheless persuade themselves that no purpose is served by 'raking up' past iniquities upon which the present leadership has turned its back.

This attitude will not do. In the first place it is treacherous: a betrayal of the memories of millions of fellow human beings who died and suffered inconceivably, unknown and unoffending – in order that Stalin could build up the power to dominate half Europe and to construct the 'material base' from which Khrushchev could launch his Sputniks. They must not be forgotten nor must those who made them suffer. Khrushchev has gone a long way towards apologising for the iniquity from which his improved model Soviet Union is arising, and he has gone still further in his efforts to ensure that such iniquity is not repeated. But in his denunciation of Stalin for his wholesale liquidation of faithful Communists and for his purges of the army command, he has not gone far enough. The great mass of the millions in Stalin's labour camps and prisons were not Communists at all: they were ordinary Soviet citizens needed for forced labour to open up the resources of the least habitable parts of the land; they were peasants who resisted the collectivisation; they were innocents denounced by informers and arrested by the political police as part of a regime of terror; they were the citizens of many lands overrun by the Soviet army and taken away to serve long terms in the interior, partly because they were needed for the vast slave labour enterprises of the

MVD, partly again as an aspect of terror – Lithuanians, Latvians, Estonians, Poles, Czechs, Slovaks, Germans, Rumanians, Bulgarians, Yugoslavs, Austrians, and Hungarians like Mr Rupert himself. Khrushchev has had nothing to say about these nameless, faceless millions, who had nothing to do with Communism, or with the domestic and foreign policies which produced victimisation on such a calamitous scale. Until books like Mr Rupert's can be translated into Russian and published in Moscow it is our duty to remember what Khrushchev prefers to forget.

Further, how except by 'raking up' the past can we hope to understand the present, which, everywhere – and not only in the Soviet Union – is the prisoner of the past? For the past is in the present, and from both the future springs.

Finally, it seems to me that the people who ask us to forgive and forget can never have understood the full enormity of what we are requested to forgive and forget. Mr Rupert can show them something of this; and that is why I warmly commend his book.

Not that his story comes as a revelation. There have, over the years, been a very considerable number of reliable and highly instructive writings about life in Soviet prison camps, including at least two classics: Elinor Lipper's *Eleven Years in Soviet Prison Camps* and Gustav Herling's *Worlds Apart*. Indeed, there has long been no excuse for ignorance of what went on all over the Soviet Union until a very few years ago. But Mr Rupert's book, as I have already said, seems to me to have a special value because of its extraordinary simplicity and unassumingness. Gustav Herling, Elinor Lipper and others in a lesser degree took their raw material as they found it and were above all concerned with exploring in their very different ways the problem of physical and spiritual survival in a wholly destructive world. They wanted to tell us something new about the human spirit, and they succeeded. But the trouble with classics is that by turning life into art, action into causes and consequences, and the particular into the universal, they offer a sort of catharsis, so that the impact of the everyday concrete is muffled. Instead of registering that such and such unspeakable events took place day after day, month after month, decade after decade, a jet flight away, just round the curvature of the earth, under our own familiar sun and moon and stars, and to human beings like us, we find ourselves wrapt in contemplation of the mysterious ways of the Almighty, seen in a grand historical perspective. Meanwhile individuals go on being hurt – and for no other reason but that some unspeakable dictator finds himself too inefficient to govern properly, and hits out savagely to cover up.

To try to appreciate and understand the Soviet Union of today without first contemplating the Russia of Mr Rupert, so different from the Russia of, for example, Sir Charles Snow (later Lord Snow), is frivolous and vain. The thing to remember about the narrative which follows is that it is almost contemporary. It begins in 1947 and it ends in 1955. Six years ago Mr Rupert, with millions of others, was still in a Soviet labour camp. Most of the camps are now closed; but, such is life in the Soviet Union, hundreds of thousands who were once prisoners and are now free, still live of their own volition (they have nowhere else to go) in and around the old camp hutments. Six years ago, although conditions were improving, the vast and intolerable network of the MVD's forced-labour system still formed a vital part of the Soviet economic system. Six years ago conditions in many parts of the Union were still such that prisoners used to send food parcels from the camps to their relatives living as free peasants outside. The Soviet Union tested her first atom bomb in 1949, quite early on, in time, in Mr Rupert's narrative. The first Sputnik went up in 1952, when Mr Rupert was still toiling away with, as far as he knew, more than twenty years of slavery ahead of him – he and millions of others. Five years ago Mr Rupert was at last sent home to Hungary (and the story of his long drawn-out release is one of the most fascinating parts of the book) – only to be seized by the political police of his own native land – and to escape, by a miracle, during the Hungarian uprising of 1956. But during all these years we have been so obsessed with the evidences of Soviet technical skill, as applied to Sputniks and nuclear fission, that we have allowed ourselves to be hypnotised into believing that the Soviet Union is peopled exclusively with budding Gagarins, Oistrakhs, Ulanovas and Botvinniks.

This misconception not only leads to a false idea of the state of the Soviet Union now, today: even worse, perhaps, it stands in the way of a proper appreciation of the vitality and the drive, the sheer magnitude of the effort now being applied to bring these people out of the abyss. In the first place, a moment's reflection will show that the Soviet Union cannot have utterly transformed itself in six years (ponder a little on the implications of Mr Rupert's chapters about the furniture factory and the collective farm). In the second place, and more importantly I think, the fact that an oppressed and shattered people, which has known such depths of degradation and humiliation, and the corruption inseparable from it, can even begin to transform itself as the Soviet people are undeniably transforming themselves today, could, through the terrible years, keep the spark of humanity burning, to be fanned, when occasion offered, into a flame, carries for us all a supremely important message about the unquenchable vitality of the human spirit. Here, in these pages, is the almost unbelievable background to the newly emerging Soviet society, which has produced, together with the first *moujik* politician, Mr Khrushchev, that host of clever and amiable diplomats, engineers, scientists, artists, writers, dancers, musicians and artisans who so fascinate us today. If this can happen, anything can happen. The problems confronting Russians working desperately and often misguidedly to escape from their own past make our own problems seem elementary and our own despondencies uncalled for.

A Long Cool Look at Lenin
Review of *The Bolsheviks*
by Adam B. Ulam
1966

Every so often a writer, a painter, a composer comes along to demonstrate that excellence is not a dream. It can happen in the most unpromising of contexts. Professor Ulam has made it happen in this biography of Lenin, which is so good that it is not merely superior in degree to any other life of Lenin, but different in kind.

The conjunction of scholar and artist is the rarest thing. We used to be told that it was worth learning Italian to read Dante, Russian to read Pushkin, German to read Goethe – at least in moderation. Here is a new one: it is worth developing an interest in Lenin to read Professor Ulam.

This, perhaps, is a tougher proposition than it sounds. Lenin was not a man, a simple foreigner; he was an alien continent. It calls for the polymath curiosity of an Edmund Wilson voluntarily to embroil oneself, as though Renaissance man were not enough, in an attempted understanding of, for example, Hindu religious art. Lenin, to us, is as foreign as that, and the fact that through Stalin, through Khrushchev, through what President Wilson once called 'the great Russian people in all their naïve majesty', his impact on us has been direct and sharp in no way diminishes his foreignness.

Thus the first particular thing to say about Professor Ulam's book is that it provides a map of the Russian culture which nurtured Lenin, seen as a foreign culture – that is to say from a detached but perfectly defined point of view, with the scene composing itself to make sense in terms understandable to us.

To write in this way of the pre-Revolutionary century is alone a rare achievement. The specialist in nineteenth-century Russian thought is almost always an enthusiast. The Decembrists, for example, are habitually glamourised and the sharp reaction of Nicholas I to the discovery that he was being betrayed by a broad cross-section of the high nobility is represented as a sign of natural wickedness. Thinkers and pamphleteers of very modest parts are offered as intellectual giants – as indeed they appeared to the muddle-heads around them. Professor Ulam gently but crisply puts the Chaadeyevs, the Belinskys, the Chernichevskys in their place, which was lowly judged by West European standards. This introduction of light and shade, contouring and relief modelling by the sharp, oblique lighting of a usually featureless landscape is of great importance. Among other things it brings out the feebleness of the ideas and the men with whom Lenin had to collaborate and contend, and it assists in an understanding of how a man of Lenin's limitations was able to succeed. Thus, for example, if one thinks of poor, wretched Plekhanov, 'the father of Russian Marxism', as a major historical figure, then one is immediately let in for an exaggerated view of the intellectual stature of Lenin himself – a view, it must be added, which may be corrected by reading Lenin's own writings.

Not, for heaven's sake, that this is a debunking biography: I doubt if Professor Ulam knows the phrase. He is wise, compassionate, just – all, be it remarked, positive qualities of an unfashionable kind which he wears unconsciously, like a skin. He is also, this time consciously, astringent, ironic and, believe it or not, profoundly humorous. He is well aware of the depths of the Russian achievement, but he knows the shadows as well.

One question about Lenin has always been how a man fired by humanitarian ideals and of such towering stature could have got a great nation into such an unmitigated mess, saddling it with a tyranny far more complete than the one from which for a brief moment, and without benefit of Lenin, it escaped – handing over to his successor the prototype of the Stalinist State.

The question, as Professor Ulam shows, was wrongly put. Lenin towered all right, but he towered only as a man of action and a tactician of extreme tenacity of purpose in a society of intellectuals who were not men of action and were infirm of purpose. He had a doctrinaire mind, tough, and good enough to invent theoretical justifications for the opportunist zigzags devised by his tactical genius. But he had to *believe*; and he was fortunate in living among people who also had to believe.

He thought he was an internationalist but he ruined the promise of socialism by unthinkingly blighting with traditional Russian expedients and Russian solutions (such as conspiracy and force) the delicate plant of the social conscience. He took the bickerings of a handful of exiled or displaced Russian intellectuals for high thinking. He turned and rent as traitors to the cause the developing thought of German Marxist revisionists – because, really, they were not Russian and absolutist, because they were not Leninist. His personality was overwhelming. He was sustained, no doubt, by a love of humanity, but he loved human beings as most people love their dogs: the kennels must be clean, the food regular and nourishing. In return it was only justice that he came to be loved by human beings as a master is loved by his dogs.

Bribes, Subsidies and Helping Hands
Review of *Soviet Foreign Aid*
by Marshall A. Goldman
1966

Dogs, as a rule, do not bite the hand that feeds them. Men, it is well known, all too often do. Americans are as aware of this individually as any other people, yet they seem unable to accept the hard fact collectively. During the past twenty years they have given away more treasure than any other people in the history of the world, more than a hundred billion dollars of it – and in return for this vast outpouring they have been treated with more contumely than any other people in the world. They should stop worrying about this. One cannot be rich and beloved, a fact which the British philosophically accepted over two hundred years ago. Americans should get used to this fact too. It is unfair that the Russians should appear – but appearances are deceptive – to make more impact with their very much smaller contribution (fourteen billion dollars over the same period), but life always was unfair. The richer Russia gets, the more her own aid will be resented. So it goes on.

What, anyway, does Russian aid amount to? It is time we knew, and Professor Goldman has performed an invaluable service in telling us, more compendiously and in greater detail than ever before, at the same time with a blessed lucidity and lightness of touch which makes his book easy reading. I hope the solemn will not be put off by this. There seems to be a widespread conviction among American scholars that nothing is worth doing unless it is made impossible to read – or that nothing can be serious and profound unless it is also murky and obscure. The Russians share this belief. Professor Goldman evidently, praise be, does not. He works hard to cast light in dark places, and he succeeds. Continent by continent, country by country, he shows just what the Russians have done, are doing, and how. This is no cold warrior's thesis, rather a determined attempt to get at the truth of an operation of extreme complexity and very wide range. With this book available there is no longer the least excuse for muddled thinking about Russia's impact on the underdeveloped countries, which is seen to be small but useful. There are also chapters, to put the whole thing in perspective, about Russia's exploitation of the satellites, which was very single minded indeed until after the Hungarian rebellion in 1956.

But I wish Professor Goldman had been more ambitious. He has limited himself too severely. It is impossible to discuss Russian aid without discussing at some length the problem of aid in general. And although Professor Goldman has many pertinent and helpful observations to make on American aid, and its impact or non-impact, these are severely incidental to his thesis. And this self-imposed limitation has, I think, caused him to waste an opportunity.

Thus one of the things that emerges from Professor Goldman's careful survey, but which he himself stresses insufficiently, is the importance of knowing just why you are disbursing. Your head should know what your hand is doing. In the bad old days, when England had the money-bags, this was easier than it is today. There was no such term as foreign aid. First there were subsidies; then there was investment. Subsidies were paid to continental powers to enable them to keep armies in the field to fight the enemies of England. At a later stage in the development of capitalism money and skills were invested in foreign railways, mines, etc. to bring in dividends. It was gratifying to know that English capital was helping to improve the lot of the naked and the hungry. But humane considerations were only secondary: dividends came first and everyone knew it. Humanitarian activities were left to the missionaries, supported by private charity frequently dependent on those dividends.

Nowadays humanitarian aims, though far from paramount, are powerful. But the old categories of subsidies and investment remain very much in being – and very difficult to sort out, so long as the convenient, absurd and inaccurate term foreign aid is used by the powers, above all by America, to cover, for example, subsidies (sometimes to very questionable governments) in the interest of the cold war, foreign investments to bring in dividends, loans to enable foreign governments to purchase American goods, food and medicines to succour the starving and the sick, money and know-how to help foreign peoples to create their own industries so that one day they may live better.

It is all a very great muddle. And it is largely because of this muddle, which Professor Goldman, I think, does not sufficiently bring out, that the Russians are able to make a more rewarding show with their relatively small contributions. The Soviet Government knows, far more exactly than the United States Administration, just what it is trying to do: to increase the prestige and influence of the Soviet Union; to create opportunities for trade and to open up markets as and when it needs them; more specifically, to keep the neutralists out of the American camp and, more recently, to counteract the influence of China. Professor Goldman correctly demonstrates that Soviet aid is concerned only minimally at present with the furtherance of revolution as such. But I think he overbalances backwards when he attributes to the Soviet Government humanitarian motives as well as political and economic ones. Governments are not humanitarian. People are. And it is so far only in the Western democracies that the people's voice in this sort of sense can make itself heard.

It is because they know what they are doing and do not have to deceive themselves, also because they do not have to take popular sentiment into consideration, that the Russians are able to distribute their largesse and to time it for the maximum effect. Thus, for example, as Professor Goldman points out, they profited by Mr Dulles's emotional blunder over the Egyptian high dam to slip in and build it themselves. And they were not deflected in this purpose by the little fact that President Nasser outlawed the Communist Party and clapped all the Egyptian Communists he could lay hands on into gaol.

Americans should read this book to see what the Russians are doing. They should then ask themselves just what they are doing and try to separate in their minds subsidies, aid with strings, investment and disinterested help.

New York Times

A Masterpiece from Russia
Review of *The First Circle*
by Alexander Solzhenitsyn
1968

This immense epic of the dark side of Soviet life in Stalin's closing years is lighted for me by endlessly exploding flares of recognition. What has to be asked is whether the illumination is such that it illuminates and throws into a coherent pattern of relief the shapes of an unknown and fantastic world so that those who have not been that way may see. Does it, in a word, work as a novel? The opening is weak and ragged. But very soon the author collects his great forces and then there is no looking back. After two remarkable books from the depths of Stalin's Russia, Solzhenitsyn has produced an unqualified masterpiece.

The central truth of the book – the truth about a huge country dominated by the Kremlin and the Lubianka prison (a medieval fortress and a converted insurance building); a country with, at the relevant period, between ten and fifteen million souls in labour camps; a landscape in which, over great areas, it was impossible to tell as one passed through it which of the ragged gangs labouring outside the wire fences were prisoners and which were free workers – is devastating in its effect.

But the centre is by no means the whole. That is to say, all Solzhenitsyn's characters, scores of them, are conditioned by this inhuman landscape; but for the duration of the narrative they are, prisoners and warders and their friends outside, partly insulated from it. They inhabit a special prison within a prison, or are in some way connected with it. All, with a solitary exception, have come in from the great camps outside or may at any moment be thrown into them. The solitary exception is Stalin himself, ill and old on a sofa in the Kremlin. For Solzhenitsyn, bolder than Tolstoy with Napoleon, has dared to put this character, living, into the limbo he created. Dared not in face of Soviet authority: Solzhenitsyn, after years of prison, must be long past caring what happens to him at the hands of administration men. Dared, much more importantly, to go the whole hog in imagination, to seize the logic of his compulsion, to declare, in effect, that it is no good calling to life the ghosts of shattered and corrupted millions without unveiling the Medusa head – an old man on a sofa – and, in so doing, facing the risk of destroying the whole illusion.

It is not destroyed. And so we can return to our First Circle, the cosy First Circle of Dante's hell, where wise men and philosophers excluded from Grace drag out a secluded eternity. It is a special prison for scientists and technicians called in from the killing drudgery, hunger and cold of ordinary labour camps and put to work on such projects as a special scrambling device for Stalin's personal use and a very special invention, a new toy for the MVD, to codify, or fingerprint, the human voice, so that a few words spoken on the telephone in a disguised tone may be taped and analysed, the speaker infallibly identified.

Indeed, the thread of the story, fragile, but armoured with irony, is provided by the furious enthusiasm of a small group of prisoners losing themselves in a scientific problem, the solution of which is to strengthen the weapons of their jailers and end in the undoing of a hopeful, normally selfish, normally corrupt, member of the new Soviet élite who yielded to an impulse of generosity and left his voice-prints. As the net closes in on him we are able to move outside the prison and penetrate into the self-regarding world of the post-war haute bourgeoisie which had so many shocks in store.

This is a far bigger canvas than anything Solzhenitsyn has so far attempted. It has all the qualities of that miniature masterpiece of ordinary labour camp life, *One Day in the Life of Ivan Denisovich* and the sprawling *Cancer Ward*. It offers the same landscape of humanity which includes jailers as well as prisoners, police generals as well as cooks and floor-sweepers, privileged as well as outcasts, philosophers as well as simple souls – virtues and vices overlapping, yet in some miraculous way sorted out into an ordered spectrum. At each end of the spectrum, near-villains and near-saints; in between, in superabundant variety, the rest, all in the grand Russian manner, rather larger, more articulate, more demonstrative than life.

I have never gone along with what seems to be a widespread idea that the violences of the twentieth century forbid treatment by novelists, poets, painters: they are too big for the frame, it is said. It depends on the frame. All that has seemed to me to be lacking is genius. Here it comes to us from a country whose rulers have sought, who still half-heartedly seek, to destroy the mind.

A word about the translation. Mr Guybon, like Solzhenitsyn himself, scratches around at the beginning, but as the narrative gathers strength so the translator rises to a great occasion.

A Light in the East
Review of *Progress, Co-existence and Intellectual Freedom* by Andrei Sakharov
1968

This inestimably important document could not have come at a better time. The Soviet leaders, riven by dissent, understandably terrified by new ideas which will one day sweep them away, shelter behind their armed might. Everywhere people have been giving up hope and despairing of any real and lasting change. To these, to all of us, the Sakharov letter, or thesis, comes as a rebuke.

It is also a challenge. It is intended, above all, as a challenge to the Government of the Soviet Union from one of that country's most honoured citizens, a scientist of genius who, when he was only thirty, put the Soviet Union ahead in the arms race with his work on the hydrogen bomb. But it is no less of a challenge to the West, to America above all, but also to the rest of us. We are all invited to think, to be our age, to be of our age, and to act to save the world from destroying itself. But although Sakharov says what many of us here already think about Vietnam, about racialism and other contemporary aberrations at the moment peculiar to the Western world, it is to Russia that he directly applies himself.

There is nothing new to us in Sakharov's catalogue of the various ways in which humanity may destroy itself in short order: we may blow ourselves up; we may ruin ourselves and the world by spending all our resources on useless anti-missile systems; we may poison ourselves by polluting our environment irredeemably in any of a variety of ways; we may starve ourselves to death; or we may cook ourselves to death under an impenetrable layer of carbon dioxide. And so on. All this has been said before in the West, but never so compendiously and with such shattering clarity and brevity, and such authority. It has not before been said in the Soviet Union, which, though Khrushchev spoke of nuclear annihilation, is officially supposed to be moving ever upwards in accordance with inexorable laws of its own patenting.

To say all this, in a short document circulated and revised after discussion with the cream of the Soviet intelligentsia and then addressed to the highest Government circles, is an act of total courage on the part of a man who is still only forty-seven, has much to live for, and could have passed the rest of his days a venerated figure, glorified, and lapped in privilege.

Sakharov comes out against that privilege. He comes out against almost everything that his political masters stand for. Whenever his criticism may be attached to Stalin it is absolute; he believes, and says so, that Stalin's excesses were worse (he says why) than Hitler's. He equates Stalinism with Fascism. He details Stalin's crimes against the Russian people, which Khrushchev never did (but he has, also bravely, a very good word for Khrushchev). He insists that before Russia can get on the right course Stalin must be formally impeached, posthumously expelled from the Communist Party, and the archives of the secret police thrown open.

But he is attacking not only Stalin. In his sharp and unanswerable plea for intellectual freedom as the first prerequisite of a society which is to survive, he is condemning the policies of the Government of the day, sometimes by implication, sometimes with perfect explicitness. And he also condemns Soviet policy, no less than the American policy in Vietnam.

I imagine that most Western readers will seize on this attack, the boldest and most comprehensive so far made publicly by any loyal Soviet citizen. But I shall not dwell on it because it is not for us but for the Russians. We know it all – though again we have never had this matter so beautifully compressed (the whole document runs to only sixty pages: Mr Harrison Salisbury's extremely helpful notes are as long) and on such absolute authority.

Because, as far as the world as a whole is concerned, this criticism is only a clearing of the decks. Sakharov believes that his own people will find it in them to set their house in order; he believes the Americans will do the same. He is not interested in attacking capitalism. It works, he says. There are gross inequities under American capitalism, which must be cleared up: there are worse in the Soviet Union. Why do we have to wait for a Soviet Marxist to tell us that 'the presence of millionaires in the United States is not a serious burden in view of their small number'? He gives some figures to show that a revolution in America simply would not pay the American workers. This, like a hundred other gems of free-thinking (a phrase we have forgotten to our great cost) is casually thrown out in the course of an argument about something else.

And all the argument, close and taut, Euclidean in its spare elegance, is centred on one problem: what the two great powers, assisted by us all, have to do to save first the world from violent annihilation, then the backward nations from starving to death, then the rest of us from poisoning ourselves to death. Naturally, it all depends on the two great nations first getting together in a limited way and instead of manoeuvring against each other manoeuvring together, each with their different systems, to present a solid front against destructive forces of all kinds. This has been said often enough before, but never so cogently by a man in Sakharov's position, never at the risk of ruin or prison, never by a Russian to his masters.

Sakharov is not content with exhortations: he offers an outline plan, a phased plan of co-operative action. It is not intended as a blue-print. It is intended to make people sit up and think. And quickly. It is impossible not to hope for Russia when this sort of thing can come out of it, when we know that these ideas are being discussed all over the place by men of influence and potential power. But how ironic to find hope for poor Russia in the appeal of a man who is convinced that humanity is finished – unless . . . .

As I observed, it comes at the right moment, at a moment when some people are so angry with the Soviet leaders, and with the Soviet people for permitting them to exist, that some of them turn, quite inexcusably, on any Russian whose fight for change stops short of total heroism. Thus poor Yevtushenko, over-valued as a poet, has nevertheless fought hard and well in circumstances impossible for those who have not experienced them to imagine. Must he be condemned for trying to live to fight another day? Must he be condemned for not being a Sakharov or a Solzhenitsyn? How many of us in condemning him for this must also condemn ourselves?

Soviet Schizophrenia
Review of *Expansion and Co-existence* by Adam B. Ulam
1969

The basic trouble with Soviet foreign policy is that it is split right down the middle. Instead of relating all its actions to a central idea, which is what it fondly imagines it is doing, the Soviet Government has doggedly pursued two separate aims, which are incompatible, even though they sometimes overlap: the encouragement of revolution and the development of Soviet, more particularly Great Russian, power. The one is inspired by a missionary ideology, the other by imperial ambition and the need for security. The two are easily confused, unconsciously by muddled thinking, consciously by tricks of dialectic.

From the earliest days of the Revolution this hopeless dichotomy, itself nourished by pre-Revolutionary historical attitudes, was embodied in two separate instititutions, both subordinate to the Politburo in the Kremlin, but working against each other: the Comintern, with its task of fomenting world revolution, and the Ministry of Foreign Affairs, which was required to achieve a working relationship, in the interests of Soviet security and aggrandisement, with the very powers which the Comintern was working to destroy. A small example of the sort of nonsense that ensued was the situation which arose when certain loyal Soviet citizens tried to stir up strikes and disrupt production in factories outside Russia making the machinery which other loyal Soviet citizens were desperately in need of.

There have been many much larger examples, sometimes involving contradictions on a vast and tragic scale: e.g. Stalin's relations with Nazi Germany. It was only for a brief moment towards the end of the Khrushchev period that the Soviet leadership showed signs of understanding that it could not for ever continue profitably in this schizoid manner. Khrushchev soon went. His successors, their brave show in Czechoslovakia notwithstanding, are so much on the defensive that for the moment they have no policy at all beyond simple self-preservation. This will not last. Sooner or later there will be a livelier leadership and the old split personality will almost certainly reassert itself.

But for the existence of this split, Soviet foreign policy would be easily predictable: the Russians try to think logically. As things are, nobody knows which side will be uppermost from one month to the next. The fact that the imbecilities of Soviet foreign policy are always carefully calculated (which is not to say well calculated), whereas the imbecilities of, for example, British foreign policy are usually achieved with an air of total and frequently regretful surprise, does not make them calculable by us for the simple reason that we don't know which of two possible boards the current chess game is being played on.

But if we cannot predict what will happen next it is usually possible to predict what will never happen, provided we stick to the general rule that the Russians are cautious to a degree, are quite good at sensing danger, and, when they do miscalculate in the grand manner, think nothing of going into reverse and cutting their losses: the dictatorship is strong enough to operate without inflaming, or being inflamed by, public opinion.

Perhaps one can only get the true feeling of this laborious and purposeful muddle by living through the years with the detailed unfolding of Soviet actions for ever under one's eyes. But Professor Ulam's latest volume, a positive monster of a book, is the next best thing to life, and, for me, offers the sensation of total recall. The whole development of Soviet foreign policy from 1917 to 1967 is set down with quite remarkable lucidity and the minimum of personal aberrations or over-elaborate interpretations. To follow his narrative, beginning with Lenin's coup, carrying on through Brest Litovsk to the period of enforced isolation and disillusionment with the revolutionary situation, through the rise of Hitler, the Nazi-Soviet pact, the two wars (the 'imperialist war' of 1939 to 1941; the 'great patriotic war' of 1941 to 1945), the beginnings of the cold war, right through to Cuba and Vietnam, is to be shown, as in no other book that I know, the real works.

Anybody who can sink himself in this narrative, for days, for weeks, according to his reading speed, will emerge with the sort of understanding which up to now could be achieved only by living the events as they unfolded. The only ingredient lacking is the part played by the deliberate lie, which introduces into all Soviet actions an element of fantasy, defying reasoned analysis.

Professor Ulam is not neutral. But his superb opening chapter about the historical backgrounds of Russia and of Marxism offers us the key to his attitude and to his personal judgement which I more or less share. He is by no means uncritical of Western policies, or the absence of them. But his subject is Russia, and here he leaves the attentive reader with no illusions. Even more importantly he dispels irrational fears.

Evolution of a Revolutionary
Review of *Memoir of a Revolutionary*
By Milovan Djilas
1973

Milovan Djilas was one of the most uncompromising and ruthless of the Yugoslav Communists. But at the height of his career, as the Party's chief intellectual, a senior member of the Revolutionary Government which he had helped to power, and one of the three men closest to Tito, he started asking questions. He went too fast and too far. One day he was President of the Federal People's Assembly; the next he was stripped of his office, expelled from the Party, imprisoned.

But nothing could stop him. Even while he sat in the very prison to which he had once been consigned by the pre-war dictatorship, he caused to be published in the West the most sweeping and closely argued indictment of Communism in theory and in practice that it is possible to imagine: *The New Class*.

One of the many remarkable things about that book was the rigorous way in which the author kept himself out of it. Other men, turning their faces against the cause for which they had fought, suffered torture and killed during the best years of their lives, would have been at pains to justify themselves. But not Djilas. There was no apologia. He had seen the light and he was now describing the Communist world as he saw it with newly opened eyes: 'I am a product of that world,' he was content to write. 'I have contributed to it. Now I am one of its critics.' There was not the least suggestion of special pleading or the self-justifying argument of a man admitting error. It made for great dignity. It also offered a glimpse of intellectual pride on a breathtaking scale.

Later he started to write his autobiography, which, when completed, will presumably tell the whole story of his life, including the unfolding of the mental processes which led to his great reversal. But not yet. The first volume, *Land Without Justice*, was a moving and beautifully written account of peasant childhood in the poverty-stricken, violence-ridden mountains of Montenegro. It was as though the poet that Djilas had aspired to be before he was ensnared by revolutionary politics had been reborn, purged of vanities and illusions by suffering heroically endured.

This second volume is in a different key. It is the story of the making of a revolutionary. Told with what appears to be total recall and with remarkable objectivity, it begins with the journey of the half-starving peasant youth from his mountain home to Belgrade; after a decade of underground struggle against the regime, it ends with the German onslaught which was to lead to the collapse of the monarchy and to the partisan war which brought Tito to power.

At first the young Djilas rebels without real direction. But soon, fanatical in his devotion to the task at hand, passionate and angry, but also puritanical, he finds himself a Communist –

looking to Moscow and to Stalin as to the light of the world. Marxist-Leninism appeals to the intellectual in him. The painful and stern rigidities of Party discipline satisfy in a most insidious form his own need to mortify the flesh and, at the same time, license him, the heir to a long tradition of tribal violence, to pursue and punish with a face closed against pity all those who are found wanting in their service to the cause.

Not that Djilas put it that way. It is impossible to know whether he realises it or not. For again in this volume there is no self-justification. We are simply told what happened. And what a story it is!

While we read, there is no other world than the world of ruthlessly driving, ruthlessly harried conspiratorial activity. It is a world of police bullying and torture, described with almost unbearable matter-of-factness; a world of informers, traitors, secret heroes; a world in which the first thing asked about a new comrade is whether he will stand up well to police pressure, the second, whether he will submit to Party discipline; a world in which even in prison revolutionary tribunals solemnly investigate the behaviour of comrades under stress and pronounce verdicts of expulsion and anathema upon those who are found wanting; a world of primitive values crazily interwoven with the endless exercise of seeking to anticipate the Moscow line and to square it with reality.

But it is not an inhuman world. Djilas the poet is incapable of mentioning an individual, friend of foe, without bringing him alive. He was in love, and like all dedicated Communists in their days of struggle felt guilty about it; an emotional entanglement of any kind must surely dilute religious zeal? He need not have worried. He went on fighting with total single-mindedness, and his girl, whom he later married, did not try to weaken him: she managed to track down his prison cell and stood outside each day in a red sweater which he could just make out. She could not see his face in the shadows, but only his hands through the bars.

It is a wholly closed world into which we are drawn. We are made a part of it and know what it is like to be a revolutionary fighting against odds in a very rough society, what it is like to be one of a tight circle of devotees looking to the Kremlin in Moscow as to the Ark of the Covenant. Only when we look up for a moment do we realise how completely immersed we have been in this claustrophobic, inward-gazing world and recognise with a sense of shock the insufferable assumption upon which it is based – that a human being, a Djilas, a Tito, a Lenin is justified not only in sacrificing himself but in imposing suffering, death and destruction on his fellows in the realisation of a dream which he calls truth.

Memories of a Former Person
Review of *As I Remember Them*
by Galina von Meck
1974

The Russians had an Orwellian term for cultivated survivors from the old regime: 'former people', they were called. Perhaps they still are, but there can be very few of them left. On the eve of the last war a surprising number of them still hung on, somehow keeping body and soul together while history noisily passed them by. Many were starved or frozen to death in the course of the war.

These were the people who had seen everything and could have described in detail the impact of the Revolution and its consequences on the society it destroyed. But they took their memories with them to the grave. Most of the books by victims of Soviet rule since very early days have come either from foreigners or from Russians who knew little or nothing of life before the Revolution. The result has been that we are inclined to attribute all atrocity to Stalin, forgetting the scope and magnitude of the destructive acts planned and carried out by Lenin when he set out to make sure that there should be no democracy of any kind.

The life story of Galina von Meck provides just the sort of continuous view we so badly need. Born to riches under the old regime, old enough to remember vividly its closing years (she was twenty-six and married by 1917), she lived on through the

Revolution into the height of the Stalin era and survived to write this book. In so doing she has given measure, perspective, distance, to Lenin's Revolution and its aftermath as part of a vast human process, still continuing, in a way that has not, in my experience, been done before.

It is a remarkable achievement on the part not of a detached observer but of one who found herself in the direct path of the avalanche and almost obliterated by it. The achievement owes much to her natural gifts, her strength of character, her ability to take the most fearful punishment without being soured by it or lapsing into self-pity. It also owes a good deal to the accident of her birth.

The Mecks were Baltic Germans who threw up one of the first great railway kings in the mid-nineteenth century; and it was our author's grandmother, Nadezhda, the widow of the railway millionaire, who became celebrated as the patroness, support and long-range confidante of the composer Tchaikovsky. The family tradition also included one of the most brilliant and colourful clans in Russian history, the Davydovs. A Davydov, poet and soldier, organised and commanded the partisan formations which caused Napoleon such woe on the retreat from Moscow; another Davydov was active in the Decembrist conspiracy of 1825 and condemned to exile. Pushkin was in love with the whole Davydov family of his day and stayed often in their home at Kamenka.

Thus it was that the high dreaming Russia of the early nineteenth century became merged in this family with the new industrial Russia to give the author of this book an immensely strong background and a deep sense of belonging. She grew up in a world of great wealth, but also with a sense of purpose. Her father was a second-generation railway tycoon, who might enjoy possessing the first motorcar in Russia and his private railway carriage, but who also had a social conscience. He decided to stay on and offer his services to the new Russia after the Revolution. The more intelligent Bolsheviks tried rather ineffectively to use his expertise, but the less intelligent, stronger and more numerous, kept on putting him in prison and finally shot him in 1928.

It needs a family background of this kind to bring the hopeful Russia of the nineteenth century into the heart of the Russia of

Stalin's camps and prisons. We proceed by almost impercep-
tible steps. From the world of country estates and strawberries
and cream for tea we move, almost without knowing it, into the
chaos of hunger, cold and total deprivation – as in real life the
Mecks themselves lived from one day to the next; from the
world of hand-to-mouth existence stripped of all possessions – a
detail which the author finds hardly worth recording – to
sudden arrests, of long queues of wives and daughters outside
the Moscow prisons trying to discover whether husbands and
fathers are still alive, and where; from this to the world of
shootings without trial, of transit prisons and forced labour
camps, haphazard at first, then hardening into the now all too
familiar world of Stalin's terror.

Nothing is abstract. Everything is personal and concrete.
There are no generalisations and no moralisings. When the
overseers on one of those terrible, meaningless treks from one
Siberian camp to another behave with a cruelty bordering on
the hysterical, the fact is recorded. When, from time to time, a
guard, or a camp commandant, shows unlooked-for kindness,
that is also recorded. This is how it was. Galina von Meck does
not ask how many were cruel, how many kind, or why. And
although she is writing not in her own language but in English
(her first husband was English: they parted in 1918, he to
return to England), she has that extraordinary power shared by
so many Russians from Aksakov to Nabokov, of compressing
into a paragraph a lyrical experience which makes the universe
stand still. Such moments may come over her when she is
recalling the sounds and odours of a summer childhood, or in
the depths of the Siberian forest, half dead with hunger and
exhaustion, on one of those dreadful night marches from one
hell to the next when she looks up for a moment through the
trees at the stars shining down in the enchanted silence of the
frozen night.

And all the time the narrative, even when it is concerned with
scenes of extreme squalor and degradation, is somehow lifted
up by the constant memory of earlier days. Pushkin and the
Davydovs and Tchaikovsky are as real to her as the princes and
the prostitutes, the thugs and the martyrs of her prison camps.

This is a book which brings home very sharply indeed the
consequences of the deliberate destruction not only of an entire

ruling class, however inadequate and inept, but also of the educated bourgeoisie, even including all members of the Revolutionary intelligentsia who would not call themselves Bolsheviks. This was Lenin's contribution. It is a phenomenon passed over as a rule in histories of the Revolution. In these the Soviet regime is presented too often as an abstraction. We are told not what actually happened when a host of illiterate and frequently drunken peasants were drafted to positions of authority (a cataclysm from which the Soviet Union has not yet recovered) but what Lenin thought he was doing, or said he thought he was doing – which was rather farther from reality than the no less irrelevant aspirations of Nicholas I.

This is a marvellous book. It is a miracle that the author survived and escaped to write it. The manner of her escape is by no means the least extraordinary episode in it.

Russian Nightmare
Review of *The Gulag Archipelago* Vol. I
by Alexander Solzhenitsyn
1974

Gulag is the Russian acronym for the Chief Administration of Corrective Labour Camps. The archipelago of Solzhenitsyn's title is the monstrous complex of these camps (now greatly reduced) scattered over the vast land. Together with the prisons that feed them and all the paraphernalia of the security police, they form what he very aptly calls 'our sewage disposal system'.

Not all the prisoners would reach the camps, of course. Hundreds and thousands were shot, often after torture, in the prison yards and basements. Millions more, too numerous to pass through the prisons and not needed for their confessions, e.g. the so-called kulaks during the collectivisation; later, whole peoples marked by Stalin for extinction – were simply rounded up in their villages, marched to the terrible trains and from these dumped in remote Siberia to be herded into camps or left to fend for themselves in the wilderness. There were also special cases, like the mass shooting of Polish officers in Katyn forest, or the cramming of unwanted prisoners into leaky barges which were towed out into the northern seas and sunk.

Much has been written about these things, from the personal experiences of survivors from the camps to elaborately documented studies of the Terror. Indeed, the Western reader who has cared to understand has been informed more fully and in greater detail of the picture as a whole than all but a handful of Russians. Solzhenitsyn did not know this when he sat down to write this book in 1958. How could he? He had been arrested at the Front in 1945 for making disparaging remarks about Stalin to a brother officer. He had served eight years in the camps and then, in 1953, been condemned to perpetual exile in Soviet Central Asia.

It was not until 1956, with formal rehabilitation as part of the de-Stalinisation campaign, that he was allowed to return to metropolitan Russia and embark on the work which proved his genius, won him brief glory in Russia, transformed him into a world figure, and led to his arrest and expulsion to the West in February of this year. So that what he was doing when he sat down to write *The Gulag Archipelago* was, as far as he knew, telling a story that had never been told.

In a deeper sense this is precisely what he has done. Because, in spite of all that has been written by others, this is the first attempt to encompass the whole story, drawing on the personal experiences of hundreds of individual prisoners and relating them to the slow movement of the entire post-Revolutionary epoch. His book is thus much more than yet another inside story of prison and camp life, of torture and shooting and starvation, of the vileness of the secret police and the men who gave them their orders. To judge from this first volume of three, it is nothing less than a comprehensive history of the rule of violence and terror to which the people of Soviet Russia have been submitted since Lenin's seizure of power. It is a history in which the spectacular passages most familiar to the West (publicised, too, by Khrushchev), above all the great purges of the 1930s, are seen as no more than especially menacing crests in an apparently endless succession of waves of iniquity which started with Lenin's formal invocation of terror in 1918 and is still not wholly spent.

The beginning is Solzhenitsyn's own arrest. And to explain this he has to go back and show through a long series of chapters, and with a wealth of circumstantial detail, the development of the system which made that arrest possible, indeed natural, and of the apparatus conjured into being for the purpose of making it. In no time at all we are looking back to the far-off, forgotten actions which led, inevitably as Solzhenitsyn sees it (as I see it too, although others, including some to whom great respect is owing, see otherwise), to the systematic destruction of the finest human material, the men and women most needed to build a new Russia (as well, of course, of much that was not fine at all) and its replacement by the destroyers and their hangers-on.

The destruction took place; and it started under Lenin, whether or not one holds him responsible for what followed. We have forgotten now the banishings, the imprisonments, the shootings of virtually all those members of the educated classes who, for better or for worse, provided the civilised element in Russian society in 1917, then of all those devoted revolutionaries who sought a better world, and had sacrificed their lives for it, on lines other than those prescribed by Lenin. But Solzhenitsyn, who never knew them, who was not born until December 1918, has not forgotten them. With heaven knows what labours, he has managed to dig their names out of old newspapers, forgotten documents, testaments, eye-witness accounts, and rescue them from oblivion.

And then on through the modest but vicious trials of the 1920s, a cortège of ghosts; the engineers, wreckers all, wave after wave of them; the 'churchmen' – the survivors, actual or alleged, from the historical revolutionary parties – all caught for a moment in the limelight to be crushed and thrown into outer darkness.

And so on to the first grand climax, which was the deliberate extermination of the Russian peasantry as a coherent class. And so on to Stalin's apogee and what came to be known as the Great Terror of the 1930s. And while on the one hand Solzhenitsyn breathes his own life into the dead, on the other he is

216

showing, step by step, the progress of the men, from the most primitive thuggery of the Chekists and the illiterate stupidity of innumerable Party bosses of the middle ranks, to the fathomless corruption and cynicism of a Vyshinsky, who rose under their master's protection (when he did not turn and rend them too) to dominate the country and infect it with their own corruption. The master himself is rarely mentioned in this volume: it is assumed that the reader knows enough about him to be going on with.

But it is not as simple as all that. Solzhenitsyn set himself the task, single-handed and working in the most difficult conditions, of raising a memorial, a cenotaph, to the millions who suffered and died to build the world's first socialist country – or to sustain a handful of men in power. It is a memorial which is also a stake driven through the heart of the monster – which, however, has life in it yet. It is also a personal statement spoken out of a whirlwind of anger, scorn and pity.

So very far removed is it from our more accustomed idiom of understatement, with its laudable aim of putting down the facts and letting them speak for themselves, that the English reader may well be disconcerted by the shriek and roar of the high wind, the sustained passion of the irony, the violence of apostrophe and invocation. Indeed, were Solzhenitsyn concerned merely with compiling a record of horror this would be legitimate criticism. The record is there, illustrated with a thousand unknown details. But what he is doing is re-creating horror, and the result is a phantasmagoria of good and evil, the intensity of experience refuelled periodically by injections of the author's personal emotions when confronted in his own life by certain crimes which appeared to him to reflect the very essence of the evil: most notably Stalin's betrayal of the Red Army – the wanton sacrifice of millions in the field, the deliberate abandonment of all those who were taken prisoner, and the arrest and punishment of those who managed to survive the Nazi camps. There are scenes from Goya, infinitely magnified; there is more than a flavour of Hieronymus Bosch.

It is thus not an ordinary book, it is a book which will one day provide basic material for innumerable ordinary books. It is an elegy and an indictment. It is also an act of contrition on the part of Solzhenitsyn himself for the heedlessness of his own

217

youth, an act in which he invites his whole people, who will one day read these pages, to join – and not only his own people.

Bolshevism's Lost Soul
Review of *Bukharin and the Bolshevik Revolution* by Stephen F. Cohen
1974

How on earth did Lenin and his handful of quarrelsome revolutionaries ever imagine that they could take over Russia and run it effectively, let alone socialise in short order a backward peasant country? The answer, of course, is that they did not. Some of them opposed the very idea of the Bolshevik coup, and even Lenin, recklessly seizing an unlooked-for opportunity, took it for granted that his Revolution could succeed only if a number of advanced Western countries, Germany above all, made their own revolutions and came to the support of their Russian comrades. In those early days it was a question of importing revolution, not exporting it.

By the time the awful truth dawned that Bolshevik Russia stood alone, and in ruins, the Party had greatly increased its membership, unified itself and secured an iron grip under the impact of civil war and intervention. But socialism seemed farther away than ever and nobody knew what to do next. Lenin needed all his unique authority to lead his followers into ideological retreat and introduce the New Economic Policy with its concessions to private enterprise. Many saw in this a great betrayal.

But the NEP started paying off and the country pulled itself painfully together. How things would have developed had Lenin not died prematurely nobody can tell. There were plenty of men, like Bukharin, who had been at one time or another doctrinaire radicals, or passionate exponents of 'statism', who were now convinced that the way to socialism must lead through the gradual and harmonious development of the country's natural resources and the education of its people. But the relatively unconsidered General Secretary, Joseph Stalin, had embarked on that bid for absolute power which started with an appeal to commonsense and moderation, involved the playing off of one faction against another, and ended, after a series of convulsive assaults upon the status quo, in absolute terror.

All this is a familiar story. But what Professor Cohen has done in this very important book is to bring out more sharply than ever before the essential unpreparedness, the chronic indecisiveness, waverings, shifts of emphasis, which marked the early days of Bolshevik rule: the vagueness and uncertainty of the aim, the fragmentation of a supposedly disciplined party, the failure to think seriously about the most immediate and elementary problems of government and economic life.

Hitherto most of the best writing on Soviet Russia has flood-lit the great 'historic' figures – Lenin and Stalin. The drama of Stalin's capture and destruction of the Party has centred on the fight with Trotsky – a presentation which suited both men. It suited Trotsky because it flattered his vanity, and it suited Stalin because it concealed the truth. It was very convenient for Stalin to be able to pretend that what he was fighting was Trotsky and Trotskyism; and Trotsky, by also insisting on this (even when his importance was marginal), played straight into the hands of the man who was quietly engaged in the destruction of all the forces of decency in the land – a task made easier by the fact that at one time or another the chief victims had themselves been associated with the policies of terror and repression inaugurated by Lenin and now used by Stalin with such brio.

The most interesting of these victims, and in some ways the most important, was Nikolai Bukharin, the youngest of all the early Bolsheviks – indeed, the Party's favourite son – the most gifted intellectually, the most charming. It was Bukharin whose attempts to save the soul of the Party (and himself) from Stalin's violence, now by fighting him, now by misguidedly co-operating with him, always by trying, hopelessly, to out-manoeuvre him, epitomised the desperate flounderings of all those who allowed themselves, by weakness, vanity, short-sightedness, to be trapped by Stalin and tainted by his poison.

It was Bukharin whose trial and execution in 1938 were to set the final seal on Stalin's victory.

Professor Cohen, in this brilliantly written, meticulously documented monograph, has not only reconstructed the tragedy of a fascinating man who ought to have known better than to pretend to government, he has also produced a classic study of the intellectual development of the foremost Bolshevik theoretician. Still more, by contemplating the whole Soviet arena through Bukharin's eyes he illuminates areas hitherto left in shadow, makes sense where there was none before, and, without in the least diminishing their importance, allows us to see Lenin and Stalin as they were, men among men.

He has, in a word, achieved a breakthrough in Soviet studies. Let us hope it is an omen. Professor Cohen was only fifteen when Stalin died. He thus belongs to a new generation unawed by Lenin, unimpressed by Trotsky, untraumatised by Stalin. His book shows the way to the rediscovery of an important part of the Russian reality long forgotten, which now, for good or ill, and after many believed it had been destroyed by Stalin for ever, is reasserting itself as we watch.

Lady with a Camera
Review of *With the Armies of the Tsar* by Florence Farmborough
1974

In August 1914 a young Englishwoman, Miss Farmborough, was living without a care in the world in the bosom of one of those cheerfully expansive Russian families, teaching English to the daughters of a distinguished Moscow heart-specialist. Six months later, after working hard and pulling strings, she found herself, a barely qualified Red Cross nursing sister, caught up in one of the most terrible actions of the war and in the very thick of a process which was eventually to reach its climax in the October Revolution.

Early in the war the Russians (full of confidence, in spite of

Tannenberg) had broken the Austro-Hungarian army in Galicia and pushed on across the River San to Gorlice in the foothills of the Carpathians and beyond. But in the spring of 1915 the Germans under Mackensen took charge and turned the tide, beating back the Russians and not stopping until, weeks later, practically all the lost ground had been regained. It was on the eve of this great retreat that Miss Farmborough arrived at Gorlice with her front-line surgical unit.

It should have been a tiny world in itself, a haven of sanity and solace on the very fringe of organised violence. But it was itself caught up in violence, overwhelmed by the shattered bodies from another world on the run, condemned to endless movement by night in primitive transport on murderous roads, overrun by all the paraphernalia of a defeated army, stopping to set up shop again and again, only to be closed down and put once more on the road under shellfire from the advancing Germans, hungry and cold and dazed with lack of sleep, beseiged not only by the walking wounded while they tended the dying but also by a ravaged and starving peasantry.

It is a forgotten war. Certainly Tannenberg is remembered. But who remembers the fighting in Volhynia, Galicia, Romania, the Carpathians? Here nobody won, and all public memory of some of the longest and bloodiest battles in history was wiped out by the disintegration of imperial Russia and imperial Austria-Hungary. Spectacular advances and retreats of a kind unknown on the Western front between 1914 and 1918 alternated with spells of trench warfare in appalling conditions. Time and again a million men on either side were thrown into head-on collision. And through it all Miss Farmborough kept a diary.

She not only noted with a keen, unsentimental eye everything she saw and did; amazingly, she also took photographs, and not with a box Brownie, but with a heavy plate camera on a tripod which she managed to lug round and set up whenever she had a spare moment, developing the plates in improvised dark-rooms and sending them back across half a continent to Moscow. That diary and a good selection of those photographs form this enthralling record of a lost epoch, worked over, tidied up and heavily cut by Miss Farmborough herself in the tranquillity of her eighty-seventh year.

She cannot give us the scale of the violence in which she was involved. Nobody can do that. But with a fine eye for speaking detail she shows what it was like, the fluctuating intensity of the fighting measured by the fluctuations in the stream of shattered bodies that passed through her hands. This is the underside of war, with a vengeance. But more than this, with greater exactitude than I have encountered elsewhere, she shows, unconscious of how it will all end, step by step the collapse of a fighting army.

The first ominous signs, not understood for what they were, were seen in 1916 when troops started arriving without rifles to reinforce the great summer offensive. Soon there are rumours, not believed at first, of demonstrations and riots in Moscow and Petrograd; then news of the abdication of the Czar – news so remote from all comprehension that at first it made no difference to the mood of the fighting troops. Kerensky, nothing but a name at first, begins to emerge as a hero figure. Then he is more than a name. He turns up to address the front-line troops in Miss Farmborough's sector, and she is dazzled by his rhetoric.

But discipline is slackening, and there are other mysterious agitators, urging the troops to defy their officers, to lay down their arms. Petrograd is very far away. Miss Farmborough is deep in Romania now, her unit in support of the army threatening Austria in the Balkans. But there is no more central leadership and when the end comes the front is simply not there.

It was only by a series of miracles that this now solitary Englishwoman was able to make her way through chaos first to Moscow, then across Siberia to Vladivostok, somehow hanging on not only to her diary and her photographs, but also to her monstrous camera, to take one last photograph of the great harbour dominated by British cruisers under the protection of whose guns she was thankful to embark on a waiting American transport. It had been a rough ride. It is not only a most moving story of human endurance and courage; it is also a close-up of the transformation, almost overnight, of a disciplined society into a barbarian rabble.

Workers' Purgatory
Review of *The Seven Days of Creation*
by Vladimir Maximov
1975

The fact that rebellious writers, novelists above all, form almost the only articulate opposition in the Soviet Union places on the backs of generally contemplative and unmeddling individuals a very heavy burden. Once in a way a man or a woman comes along who is strong enough to bear it: a Solzhenitsyn. But as a rule it is too much. For a Soviet novelist with an active social conscience must not only find the courage to fight a more or less single-handed campaign against the embattled state; he has also to express in his work an immense range of protest against the failures and iniquities of state and society which in the West is conveniently shared among hundreds of reforming societies, pressure groups, periodicals, and countless thousands of agitating individuals.

Imagine the whole burden of trying to tell the truth, or part of it, about our own society falling on half a dozen novelists who will sooner or later be thrown out of their union (a closed shop as recommended by our incomparably silly Mr Foot) and, unless they are very lucky, into concentration camps or worse.

That is why the frequent complaint that Soviet writers critical of their country's regime are discussed too much in political terms is so nonsensical. Of course they are, and have been ever since the reign of Nicholas I, and will continue to be until the proper people take over the business of opposition and somebody gets up in the Supreme Soviet, denounces Brezhnev and all his works, and is not led away in chains.

With this sort of background it is not to be wondered at if dissident writers tend to bite off more than they can chew. Vladimir Maximov, it seems to me, is driven and oppressed by so much that he feels he must say that his powerful talents are stretched to their limit and sometimes beyond. He has attempted nothing less than a panoramic view of the fate, the suffering and the corruption, of the Russian working class through three generations of Soviet rule. It is as though he were determined to work into this one book, directly or obliquely, the whole of his experience because tomorrow he might die.

His strength is that he himself was born a proletarian among proletarians. His father was imprisoned by Stalin, then killed in the war. Maximov at twelve years old, in 1944, was on his own and on the run, in and out of children's homes and reformatories, drifting from one odd job to another, then, as a bricklayer, following the money to remote areas all over Russia. Against this sort of background the roughness, drunkenness and degradation of millions of Maximov's countrymen is reflected in these pages. But the core of the book is on a higher level, centred on the painful awakening of the elderly hero, a retired railwayman once proud of his uniform and a devoted Party member, to the fact that he has sacrificed everything, family, love, friendship, human warmth in his dedication to a soulless Moloch that has devoured his own life and the life of a great people.

The strength of the book is in its episodes. It is unfair to compare Maximov with either Solzhenitsyn or Pasternak, as has been done. He is a desperately honest writer of great gifts who has put himself outside the pale of Soviet society and now lives in exile. But he is not a born novelist. His characterisation is weak and the devices he uses to contain and connect up his episodes – dreams, the convenient outpouring of life stories, coincidences, etc. – are outworn. He has a marvellous eye, however, an exact ear for dialogue, and the power to make a scene live.

His scenes range far and wide: from glimpses of the lower depths in the worst kind of contemporary Moscow slum to the building of a new prison in the Central Asian desert; from the forced evacuation of a herd of cattle across half Russia in face of the advancing Germans to a hospital for hopeless cases. And through the hero's memories and through the exploration of the lives of the relatives and acquaintances he rediscovers in his belated search for a human purpose, the whole period of Soviet history is covered. It is the step-by-step revelation of the pursuit of a false idol. It is a bleak revelation. Here are Russian working men and women, the very people who were to inherit the earth, and here, soaked in vodka, is their inheritance. No wonder some of them start turning to religion.

The book suffers terribly in translation. Maximov's leaping style, full of vitality, rejoicing in words, is flattened; his gutter dialogue loses all its tang. Since the translation is anonymous the publishers must take the whole blame for spoiling an important book. And also, it seems to me, for tolerating the slavish adherence to the Russian use of Christian names and patronymics, to say nothing of pet names, which must make it almost impossible for an English reader unfamiliar with these usages to know for some of the time who is who.

A World of Evil
Review of *The Gulag Archipelago* Vol. II by Alexander Solzhenitsyn
1975

There is no need, as there was eighteen months ago when the first volume of *The Gulag Archipelago* appeared, to explain the title: like the Final Solution it has gone into the language. And Solzhenitsyn put it there by virtue of his genius.

About that genius there can be no mistake. Certainly it is flawed. One may disagree with some of Solzhenitsyn's views, catch him out in inaccuracies, find him at times grossly unfair, hold reservations about his actual writing, feel unease in face of a certain moral arrogance. But with all that he is one of the towering figures of the age, as writer, as moralist, as hero. Leaving aside all his other work, in *The Gulag Archipelago* he has achieved the impossible.

He has done this by rendering in words, by re-creating within the covers of a book, a world as remote from most of us as Mars: an immense world of limitless suffering, corruption and degradation, inhabited by millions who dragged out shattered lives, starving, sick, exhausted by impossible labours in the harshest climate in the world until death mercifully took most of them; a world ruled over by an army of slave-drivers of almost unrelieved brutality and vileness, themselves commanded by a police bureaucracy nurtured in cynicism, greed and sadism in the service of a monster.

And this world, here made so real, is still by no means wholly cleared away. Twenty-two years after the monster's death, even at this very moment, many of our own contemporaries are condemned to live as here described, some well known, most not. There they are, as all these millions were before them, not far away, just a little way round the curvature of the earth, so that the sun rises and sets on their misery only a few hours earlier than here, and the same cold moon and stars stare down on them.

Until Solzhenitsyn, it could be taken for granted that nobody would ever be able to convey anything like a complete picture of the supreme barbarities of our time. This is not to say that nobody has written about them. Of course, many have done so, and sometimes with great power. But such writings have all been severely limited in range. The Olympian view was absent. We were given not Evil enthroned but, as it were, bits and pieces of the Devil's work.

Some of the bits about prison and forced labour in the Soviet Union have been so outstandingly good that, given a strong enough imagination, the whole could be deduced from the parts. But imagination faltered. The mind refused to grasp the whole – still more to develop a coherent picture of the organisation, getting for a million strong (and rich!) of which these camps and prisons were the proud end-products; or of the Government which conjured up that organisation (Cheka, GPU, NKVD, etc.).

Solzhenitsyn has achieved the impossible by helping us to grasp the whole.

How difficult that is I can testify from personal experience, having had the unusual advantage of glimpsing at first hand some of the commonplaces of these books – the casual shooting by the guard of a prisoner falling out of convoy to snatch a crust out of the snow; packed prison-vans standing in sidings with the guards refusing water to the desperate mouths forced against tiny gratings; frozen corpses unloaded from prison trains and stacked like cord-wood; prisoners set to ship logs (whole trees) out of river ice with broken picks and left to die in the snow where they fell with exhaustion. And so on.

Even with these advantages, and knowing much more from reliable sources, I found it for many years virtually impossible to grasp the *scale* of the iniquity. The mind rejected even what the eyes – and the heart – perceived. Part of the trouble, I think, has been that for a number of generations Western man had lost the sense of evil. Faced with manifestations that were clearly evil, his instinct was to treat them as aberrations. But now we know that evil can be everywhere at once.

Solzhenitsyn has had the greatness to show evil in operation on a continental scale and with a crudeness special to a rough and backward country which has a weakness for extremes and which, with the Revolution, destroyed with certain hated taskmasters virtually the entire civilising element.

In the first volume of his masterpiece he was writing from the centre outwards – the centre being the point he himself occupied after the shock of his arrest and sentencing. In the second volume he works from the outside to the centre, showing the birth of the system under Lenin and tracing its cancerous spread until it had subjugated and morally ruined a great people – finishing with chapter after chapter dealing with special aspects of life and society in that fearful imperium.

But even Solzhenitsyn, it seems to me, shies away from the ultimate truth. Stalin, of course, was a monster, and without the provision of a monster of that calibre the Archipelago could not have become what it did become. But Solzhenitsyn tells himself, and us, that the extermination of millions by the various means so exactly described in these pages was deliberately planned by the monster, stage by stage. This I should like to believe. But I think the truth was worse: the monster lurched from muddle to muddle, not seeing clearly where he was going, not (at any rate for some years) the unchallenged tyrant, but positively sustained in his extemporised villainy by men and women of good will as well as by dedicated rogues – most of whom, of course, were themselves doomed to extinction, though again not as part of a plan.

To look at the problem like this is to make it harder. Solzhenitsyn begins to approach it in his final section, particularly in his chapter about corruption. But that section needs to be carried further. Too many of his fellow-countrymen gave way too easily. Why? Too many of the survivors are rediscovering decency very slowly. Why? If Solzhenitsyn could give us useful answers to these questions he could help the rest of us to a better understanding of our own vulnerability. In fact, Solzhenitsyn's one major weakness, it seems to me, is his lack of sympathy with human vulnerability. He is too hard, for example, on some of his fellow writers, apparently failing to understand the paralysing nature of the pressures brought to bear on them under Stalin. The few heroes he salutes. But he fails to distinguish between the wicked, the venal, the sycophantic, the weak, the silly and the muddled. Perhaps he is a little too much inclined to confuse the terrifying certainty of genius, which he possesses, with moral integrity.

Introduction to *The Grigorenko Papers* by Peter Grigorenko 1976

I suppose most people who are likely to read this book are by now familiar with at least some part of the Grigorenko story. They will know, that is to say, that Major-General Peter Grigorenko, a distinguished Soviet Army officer, has long been prominent among those critics of certain aspects of their Government's behaviour who have been arrested by the KGB, declared insane by KGB psychiatrists, and shut up in lunatic asylums. Far fewer are likely to have a clear idea of the precise nature of General Grigorenko's offences against authority and of the processes whereby he found himself stripped of rank, civil rights and means of livelihood and subjected to a sustained and long-drawn-out attempt to destroy him mentally and physically.

This is what this book is very largely about, but it is about much more besides. Grigorenko has for many years lived not for

228

himself but for others. It was for helping others in distress that he found himself repeatedly in trouble and finally arrested and put away. In this collection of papers Grigorenko is less concerned with his own case than with winning justice, or mercy, for others. As a rule he cites his own appalling case only to make a point, to draw a moral or a parallel. But all the time, unconsciously, he is showing what sort of a man he is, revealing absolute integrity and almost unimaginable depths of courage in his refusal to give an inch in face of the most dire warnings. So that when, turning from these pleas, demands, tirades, indictments on behalf of this or that victim of this or that iniquity, we read the more impersonal documents bearing directly on his own fate – his case-history, for example, as recorded by the official psychiatrists, their diagnoses and the reasons for them, the unofficial analysis of those diagnoses by independent Russian psychiatrists (one of whom, Semyon Gluzman, was himself arrested and sentenced to a labour camp for daring to put his name to it) – Grigorenko has been brought close enough to us to appear in all his very remarkable individuality as a living man, not as an abstract figure in an obscure, faraway and recondite argument about justice.

Not only a remarkable man but a quite unusually clearheaded and lucid one. As one reads, one is struck by the mental vigour and the sheer hard thinking of this man who was educated and brought up in a Communist society, working his way up from his peasant background and somehow learning to think for himself, even though his whole conscious life was lived in the bosom of the Party. That ardent but independently minded Marxist-Leninist, Roy Medvedev (whose celebrated brother, Zhores, was himself locked up in a madhouse for a time) wrote of Grigorenko that nobody could have been more sane:

We had a particularly long and involved conversation at the end of April 1969, that is, only a few days before his arrest. He is clearly an extraordinary and absolutely normal man in complete command of his faculties. Much of what he said seemed to me mistaken, and I told him so . . . . He argued with me, but without a trace of intolerance and agreed with some of my objections. He made no attempt to impose his

229

own views on me and recognised that there could be other approaches to the problems that concerned him.

This seems to me an extremely important statement, to be borne in mind when perusing the unblushing and sinister tomfoolery of the so-called 'forensic psychiatrical examinations' conducted under the auspices of the infamous Professors Luns and Morozov of the equally infamous Serbsky Institute.

Even so, it is not so important as the direct impression which Grigorenko's own writing will make upon the readers. I myself found it impossible to read without a twinge of sympathy for the Soviet leaders: how best to defend themselves against this terrible little man who kept on telling the truth?

I say the Soviet leaders, the Government of the Soviet Union, because the men ultimately responsible for the atrocities which declare themselves in the following pages were not the faceless officers of this or that department of the KGB nor even Professors Lunts, Morozov and their *confrères*. These men, vile as some of them are, were acting under orders, and the orders came from the leadership of the Communist Party, whose instrument is the KGB. When Grigorenko was first declared insane the KGB was acting on behalf of Khrushchev; during his second and much longer more brutal incarceration, beginning in 1969 and lasting five years, it was acting for Brezhnev. I stress this matter of responsibility because there is a tendency to hold the KGB itself responsible, as it were, in a vacuum, detached from the actual business of government. And I hope it is not asking too much of the reader to suggest that when he reads in these pages of what was being done to General Grigorenko as recently as last year he should bear in mind that it was done with the sanction, if not on the direct instructions of, Leonid Brezhnev, that jovially beaming exponent of détente.

The story unfolded in these pages is more than deeply moving; it is a story of the greatest importance for a proper understanding of the realities of life in the Soviet Union twenty years after the death of Stalin. It is particularly revealing about the almost total inability of Soviet officialdom, from the highest to the lowest, nurtured for so long on lies and driven for so long by fear, to distinguish right from wrong, to sustain a logical argument (even, perhaps, to perceive the desirability of logical thinking) or to understand what is meant by the rule of law.

The story is also a monument to a hero of our time.

The idea has been spread around that General Grigorenko's involvement in what may broadly be called the Human Rights movement in the Soviet Union resulted from a softening of the brain, sad and regrettable, of a man who until the 1960s had been an exemplary soldier. In fact he began skirmishing with authority a quarter of a century ago when he was only thirty-four. He was deeply critical of Stalin's military shortsightedness and bungling which cost Russia so dear when the Red Army crumpled up under Hitler's onslaught in that terrible summer of 1941. And he dared express his feelings – not in public, of course, but in the privacy of a Party meeting. For this he was formally reprimanded and marked for life. But he was so good at his job that it was not until after the war, in which he was twice wounded and several times decorated, that the reprimand was held against him, retarding farther promotion. By then he had emerged as a leading military thinker holding important positions at the Frunze Academy, the equivalent of the British Staff College. But it was not until some time after Khrushchev's denunciation of Stalin in 1956 that he was promoted to Major-General.

Grigorenko's criticism of Stalin, an almost unheard of liberty in 1941, was all of a piece with what was to happen publicly twenty years later. His individualism came out in other matters. For example, he offended authority by marrying a woman whose family had been virtually wiped out by Stalin and was therefore herself to be considered untouchable. After the war, in 1949, he paid a visit to his home village in the Ukraine and was so appalled by the conditions there and made so sick at heart by the way in which the villagers clung to him, the distinguished soldier-son, as their great hope and redeemer, that he stirred up deep resentments against himself among Party officials for doing what he could to help. Later, in 1976, as so often in the van of current military thinking, he started preaching the new science of cybernetics, today regarded by Soviet authority, almost totemistically, with a holy hush, but then officially banned.

What I am trying to show is that Grigorenko even in his palmiest days was known as an awkward customer, and his subsequent conduct has been really all of a piece with what went before. In those early days, while possessing a mind of his own and refusing to be frightened into sycophancy, he was selective in his indiscretions, only letting himself go when he believed that silence was the coward's way, and that something might be achieved by speaking out. It was not until much later, the period illumined by this book, that, with nothing to lose but his sanity or his life, he went over to the attack with a boldness and a recklessness (in the literal sense of the word) rarely equalled and never excelled in the history of protest and nonconformity. For towards the end of the 1960s it must have seemed to him that there was nothing at all to be gained from circumspection and discretion, that he might just as well be hung for a sheep as for a lamb.

It was not until 1961 that General Grigorenko began to become a serious problem to the Soviet leadership. By that time he was a figure of very considerable standing, a Major-General, an active member of the Communist Party, a leading military theoretician and instructor, and still only fifty-four years old. He was disturbed in general by the slow and erratic progress of the de-Stalinisation movement and in particular by signs that a new 'personality cult' was being built up round the figure of Khrushchev. As a delegate to one of the many regional Party conferences held all over the land to prepare for the full Party Congress, he made a speech suggesting that it was high time that all 'elective offices', including, of course, the First Secretaryship of the Party and the Premiership (both then held by Khrushchev), and including the entire higher leadership, should be held on a rota system, precluding any one individual from perpetuating his authority. For good measure, he urged that the said higher leadership should be paid a great deal less. The interesting thing is that the first reaction of the majority of his fellow delegates was to reject the immediate proposal of a senior official that Grigorenko should be punished by being deprived of his mandate (i.e. shown the door); it was only after a great deal of coming and going behind the scenes that a vote was rigged against him. He was afterwards officially reprimanded by the Party and transferred to the reserve. After six months in limbo he suffered a reduction in rank and was posted to the Far East.

But now his blood was up. All he had ever done was to take at their face value the Party rules which allowed free and open discussion of all problems in the privacy of Party meetings. Stalin had made nonsense of these rules, but Khrushchev talked a great deal about returning to Leninism. If Khrushchev could not live up to his own declarations, it was time somebody else did. So in November 1963 Grigorenko formed his 'Action Group for the Revival of Leninism' – one of many such short-lived societies, or pressure groups, which cropped up in that comparatively liberal era, which issued leaflets calling for a return to the spirit of Lenin and citing as examples of anti-Leninist behaviour such unmentionable events as the brutal suppression of food riots in Tiflis, Novocherkask and else-where. Within three months he was arrested, found insane, locked up and reduced to the ranks.

That was in February 1964, just eight months before Khrushchev himself was deposed. Soon after that event, in March 1965, Grigorenko was discharged as 'cured', but he could not get back into the army and was forced to work as a manual labourer to supplement his greatly reduced army pension. It was from 1965 onwards that he must have felt that he had nothing to lose but his life.

I do not propose to outline his career from then on. The facts are best and most vividly exposed in the documents that follow – not least in the self-incriminating nonsense-talk of the KGB psychiatrists so full of contradictions and remarkable for the diagnosis: 'mental illness in the form of pathological (paranoid) development of the personality, *accompanied by reformist ideas* [my italics] and by early signs of cerebral arterio-sclerosis.' Indeed, the long reports on Grigorenko as out-patient and in-patient tell us as much about the sad state of Russia as any hostile commentary, and Grigorenko's own notes about his treatment in various asylums make what would otherwise seem a product of fantasy most chillingly real.

It was Alexander Solzhenitsyn, protesting in 1970 against the imprisonment in an asylum of Zhores Medvedev, who offered the most searing indictment of these people, and the system which sanctioned their behaviour:

Servile psychiatrists, who break their Hippocratic oath and are able to describe concern for social problems as 'mental illness', can declare a man insane for being too passionate or for being too calm, for the brightness of his talents or for his lack of them . . . .

It is time to understand that the imprisonment of sane persons in madhouses because they have minds of their own is *spiritual murder*, a variation on the *gas chambers* and even more cruel: the condemned suffer torments more fruitful and prolonged. Like the gas chambers, these crimes will never be forgotten, and those involved will be condemned for all time, during their life and after death, without benefit of moratorium.

Grigorenko gives us a very vivid idea of the fearful effect on a sane man of being confined by force among genuine lunatics and treated as one of them. But even so, he is not able to tell us from his own experience of the crimes committed against certain individuals (as they are being committed at this moment of writing against the mathematician, Plyush) whose minds are systematically destroyed by murderous drugging.

As Solzhenitsyn prophesies, those concerned in these crimes, from Messrs Brezhnev and Kosygin to the assistants of Professors Lunts and Morozov, will be condemned for all time. The Czar Nicholas I had the philosopher Chaadeyev declared insane for comparing the development of Russia unfavourably with that of Western Europe. But, although much is nowadays made of the old Russian custom of locking up nonconformists in lunatic asylums, in fact this happened very seldom under the Czars, and Chaadeyev himself was not even imprisoned. He was declared insane, but he was not sent to an asylum, being confined to his own house under medical supervision. Before very long he was out again and moving freely about St Petersburg. And yet Nicholas is still remembered, and always will be, for this act.

Nicholas almost certainly genuinely believed that anyone who thought of Russia as Chaadeyev said he did must be mad. I am quite sure that thousands upon thousands of conformist Russians would regard Grigorenko as mad for setting himself up against the autocratic will of the Soviet leadership. What would seem to them particularly mad is precisely what seems to us to be particularly noble – the repeated intervention of this lonely and persecuted man, who had enough troubles nearer home, not only on behalf of unknown youngsters who were being crushed by the immense apparatus of state for learning to think and conduct themselves like decent and responsible human beings, but also for a virtually unknown nation – the unfortunate Tartars of the Crimea violently dispossessed and removed from their homeland by Stalin and then cruelly disappointed in their hopes of better times when Stalin had gone. It was Grigorenko's perfectly disinterested concern for these unfortunates for whom nobody cared which the Government of Brezhnev and Kosygin exploited in their desire to put him away for the second time with the least possible publicity. He flew secretly to Tashkent in May 1969 in response to a message asking him to appear as a witness for the defence in the Tartar cause. The message in fact originated from the KGB who wanted him out of Moscow so that he could be arrested and put away far from home and friends. That was the beginning of the long agony in which every effort was made to break Grigorenko's will and force him to recant – until, in the summer of 1974 after he had suffered a succession of severe heart attacks, the authorities, not wanting him to die on their hands, ordered his release. But others, whom we must never forget, are still being tortured by the men whose names will live in the archives of dishonour.

Limits of Imagination
Review of *Lenin in Zürich*
by Alexander Solzhenitsyn
1976

When a respectable novelist sets out to re-create a character from recent history he must obviously be driven by the conviction that he can do better by the truth than any memoirist historian, or biographer. And he must stand or fall by his success or failure in imposing his own truth upon the reader, whose acceptance must be no less total and everlasting than his acceptance of characters having no existence outside the novelist's mind – until they live again in the reader's mind. There is no room for relativities here: only the absolute will do. It is not enough to offer a view of Napoleon which convinces for the time it takes to read the book, then fades. The reader must feel that it is the only possible view: he has at last seen the real Napoleon, and there is nothing more to be said.

Can this be done? Tolstoy tried it with Napoleon and failed. Certainly he succeeded in making the titan look small, but he offered no convincing vision of what was left. But Kutusov? I imagine that pretty well every reader of *War and Peace* happily accepts Kutusov as he stands. Surely this miraculous piece of characterisation must indicate that it is indeed possible for a gifted novelist to weave a real-life character into his fictional design? Alas no, for Tolstoy's Kutusov is almost wholly imaginary, more imaginary than many of the ostensibly invented characters in that great gallery. Tolstoy's benevolent, indolent, infinitely patient embodiment of all the Russian virtues is as far as possible removed from the historical Kutusov, lecherous, lazily corrupt. We accept him because he falls so perfectly into place in Tolstoy's narrative. But a close look at that narrative soon shows that its author is not in the least interested in seeking the truth about his historical characters but only in using them to dramatise and advertise a theory, his own personal view of life and the historical process and the nature of legendary heroes. This is art employed not in the search for truth but in the interests of propaganda.

Now Solzhenitsyn gives us Lenin. Can he succeed where Tolstoy failed? It would seem to be improbable, for magnificent writer as he can be (and a heroic figure it goes without saying), Solzhenitsyn as artist lacks the iron-hard discipline and self-criticism of Tolstoy, as well as that terrible, all-seeing eye.

Lenin in Zürich consists of eleven chapters from three volumes, two of them far from being completed, of the author's work in progress, a series of self-contained but interlocking novels dealing with the death of the old Russia and the birth of the new; 'the chief artistic design of my life', Solzhenitsyn has called it. A vast work it certainly will be. So far only the first volume has been published, *August 1914*. Volume Two will be called *October 1916*, Volume Three *March 1917*. I have no idea how many more there will be. A key to Solzhenitsyn's line of thought is his decision to call these volumes 'Knots' (*Uzel*, in Russian). He might have called them 'Conjunctures', for they are evidently arranged in time to fix moments of crisis when conflicting forces from many sides converge. One of those forces was Lenin. His first appearance should have been in Chapter Twenty-two of *August 1914* (Chapter One in *Lenin in Zürich*) which was omitted on the author's instructions when the English translation was published in 1972. Seven of the remaining ten chapters will take their places in *October 1916*, the other three in *March 1917*.

The first thing to be said is that these eleven chapters in preview read clearly and consecutively. From the mechanical point of view Solzhenitsyn was justified in grouping together these scattered extracts from an unfinished work in progress and publishing them out of context and in advance. Evidently what happened was that after his arrest and expulsion from Russia, Solzhenitsyn, fetching up in Zürich, very soon began to find out all sorts of things about Lenin unknown to him before though well known in the West. Because of this he had to rewrite Chapter Twenty-two of *August 1914* – which is why that chapter remained unpublished. More than that, he must have found himself for a time very deeply absorbed in his detective work on Lenin. This led him to a weird story (grimly suppressed in Russia, but explored in detail by Western scholars) of the remarkable millionaire revolutionary Parvus/Helphand, whose connections with the Wilhelmstrasse enabled him to persuade the German Foreign Office not only to organise the transit of Lenin and his companions in the notorious sealed train through Germany, but also to finance the tiny Bolshevik Party during the critical months of 1917 when Lenin was manoeuvring and plotting to destroy the Provisional Government and take Russia out of the war.

Soon Solzhenitsyn had become so deeply sunk in his reconstruction of Lenin's Zürich existence that he seems in some sense almost to have become Lenin. He sought out Lenin's old haunts, worked in the Zwingli library, as Lenin had worked there, made the same lakeside and mountain excursions, experienced the same homesickness for Russia. Above all he suffered the same sense of frustration and disgust with his surroundings. With Lenin this was a complex of emotions: hatred of the smug Swiss bourgeoisie, contempt for, and fury with, the cowardice and treachery of his fellow-revolutionaries who had forgotten their internationalism under the impact of war. With Solzhenitsyn it was above all anger, contempt and despair when faced with the frivolity and corruption of the bourgeois West, the 'free world' which was betraying not only itself but also his, Solzhenitsyn's, dream. Added to this was the unexpected realisation that here in twentieth-century Zürich he was closer to Lenin than to almost anyone else. He, too, exiled from Russia, lived and laboured with ruthless and fanatical devotion to his cause, grudging the time for eating and sleeping, resenting every call that distracted him from his work, dedicated no less absolutely to the salvation of Russia from the consequences of revolution than Lenin had been to making revolution. The extremely high voltage induced in this narrative by the novelist's emotional relationship with the ghost of the man seen by him as an agent of destruction whose legend it was his mission to destroy, produces in these chapters an incandescence which for moments seems to justify Solzhenitsyn's method. But, to my mind, only for moments.

The book opens with a failed revolutionary of forty-four, slipping out of Austrian Poland and to neutral Switzerland immediately after the outbreak of war. It closes, two and a half years later, with Lenin's miraculous return to Russia when all had been given up for lost – so much so that he refused at first to believe that the Revolution had taken place (without Bolshevik assistance), the imperial throne abandoned.

Because of these narrow time limits, if Solzhenitsyn is to make sense of Lenin's character and revolutionary past and of the revolutionary movement as a whole in Russia (or as much of these as seems vital to him) he is forced to make full and elaborate use of retrospect, of flashback. And the method he has chosen, which gives him almost perfect freedom to range backwards and forward in time and laterally in space, is to get inside Lenin's skull and render his thoughts, fears, hopes, impressions, plans, as a rushing, brawling stream of consciousness only occasionally interrupted. With the result, inevitable it seems to me, that as one reads one is constantly demanding: Did Lenin really think that? What authority has the author for making him say, do, think, feel, the other? Yes, by all means such and such a statement is true as far as it goes; but is that how it really looked to Lenin himself? Certainly he rejoiced in the war and hoped desperately for it to be turned into a civil war – by all means; but did he in fact, as Solzhenitsyn insists, actually gloat over the thought of all those ruined and mutilated bodies?

Perhaps I should say at this point that I have for long regarded Lenin as one of the most detestable men who ever lived, his victory, his contemptuous dictatorship, a disaster for Russia and mankind. Solzhenitsyn's presentation brings out many of the characteristics which I find insupportable, but except for two or three flashes of superb perceptiveness (over almost before they are recorded, and lost in a welter of detail about the activity of fourth-rate conspirators), it fails to show his power over men. In a word, although this Lenin portrait is true as far as it goes, it is very far from complete. Certainly Lenin dithered over the 1905 revolution and then made a fool of himself; hated the young Trotsky because Trotsky could, and did, address multitudes, while Lenin had never talked to more than a dozen or so at a time; again and again showed malice; spent most of his time first quarrelling with friends and allies, then organising factions against them, then blackguarding them with Goebbels-like invective, turning them into enemies pursued with far more venom than their common enemy. Certainly he has an inspired political opportunist who passed for a political philosopher because he knew how to dress up his calculations in Marxist jargon. All this is true and Solzhenitsyn shows it. He also shows the consuming drive for power which went with so much pettifoggery, the slyness and the cunning which went with the head-on collisions, the almost insane strength of will which enabled him to hang on and declare that the Bolshevik Party was the sole repository of truth among all other revolutionary parties, even when, on occasion, that party was effectively reduced to two – he and his almost unimaginably boring helpmeet, Krupskaya; the contempt for the people, for fellow intellectuals too, displayed in his preference for lying

239

slogans, mercilessly repeated, over persuasion and argument. What Solzhenitsyn fails to do is to show how this man commanded others, recalling them to his side when they thought they had left him for ever. What he quite fails to suggest is the man who in spite of his ruthlessness and his really appalling cynicism was able to make himself a beloved father-figure in his own lifetime.

This, it seems to me, is a failure of method as much as of perception – though it might be said that the choice of method was itself a failure of perception. How can you convey the impact of a powerful personality if you limit yourself to a record of his private thoughts and feelings and the words with which he expresses some of them? It is worth recording that there is one passage in the book in which we suddenly begin to see Lenin whole. This is in the entirely imaginary episode when Lenin in his dreary bedsitter is visited by the amazing Parvus, a huge looming bulk of a man offering Lenin all the kingdoms of the earth if he will go back to Russia now, in 1916, under German sponsorship, and start a revolution which, he, Parvus, will finance. Lenin, crowded almost off the bed by this accomplished bounder, resists temptation and defeats him with a look – a look not of haughty nobility but of sleek Tartar cunning, which reduces Parvus, this conman who is used to having governments eating out of his hand, to amateur status. Lenin's look, of course, is seen from the outside. And for once the man is real and whole, as real and whole as in Bertrand Russell's unforgettable and prophetic description: for it may surprise Solzhenitsyn that it was his *bête-noir*, Bertrand Russell, who in 1918 visited Lenin and afterwards showed him for the first time as he really was – a self-satisfied tyrant, a man who enjoyed the exercise of cunning for its own sake and preferred the lie to the truth even if the truth might serve his purpose better . . . . Self-satisfaction is a key quality here, I think, and it is one of the qualities missing in Solzhenitsyn's Lenin except in a fairly primitive form. As Tolstoy knew so well, self-satisfaction to a very high degree is a *sine qua non* of the dominant male. Lenin positively exuded it. Solzhenitsyn has him worrying too much. Of course he worried, but he was for all practical purposes the man who *knew* and was pleased with himself for knowing, because he *knew better than anybody else in the history of the world.*

Lenin is not the only character from history in this great work in progress. The crux of *August 1914* is the battle of Tannenberg, in which the Russian high command and the treachery of General Rennenkampf allowed General Samsonov and his army to be cut off, surrounded, and systematically annihilated. Samsonov is presented as a heroic figure, the embodiment of Russia betrayed, and Solzhenitsyn's handling of him seemed to me three years ago highly suspect. So it does still. It would have been one thing to show Samsonov from the outside, a kind of Russian Laocoon, wrestling with many-headed evil and driven to suicide by the destruction of his army. In this way he could have been presented as a central and symbolic character, pulled down by Lilliputian jealousies and intrigues, the inefficiency and the corruption of colleagues and superiors. But Solzhenitsyn was not content with that. For long periods the action is seen and described through Samsonov's own eyes, through the eyes of an established historical figure, that is to say, whose thoughts and motives the author purports to expose as any novelist exposes the thoughts and motives of characters of his own imagining. So that, as now with Lenin, I found myself constantly asking questions that weakened the impact of the narrative.

I also found it presumption on the part of a novelist to pretend to exact knowledge of what went on in poor Samsonov's mind as he prepared to kill himself, alone in the deep forest.

If Solzhenitsyn wishes to imagine himself into the skin of a distinguished soldier driven to suicide, well and good: let him imagine Samsonov, by all means, or any other individual so situated, and give his creation another name. If, on the other hand, he wishes to reconstruct a historical drama and is thus compelled to portray the actual characters in that drama, when he should present those characters from the outside, in their speech, their appearance, their behaviour, their impact upon others. With all his skill, focusing the rays of his genius, he could give to any figure a three-dimensional look with the illusion of total revelation.

This, it seems to me, applies even more to Lenin, about whom we know so much. I have never been more acutely aware of the virtues of documented scholarship, its sterilities and excesses notwithstanding, than while reading this freehand contrivance presented by a great writer as a deeper truth than any historian or biographer can hope to achieve. I have never more acutely appreciated the magic of the novelist's imagination than when driven by contemplation of these chapters which make the worst of both worlds – the world of imagination and the world of hard fact – into considering what a magnificent novel could be written round an imaginary revolutionary based on Lenin.

It will be interesting to see whether Solzhenitsyn revises and improves these chapters radically before they reappear in their predetermined places. They are not good Solzhenitsyn, although they contain superb moments. As one reads one feels that the author's desperate need to shatter the Lenin myth has driven him to work too fast. Much of the narrative is curiously perfunctory, the stream of consciousness rattles on with little variation of tempo and all too often with the sketchiest obeisance to verisimilitude: sometimes it reads like a provisional draft, as though the author's mind is racing ahead. I refer particularly to those very long stretches when Solzhenitsyn is dutifully 'getting in' Lenin's past and fixing him in the revolutionary scene with his rag-tag companions of the junior league of European revolutionaries and their silly plots and aspirations. The narrative comes alive and brilliant all too rarely. It does so when Solzhenitsyn is *living* in Lenin's unpolitical thoughts about Zürich and his destiny and the cross he has to bear – then, as suggested above, coming virtually to identify himself with his hero. It does so again when he is describing *from the outside*, and out of his own imagination, the encounters between Lenin and Parvus. Here at last the novelist is set free.

I think it would be out of place at this stage to discuss Solzhenitsyn's view of the causes of the Revolution and what came after. This, really, is what the whole immense project is about: there will be time for judgement later. I do not think it out of place to enter one more reservation about Solzhenitsyn as a novelist. Of course he stands head and shoulders above the ruck. He has proved himself in *Cancer Ward* and *The First Circle*, to say nothing of *The Gulag Archipelago*, as a documentary writer of genius, *sui generis*. But has it escaped general notice that this great writer has yet to show that he can write about women?

242

The sentimentalities which spoilt the love affair in *Cancer Ward* fleetingly repeat themselves here again, in, of all things, Lenin's love life. Lenin had a well-documented affair with a fellow revolutionary, Inessa Armand. Solzhenitsyn may or may not make too much of this (I think he does); but he certainly makes a remarkable hash of it. Here we are, allegedly, inside Lenin's mind as he thinks about Inessa: 'From where she was, from Sorenberg in the south, he felt her love calling to him. He remembered the flutter of eyelids over half closed eyes, the quick gleam of her white teeth . . . .'

Shades of Anna and Natasha!

Books and Bookmen

A Very Brave Conversion
Review of *To Be Preserved Forever* by Lev Kopelev
1977

Readers of *The First Circle* will remember the strange prisoner, Lev Rubin, a large, boisterous, bearded extrovert who was also a gifted philologist. It was Rubin at Mavrino who developed the technique of voice-printing to identify unknown speakers, thus making himself (Stalin's victim) into Stalin's willing agent – enthusiastically working to perfect a device which he knew would be used by Stalin's police to catch more innocents as he himself had been caught.

The thing about Rubin was that although his life had been destroyed by Stalin he remained a convinced Communist – or, more accurately, a blind believer in the Soviet system.

We now discover that Solzhenitsyn's Rubin was in fact based upon the real-life Lev Kopelev, the author of this book. And it should be said at once that Kopelev's narrative is a resounding, though quite unconscious, tribute to the power and sharpness of Solzhenitsyn's vision. There are moments in *The First Circle* when Rubin, blithely and argumentatively working away to deliver one more instrument of terror into the hands of his jailers, seems almost too much of a good thing. But now we see that Solzhenitsyn's portrait has nothing of the caricature about it. It goes straight to the essence of the man as he submitted to the orders of corrupt and repellent thugs whom he despised and hated: because the infallible historical movement in which he believed used these unworthy monsters as its vehicle, he must rise above his own personal feelings . . . .

One of the most valuable features of Kopelev's absorbing narrative is the unique insight it offers into the mind of an intelligent (but not very perceptive) young man who actively assisted in the commission of some of Stalin's worst crimes, glorying in his part, totally convinced that the means, any means, are justified by the end – and sticking to this insane conviction even when he sees at his feet the broken human bodies which bear witness to the atrocity of those means, as when he euphorically took part in the violent seizure of grain from starving peasants, certain that he was engaged in a heroic action to transform society.

The second valuable feature is the light the book throws on the moral and mental squalor of the middle ranks of Soviet officialdom, whether in uniform, attached like toxic parasites to the unfortunate Red Army, or in civilian clothes. This is a milieu almost impossible for the foreigner to present to his own countrymen. I have had to work with such officials in war and peace. Their sycophancy, their barefaced lying, their treachery, their cowardice, are so blatant, their ignorance so stultifying, their stupidity so absolute, that I have found it impossible to convey it with any credibility to those fortunate enough never to have encountered it. Kopelev manages to bring them to life in all their horror because until he went to prison they seemed quite ordinary to him. These are the people we are still up against in a society which changes with glacial slowness.

Kopelev went to prison for being decent. He had done his level best to turn himself into a good Soviet official, but in the end he failed. As a trained philologist and a natural linguist he found himself in that Red Army department responsible for processing selected German prisoners, turning them against Hitler, and engaging them in various quite dangerous front-line propaganda escapades. He had always been impetuous and outspoken, but hitherto his outspokenness had hardly amounted to much more than 'down with the fascist hyaenas!' (meaning also you and me). He had usually agreed with authority, even during the years of the purges.

He went into battle yelling 'For Stalin! For the Motherland!' (Readers who are not acquainted with the unembarrassed manner in which quite educated Soviet citizens are apt to express their patriotic emotions are in for a shock.) But now he began to disagree with his superiors about the behaviour of Soviet troops in occupied Germany. At a time when the writer Ilya Ehrenburg far, far from the front was still yelling for total destruction and annihilation, Kopelev was finding that some of the Germans he encountered in the line of duty were human beings. And when the Soviet advance became an avalanche he was revolted by the atrocities committed by his own country-men, while never forgetting the unspeakable behaviour of the Nazis.

He spoke out, demanding punishment for murder and rape. In no time at all he was charged with giving comfort to the enemy and after a sickening process of interrogations and rigged trials during which he fought back hard, found himself faced with a ten-year sentence. The fact that Marshal Rokos-sowski had himself instructed that troops under his command must be shot for looting made no difference. We know, of course, all about the way those troops in fact behaved. What Kopelev does is to take us into the minds of the officers who allowed such behaviour, or even encouraged it.

Some parts of the book cover familiar ground – everything to do with Soviet prisons and camps, for example. What makes this narrative outstanding is the unique picture of the sort of men who made Stalin's Russia what it was. There is also the character of the author himself – a man who tried to turn himself into a zombie but failed because of an inner decency allied with great courage – and, when that decency was quick-ened by the experience of prison, blossomed into one of those outgoing Russian eccentrics who make friends everywhere and cannot be put down except by naked force.

Seeds of Dr Zhivago
Review of *Meetings with Pasternak*
by Alexander Gladkov
1977

Art may be long, but there are times when politics seems longer. It may be salutary to reflect that the Government of the Soviet Union is today still run (a few casualties excepted) by the very men who presided over the banning in their great, warm Motherland of *Dr Zhivago*, and inspired the unspeakable onslaught on the author when he so far forgot himself as to win a Nobel prize. These men, Mr Brezhnev and Mr Kosygin high among them, refused to allow a single obituary notice to appear, let alone permit a public funeral, for the greatest Russian writer since Chekhov, when he died in 1960.

Since then admirers among his contemporaries and disciples have been inhibited from coming forward with their personal memories. The most revealing impressions so far published (not, of course, in the Soviet Union) have been Nadezhda Mandelstam's in her two-volume masterpiece, *Hope against Hope* and *Hope Abandoned*. But to Mrs Mandelstam Pasternak was her husband's friend, champion, contemporary and more or less equal, very much to be taken for granted and while something of his stature and extraordinary quality emerges from her exasperated affection and respect, he does not appear in her pages as the towering figure who loomed, still looms, an unseen and beneficent presence over younger generations of Soviet writers.

This is why Alexander Gladkov's contribution is so valuable and enthralling. Gladkov, who died last year, was over twenty years younger than Pasternak, and while not in the least intimidated by the great man's reputation, he was not afraid of admitting to his proper veneration. What really brought them together was the wartime evacuation of most of the Moscow writers to a one-horse provincial town on the Kama River, Chistopol, where they were thrown up against each other to a degree that even Soviet writers, who are given to living in each other's pockets, must have found almost intolerable.

246

Some lived fairly fatly, with their expensive fur coats, comparatively warm apartments and special rations. Others did not. Pasternak, the supreme outsider, did not, and Gladkov gives a pretty vivid indication of the desperate existence of all but the highly privileged in that terrible winter of 1941 to 1942. Pasternak was working at his Shakespeare translations, and rather glorying in the almost killing austerities of his daily life. But he liked to talk to someone, and that someone was Gladkov, whom he had met a few years earlier as a young disciple of Meyerhold and an aspiring playwright. Now he was on the verge of success, and to Pasternak, who suffered from that first infirmity of unworldly genius and saw himself as a famous dramatist, embarking on the primrose path to glory, vast audiences and a financial beano, he was a useful contact. But quite obviously he very much liked the younger man and trusted him as he trusted one of his grander colleagues.

All the talk recorded here is fascinating, some of it is historically important. The Chistopol experience did not last long, but the men stayed friends when they came back to Moscow, meeting intermittently; and the most important conversation of all came from a chance meeting in the Alexandrovsky Garden in 1947.

At that time Stalin was bringing his post-war terror to the boil and nobody who stood out from the ruck was safe; Pasternak himself feared the worst, in spite of the mysterious respect in which Stalin held him. But he was fighting back, and now, seated on a park bench in the very shadow of the Moscow Kremlin, he talked about the big novel which was to be *Dr Zhivago*, why he was writing it, what he wished to achieve with it, why he, a poet, had felt compelled to turn to prose, why he, indifferent to politics, had come to feel an imperative need to give expression to his opposition.

It was dangerous to talk like this, but Gladkov did not betray him. And it is somehow characteristic of that strange country that Pasternak, who had defied authority almost casually and at pointblank range again and again, and then turned away unheedingly to get on with whatever he was doing, kept out of prison and went on to write his masterpiece, while Gladkov, for no particular reason except that he was human, was arrested in the following year and sent off to a camp, where he stayed until Stalin was dead.

I don't want to suggest that the book is all veneration. On the

247

contrary, Gladkov captures quite beautifully the sometimes tiresomely elusive quality of his hero, who could never be pinned down even by those who loved him most (he himself was pinned, as it were, to a vision out of other men's sight). He is quite funny too, which is right, because Pasternak himself, with his abstractions, his dithering, his gaucheries and maddening lack of practical sense was in one aspect a comic figure. Courage, steadfastness and loftiness of purpose, nobility of character, extreme modesty accompanied by extreme self-respect (saintly innocence one might have been tempted to add until the recent devaluation of the phrase) – an alliance of these qualities is bound to prove almost too much for the mortal integument and to push it irresistibly into the realms of Quixotry.

It is a beautiful balance that Gladkov achieves. Only his undervaluing of *Zhivago* quite misses the point, and here he echoes the feeling of so many Russian worshippers at the shrine of the great poet, who makes things so hard for them by insisting that much of his early poetry is inferior and all of it no more than a preparation for this crowning work. When you have been sustained all your life by the secret power of that poetry it is hard to be told by the author that he has no use for it.

Mr Max Hayward, introducing his admirable translation, writes as perceptively as it is possible to imagine about this situation, and at the same time fills out our view of Pasternak the man. His 'Notes and Comments' at the end are a model of their kind.

Inquest on Our Haunting Shame

Discussion of *The Secret Betrayal* by Nikolai Tolstoy
1978

The story of the enforced repatriation of a host of unfortunate Soviet citizens, left stranded and abandoned in Hitler's Europe at the end of the Second World War and sent home to be shot, starved, driven to death in labour camps or tortured by Stalin's police, is one of the most disgraceful chapters in our history. Anyone who cared for the good name and continued decency of this country must be deeply grateful to Nikolai Tolstoy for bringing it out into the open and documenting it so thoroughly in his long and important book *Victims of Yalta*.

But how reasonable or sensible is it to demand a public inquiry into events of over thirty years ago, sins that may be in part atoned for but can never be undone? A public inquiry would inevitably degenerate into a hunt for the 'guilty men'. This is too easy. (What do we do with them when they are identified?) There is nothing like a scapegoat for obscuring our own failures.

The men who were responsible for this horror, from Eden and the all-party War Cabinet downwards to then quite junior officials in the Foreign Office – and too-obedient Army officers – were either our freely elected representatives or a fair cross-section of British officialdom. It is British attitudes and the British way of doing things that should be on trial. A public inquiry should be a public inquest into ourselves.

The story began with the Normandy landings in the summer of 1944 when the Allied Forces found themselves overrunning and capturing large numbers of bewildered Russians in German uniforms who had been forced by the threat of starvation or shooting to take up arms in defence of Hitler's West Wall. What to do with them? The legal brains of the Foreign Office got busy and decided that they had better be treated as Russian nationals, kept separate from German prisoners, and in due course sent back to the Soviet Union.

The landings had only just taken place and much fighting lay ahead. Nobody clearly saw that before the operation of repatriation could be concluded, millions would be dragged into it and that many would kill themselves rather than go back.

Very few realised that among this host were not merely the dumb peasants in uniform pressganged by Hitler but also old men, women and children, part of the horde of displaced persons torn from their homes and taken to slave labour in Germany; anti-Soviet crusaders transformed by Stalin's atrocities into dedicated foes of the Soviet Union under General Vlasov, once a great popular hero; survivors from the dreadful prison cages, abandoned by Stalin, almost starved to death by Hitler, all of whom knew that Stalin had said that he would regard any Red Army men who allowed themselves to be taken prisoner as deserters; whole settlements of rebellious Cossacks who had somehow kept together, drifting over half Europe with the German forces; nationals of non-Russian territories of the Soviet Empire who had never accepted Russian rule.

All these were sent back – to death, prison, or remote exile, some three million who had fallen into Western hands, the deserving and the undeserving with no difference made between bewildered innocents, convinced opponents of the Stalin regime, and the worst scallywags trying to get on to the winning side. Why?

It is this 'why' that has suddenly sounded louder than ever before with the publication of Count Tolstoy's book. How did it happen? Who was to blame?

The interesting thing is that there was no such outcry when this story was told for the first time by Nicholas Bethell in *The Last Secret* nearly four years ago. Some of the worst episodes in the Tolstoy book were also described by Bethell. For example, the betrayal of the fifty thousand Cossacks, women and children included, who, in retreat from Italy, camped in the valley of the River Drau outside Lienz on the Austrian side of the Dolomites. How to get these fierce clansmen, armed to the teeth, into the trains that would take them back to Russia? Clearly they had to be disarmed. This could be done only by treachery.

Certain British officers had won the confidence of their

chieftains, and these officers were now used to lie to them, to persuade them to lay down their arms so that they could be rounded up (as though by the KGB), bludgeoned and bayoneted into the waiting trains. It was some of these unfortunates whom Solzhenitsyn met in the camps: they filled him so with indignation at the Allied treachery that he was moved, unfairly and absurdly, to equate Roosevelt and Churchill with Stalin and Hitler.

There was the story of the thirty-two thousand prisoners who were actually brought to Britain. Russian secret police agents, if you please, were allowed to scour the English countryside like jackals smelling them out. The prisoners were embarked at Liverpool (some killed themselves at the dockside) and shipped to Odessa, where many were shot out of hand on the quay, with no attempt at concealment from the British liaison officers and crews.

And so on.

When Lord Bethell's book was published he did not have access to all the documents covering the main period. This meant that the story he told, though terrible, was not so unequivocally bleak as the story now told by Tolstoy. I quote from my own review:

Besides being an important contribution to history it is an exploration of the borderland between tragic necessity and self-deluding expediency, which is the area in which so much political activity is inevitably conducted. A number of Englishmen meaning no harm, reasonably upright civil servants, reasonably honest soldiers, were committed by their political masters in the interest of an overriding necessity (the preservation of the Soviet alliance) to carry out actions which condemned hundreds of thousands of their fellow men and women to death or terrible suffering.

The political masters themselves – Churchill, Roosevelt, Eden, Bevin – were not evil men, only politicians caught in a web of evasion and expediency and faced with a situation for which they were quite unprepared and which they did not understand – driven by almost intolerable pressures to actions so unthinkable that they could not bring themselves to think.

251

In the light of Count Tolstoy's account I think this judgement was too soft. Of course there were mitigating factors. It was the end of the war and people were desperately tired; Russia was our gallant ally to whose sacrifice we owed, perhaps, our very survival. Stalin had done terrible things, but was it conceivable that there would be no relaxation after a victorious war in which he had made common cause with Britain and America?

Promises had been made and had to be kept: what would happen to British prisoners who had fallen into Russian hands if we flouted Stalin's wishes about his own nationals? Stalin apart, what on earth was to be done with all these hundreds of thousands, millions, if they stayed in the West? Who was going to feed them? Where could they live and work?

But having said this much in mitigation, the hard facts of Count Tolstoy's recital tell another story. The record is a chilling one. Eden, Churchill's Foreign Minister, clearly propelled above all by vanity, was impatiently convinced that he could get on with Stalin, apparently regardless of the human tragedy. He positively pressed these unfortunates on Stalin before Stalin was even ready to admit their existence – and then insisted that he was bound by the resulting protocol to deliver the lot.

Alexander Cadogan, then Head of the Foreign Office; Christopher Warner as Department Chief; Patrick Dean as legal adviser and later Ambassador to Washington ('We are not concerned with the fact that they may be shot or otherwise more harshly dealt with than they might be under English law'); Thomas Brimelow, one day himself to be Head of the Foreign Office, industriously stopping all possible boltholes; John Galsworthy, now our Ambassador to Mexico, who at least admitted that the crux of the matter was expediency – all these knew what they were doing.

As a small example, the exchange of Minutes about the impossibility of squaring the Liverpool Coroner when it came to trying to prevent public knowledge of the fact that Russians resisting embarcation kept on killing themselves is most revealing. So is the urgent awareness of the need to keep from the British public the fact that men from SMERSH were given a licence to roam the country.

There were also straight lies, as when Warner categorically stated that no violence had had to be used. Even more squalid was the way in which old anti-Bolsheviks who had lived outside Russia for years were bundled back to Stalin even though he had never dreamt of asking for them. This gratuitous flourish remains inexplicable, the relevant file apparently suppressed.

But why should this handful of men be singled out for the pillory? They were a dozen among thousands. For this is how the British official conducts himself habitually. For him tidiness and administrative convenience are above all important. The public he regards as a clumsy, interfering ignoramus. No doubt he is right, but on the whole, uncorrupted by authority, it remains a good-hearted ignoramus. And it needs to watch out and not to delegate the powers of good and evil to men chosen for a very particular kind of cleverness, who spend most of their time in offices.

Precisely the same sort of men are to be found in all the ministries known to me today. The shifts and evasions; the Ministry of Defence juggling with figures and lying about combat readiness; the Inland Revenue obedient to the most narrowly legalistic interpretations; the Home Office, Treasury, Department of Education and Science all busily keeping their ends up against those they are supposed to serve are all peopled by the same very clever sort of Englishmen.

It seems to me that we do not need a public inquiry into a single ministerial atrocity which nothing can repair. We need a fresh look at the way we run our institutions (including now our larger industrial complexes, private as well as nationalised). That is to say, we need an inquest on ourselves.

This does not mean that we should read this book and simply pass on. We cannot directly help the survivors and their children in the Soviet Union. But we can at least try to help those outside the Soviet Union who are in various ways victims of the Kremlin's savagery. These include the remnants of those Poles who fought with us against Hitler as well as refugees of half a dozen countries under Russian domination.

Perhaps it would also be an act of grace, as well as a salutary reminder to ourselves, to dedicate a memorial to those unfortunates we sent away – if only in part to atone for the mean-spirited resistance of our contemporary officialdom to the raising up of a memorial to the Polish officers murdered by the Russians in Katyn Forest.

In the general bleakness splendid exceptions shine out. Lord Selborne protested vigorously and movingly to his Cabinet colleagues and was snubbed by Eden for his pains: Churchill wavered. Sir James Grigg in the War Office objected very strongly to his soldiers being used by the politicians to beat and bludgeon their prisoners. Field Marshal Alexander, who had once fought alongside the Cossack leader Krasnov in the early days of the Revolution, also protested sharply. General Horatius Murray, commanding the Sixth Armoured Division, saw to it that the prisoners he was supposed to deceive and shanghai were given a chance to escape. There were obviously exceptions in the Foreign Office too, but we do not meet them in the pages of this book.

But on the whole British coldness and British rectitude prevailed, dragging the Americans with it. At the end of it all one feels one understands a little better just why Albion has so long been regarded as perfidious. Other peoples may be and are rougher and more cruel; other bureaucracies are no less lacking heart; but the particular inhumanity of British officialdom seems to lie in the fact that it brings to its more disgraceful behaviour that flavour of high-minded, distant, chilly holiness, which is also a feature of British justice at its best.

Having said all this, let us recollect ourselves. The cause of all this horror was Stalin, and the men who did the shooting and the torturing were Russians. From Russia we hear not a word of self-reproach or self-searching. If ever a book of this kind comes to be published in Russia we may begin to regard Stalin's successors as civilised human beings.

Shouts in the Mountains
Review of *The Oak and the Calf*
by Alexander Solzhenitsyn
1980

One day, fairly early in the ten-year battle with authority which ended in his being thrown out of his country, Solzhenitsyn was feeling desperate. After the false dawn which was the publication of *One Day in the Life of Ivan Denisovich*, the prison walls seemed to be closing round him once more (he had already suffered eight years in prisons and camps and another four in remote exile). None of the great works composed so laboriously in conditions of almost unimaginable adversity had appeared anywhere in the world or seemed likely to appear; but at least they had been safely hidden away, until, sudden calamity, the KGB managed to lay hands on the manuscript of *The First Circle*.

It looked as though Solzhenitsyn himself might be picked up quietly and bundled away into oblivion before he had given the world what he was passionately convinced he had been sent into the world to give. And, indeed, had he been put away then, in 1966, we should never have understood the extent of our loss. There was only one thing to do, he decided: to start shouting as hard as he could. 'A shout in the mountains has been known to start an avalanche.' And so he did. The avalanche he dreamed of, the sweeping away, the suffocation of the entire brutal, corrupt, fathomlessly stupid apparatus devised by Lenin and handed down by him for the admiration of the world, presently incorporated in Brezhnev and Co., has not taken place. But I do not think it too much to say that this one man, much larger than lifesize, has effected a change in attitudes towards the Soviet Union which is permanent and real, even though at times it may seem that we are as far away from grasping the truth about that vile regime as ever.

He has also, with a handful of others, given all those men and women in Russia who are dissenters but, for a variety of reasons, not fighting ones, a standard to bow to. What he has done above all things and all others has been to record the truth in such a manner as to render it indestructible, stamping it into the Western consciousness with all the authority of a prophet of the Lord.

He cannot really have expected the avalanche. The immediate purpose of the shouting was to cause such an uproar that he could not be quietly put away; thus time was won to complete the work he had to do in Russia and prepare for the ultimate detonation of the landmines, his great works, designed to breach the curtain of the official lie.

There was much more than shouting. Indeed, for long periods after each sortie, each uproar, he sank back in upon himself and lived as quietly as a mouse, working, working through the lull, dreading the day when he would have to break off his writing to fight another action in what was a long and elaborate one-man war, the campaigns elaborately planned and plotted, against the embattled resources of one of the two most powerful states in the world. He himself rejoiced in the fight when it was actually joined, making such rings round Brezhnev and his huge police apparatus that the one had nothing to say and the other behaved at times like the Keystone cops.

This volume is a day by day, year by year account of that battle, written more or less as it unfolded. It is marvellously easy to read (helped by an admirable translation), the best-written, the most good-humoured of all his works. Perhaps in a way also the most devastating. It would not occur to many people to go to Solzhenitsyn for laughs, but certain passages are hilariously funny. And the humour, the outcrops of farce, the general ebullience, bring home to the reader, as a more solemn and formal treatment could not, the simple fact that here we are dealing with human beings like ourselves, people who bleed when they are pricked, in the grip of an apparatus of repression which is suddenly very real through the farce, as when the trusted woman friend, forced by the KGB to reveal the hiding place of the *Gulag* manuscript, is found hanged in her own apartment, whether by her own hand or at the hands of the police nobody can be certain: we are living in Russia, and there is nobody to inquire.

If sometimes Solzhenitsyn has seemed overburdened with his sense of mission (as well he might be), with his responsibility to the dead, to history, here he is responsible only to himself; and as a result the artist in him is given his head. And what an artist! Although the narrative is in outward form a spontaneous outpouring, as it were, a situation-report from the front, written up rather breathlessly in quiet times between offensives, it is in fact most carefully and closely fashioned round a central core: the splendours and miseries of Alexander Tvardovsky, poet, still more famous in the West as editor of the monthly review, *Novi Mir*, distinguished for its relative courage during the post-Stalin thaw.

Tvardovsky's supreme moment was the publication, with Khrushchev's blessing, of *One Day in the Life of Ivan Denisovich*. From then until his death he was to be hopelessly caught up, sometimes willingly, sometimes grudgingly, in Solzhenitsyn's own struggle. It seems to me that Solzhenitsyn's account of his relations with his so different champion and critic takes the reader more directly into the very heart of the Russian tragedy than anything known to me. It also offers a superb and long drawn-out portrait of a tragi-comic individual. Anyone who has any doubts about Solzhenitsyn's potential as an artist or his eye for comedy will shed them now. Developing without fanfare on an almost Proustian scale in length and in depth, it establishes itself as one of the truly great literary portraits.

The interplay between Solzhenitsyn the hero and martyr, full of his own genius, harsh, demanding, ruthless, and the brave, weak, corrupted (but not corrupt) alcoholic, a good and rather more than averagely gifted man, struggling for ever out of his depth, is quite beautifully rendered.

Solzhenitsyn is not beyond criticism. His sniping at some of his fellow-dissidents is unworthy. His condemnation of the all too obvious sins of the West is absurdly out of perspective. But we can argue about these failings at another time.

In Memoriam:
Nadezhda Mandelstam
1981

Osip Mandelstam, the world knows now, was one of the supreme poets of a century which has produced many fine poets; but he was born in Russia in 1891 and killed by Stalin, probably in 1938, obliterated without trace, his writings banned, erased.

That his poetry survived was due to the active devotion and heroism of his wife, Nadezhda Yakovlevna, who memorised it and wrote it down and kept it through a lifetime of privation and humiliation so that she could send it out of the country. Besides this, only the rarest fraction of his published work survives.

And then, as if this was not enough, she herself composed two volumes of memoirs, published here in 1971 and 1974, *Hope Against Hope* and *Hope Abandoned*,* which told her husband's story and re-created with astonishing vividness his life and times.

She was eighty-one last November, and died last week, an astringent, formidable old lady, sardonically humorous, who made herself immortal, without thinking of it, by securing her husband's immortality. For forty-two years after the police came for him in her presence and took him away to die, she fought on.

Her husband knew it was bound to end like that. Not in the least a political animal, he could not stand the lies, and went on telling the truth as it came into his head (he would have had uncomfortable things to say about our own society had he been lucky enough to have been here). But he was far from looking for trouble.

Mrs Mandelstam would have wished for her death to serve also as a memorial to her husband, so it is not out of place to speak so much of him here. The two will be inseparable as long

* Both translated by Max Haywood (Atheneum, 1971 and 1974).

as poetry exists, as they were in life until Stalin tore them apart.

But Mrs Mandelstam's memorial to her husband is also her own memorial. No other book, I think, has quite the range and depth as a record, wholly without self-pity, of Stalin's destruction of the minds of her own people, and particularly of the painfully thin layer of civilised humanity which survived the Revolution – only to see it pulled down and trampled to death in the name of the future.

She was born in 1891 of educated professional parents (her mother was a doctor); she spent most of her youth in Kiev, marrying in 1919. Although a talented writer, she devoted herself ever after to her husband's genius.

It cannot have surprised her when her husband was sent into internal exile in 1934 for a poem in which he called Stalin a 'murderer of peasants'. But it probably surprised even her when, four years later, at the height of the great purge, he was arrested again with all the panoply of the NKVD (still happily active to this day as the KGB) and sent off to die.

She never knew for certain how, or even when or where, he died, in spite of persistent questioning of survivors from the camps when they started coming back after Stalin's death. It hardly mattered. She herself for eighteen years was condemned to exile in remote provincial towns where she managed, sometimes with excruciating difficulty, to keep body and soul together by language-teaching.

In 1956 she came back to Moscow and began a new career. She had refused to die because unless she stayed alive her husband's work would die. Now she went on, and her tiny, cramped, one-room apartment became a meeting place for much that was good in her life, in first Khrushchev's and then Brezhnev's Russia. Her memoirs, of course, have not yet been published in her native land, but some years ago a small selection of her husband's poems was brought out in Moscow.

When *Hope Against Hope* and *Hope Abandoned* are published in Russia, it will be the start of hope returning. And when that time comes, it will be, above all, due to the spirit shown by this remarkable woman and a very few others fit to be mentioned in the same breath with her.

Miracle in a Death Camp
Review of *Within the Whirlwind*
by Eugenia Ginzburg
1981

Those who remember the first instalment of Eugenia Ginz-burg's story, *Into the Whirlwind*, will need no urging to read its sequel. Fourteen years have gone by since the appearance of that first marvellous volume. Now the whole story emerges as one of the classics of twentieth-century Russian literature – but a classic still banned in its homeland.

The author, who died four years ago still hoping that her grandson if not her son might live to see this book published in Russia, was very much a child of the Revolution. Keenly intelligent but blinkered – self-blinded, indeed, one might say – a teacher and journalist, a wife and mother married to a senior member of the Kazan Regional Party Committee, a Party member herself eager to carry out the Party's will and oblivious of its crimes, she ran into trouble with tens of thousands of others soon after the murder of Kirov in 1934 which set off the great purge. A bogus confession to an imaginary offence would have got her off, at least for a time, but she believed in Soviet justice and the goodness of the Party and indignantly refused to lie her way out.

That made her a Trotskyite and a terrorist, and in 1937, in her early thirties, she was arrested, torn away from her family, and embarked upon an eighteen-year pilgrimage of sorrows – prison, camp and exile until her rehabilitation two years after Stalin's death.

Into the Whirlwind took her story from the moment when the ground, terrifyingly and inexplicably, started moving under her feet to her arrest in 1937; two years in prison (much of the time in solitary); interminable surrealist interrogations; the terrible journey across Siberia to the Pacific coast, the sea voyage in the slave ship to Magadan; then to the edge of death from exhaustion and starvation in one of the worst camps in the Kolyma goldfield. She was saved by a miracle, and *Within the Whirlwind* carries on from there.

It opens with her transfer from hell to heaven – to a hospital for children born to women prisoners in the Kolyma camps. There, in that howling arctic wilderness, stood the ramshackle huts with their labels: 'Infants' Group', 'Toddlers' Group', 'Senior Group', alive with yelling, romping children. And there among the toddlers she recovered some of her strength.

What was of especial value in the first volume was that it offered the most complete, coherent and perceptive *inside view* of arrest, interrogation, imprisonment and transportation as practised under Stalin. It showed for the first time the operations of a lunatic system as they affected an intelligent Russian who thought she was part of that system and thus helping to transform the world.

Until then, with the brief exception of *One Day in the Life of Ivan Denisovich*, we had only the accounts of foreign survivors – Poles and Germans above all, aliens in an alien land, lost in unknown territory, uncomprehending, with no means of telling the normal from the abnormal. The German Communist Margarethe Buber-Neumann, imprisoned by Stalin for being a Communist, then handed over to Hitler, found her heart bursting with mingled relief and pride at the contrast between Gulag and, if you please, Ravensbrueck (where Hitler put her) with its neatness and order and colourful flowerbeds . . . .

But Eugenia Ginzburg was on her home ground. The men who tricked her, betrayed her, informed against her, bore false witness against her, sold her, were men she had worked with in what she believed to be a common cause. Having been expelled in due form from the Party and handed over to the secular arm, she found herself being interrogated in a familiar building quite close to her home, and she could hear the dear old familiar trams clanking by outside. All around her were familiar faces. She was not, as foreigners were, lost in an unfathomable jungle inhabited by monsters: she was among her own people, taking for granted aspects of the scene which strike unpractised foreigners dumb with bewilderment, but able as no foreigner could to point up the deviant wickedness.

This applies no less to this second volume, which is an account of life in the Kolyma camps of the farthest northeast, part of that unspeakable empire of slaves so elaborately mapped and charted by Solzhenitsyn. Eugenia Ginzburg adds to Solzhenitsyn, however. For even he came to write in some sense as an outsider in a positive fury of alienation. Eugenia Ginzburg is the voice of humanity itself. Her character commanded a combination of qualities which stamps every detail of her story with a sort of radiance.

Out of the pit she can laugh, her sense of humour tempered with the most delicate irony, giving life and shape to a society of what from the outside looked like living dead. She can face and register without a flicker of hysteria or despair the worst that human nature can devise – and still be filled with purposeful indignation and compassion. She moves through this appalling landscape fully aware but protected by a sort of impenetrable innocence.

The horror and farce are all there. The society of the dying; the women compelled to work in that fearful cold so long as the temperature was a degree less than fifty below; the sick gravedigger declared dead and laid under a pile of frozen corpses on the mortuary slab – who came to life and was furiously asked what he meant by breaking into the morgue before he was dead; the doomed young actor from the Meyerhold theatre and his ballerina sweetheart who contrived to come together from separate camps when he was detailed for an errand with a horse and cart: 'Relations between a male and a female convict involving a horse standing idle for two hours' the charge ran when they were caught, and that was the end for them; the lunatic system of rationing, so that the less you fulfilled your output norm the smaller the ration, until in the end there was no output at all, and no food.

And to turn prose into poetry, there runs a thread distinguishing this terrible story from all others of its kind: the uncovenanted solace of a profound and slowly growing love affair with a fellow prisoner, a German, a Catholic and a homeopath, himself some sort of a saint dispensing healing to good and evil with perfect absence of self-consciousness.

Where Angels Fear to Tread–
Political Pilgrims

Review of *Travels of Western Intellectuals
to the Soviet Union, China and Cuba*
by Paul Hollander
1982

Paul Hollander has had the very good idea of examining *in
extenso* and in depth the imbecilities of successive waves of
intellectuals returning from the holy places of the twentieth
century with their tidings of great joy: Moscow, Havana,
Peking, Hanoi – the very names are like a knell.

I think if one had to single out the worst offence common to
the many varied individuals who make up this cloud of false
witnesses it would be their inhumanity. And yet it has been
precisely on their humaneness that most of them have preened
themselves, up and down the scale of intellectual eminence:
Julian Huxley, Jean-Paul Sartre, Edmund Wilson, Pablo
Neruda (perhaps the most frivolous of them all), the super-
humanly vain Hewlett Johnson (the Dean of Canterbury),
Norman Mailer, innocents like Mary McCarthy and Susan
Sontag, occasional rogue elephants like H. G. Wells and Ber-
nard Shaw, and many, many more.

They showed their inhumanity by holding their own preconceptions, their own desires, in higher esteem than the search for
truth; and even when the truth was thrust upon them by the
victims of one tyranny after another, they refused for too long to
believe: the victim, they thought, is by definition biased; but the
jailer is not – not when he is Stalin, or Mao, or whoever else is
leading the vanguard of progress.

Professor Hollander brings this home with salutary force. He
has produced a work of illumination which is to a high degree
entertaining. Malcolm Muggeridge, Robert Conquest and
others have long familiarised us with the more hilarious pro-
nouncements on Stalin's Russia by the first batch of pilgrims in
the early 1930s; Hollander explores the assumptions behind the
nonsense, and brings to his task a useful detachment arising

from his special background – schooldays in Communist Hungary, followed by student days in London, followed by a distinguished academic career in the United States.

While he recaptures and records unmercifully those first far from careless raptures over the great socialist experiment he is especially instructive in showing up the scale on which these follies have since been repeated in the Far East and the Caribbean – sometimes by the same men and women who earlier made fools of themselves in Moscow.

Here we are dealing for the most part with Americans either in revolt against their own society or justifiably outraged by the crass brutality of the Vietnam adventure. The emphasis has shifted since the Thirties. Then it was taken for granted by the pilgrims that the capitalist West was finished (which it certainly appeared to be at the time) and that by aligning themselves with Stalin they were aligning themselves with the one man who knew where he was, with power and purpose. Stalin had to be benign because he was lord and architect of the future, and the future was Utopia, with special luxury apartments for philosophers, scientists, artists so undervalued in the West.

There was no agonising. Stalin was positively softhearted (except to Shaw who saw him as the timely scourge of the incompetent). To Harold Laski the labour camps were beneficient institutions gently straightening the crooked; the Webbs announced that Stalin had far less power than the President of the United States, was no more, in fact, than the instrument of the Central Committee's will; Julian Huxley reported wide-eyed at the height of the famine years on the magnificent physique and bearing of Soviet youth; Wells decided that everyone trusted Stalin, nobody feared him; even the inescapable dinginess and smelliness and general dilapidation of the material apparatus of Muscovite life was exalted as a necessary and glorious proof of spiritual virtue.

Something of this spirit was recaptured when Castro took over Cuba – though even here the emphasis was on the ruthless destruction of Americana rather than on the pious building of a new society with the leader as Sunday-school teacher. But doubts were creeping in. Mailer had to shout down his own doubts with invocations of a Zapata-like redeemer on a white horse. Mary McCarthy gave the whole game away in one small *cri du coeur*, which seems to me the saddest thing in the book: commenting on the Húe massacre in Vietnam she wrote: 'There is no way of knowing what really happened .... I should prefer to think it was the Americans.'

My only major criticism of Professor Hollander is that he takes these people too much at their own valuation; and although he tries patiently and often successfuly to sort out their tangle of motives, he seems to me to shy away from the main point: namely that pretty well all those mentioned and quoted behaved, *not as intellectuals in the proper sense* (men and women of reason), but only as left-wing publicists, politicians *manqués* dealing with abstractions, members of an exclusive and highly conformist congregation.

The fact that some of them had, or have, first-class brains is neither here nor there: they were, or are, above all performers. There have been plenty of intellectuals, both left and right inclined, sickened and appalled by too many aspects of Western society, who have at least tried to use their brains instead of surrendering them to the miracle man of the moment.

How It All Began
Review of *The Cheka*
by George Leggett
1981

Previous volumes in the splendid Oxford History of Modern Europe have been wide-ranging affairs (Zeldin on France, Raymond Carr on Spain, Taylor on Europe). In this latest addition to the series, however, Mr Leggett confines himself to the genesis, development and activity of a single institution over a span of only four years: the Soviet Secret Police in its first incarnation as the Cheka.

If at first sight this seems a little odd, in fact it turns out to be a brilliant idea. For Mr Leggett's compressed but lucid and refreshingly unassuming narrative is seen as it takes shape to be something very like an account of the foundation and early development of the Soviet state as we know it – as distinct from the Soviet state as its leaders have imagined it to be and as it has been taken more or less at face value in most histories, from E. H. Carr's colossal essay in monumental architecture downwards.

It is commonplace to refer to the Soviet Secret Police as a state within the state. I have done this myself. But it is wrong, because for all practical purposes it *is* the state. And it began with the Cheka and Lenin's invocation of mass terror as an instrument of government.

Mr Leggett does not go in for conclusions of this kind. He offers the facts and leaves it to us to make what we can of them. I do not know whether he had it in mind to show that the Soviet Union in all its nastiness was the creation not of Stalin but of Lenin – who, of course, created Stalin too. It does not matter. His carefully documented account of Lenin's embracing of terror and his subsequent unplanned institutionalisation of it is a reminder that Lenin was the inspiration of the arbitrary violence of his day and has remained so ever since, his absolute responsibility obscured by Stalin's hysteria, Trotsky's special pleading, Brezhnev's dull brutality – to say nothing of the hosannas of Western historians who should have known better. One of the troubles in all attempts to write the history of the Soviet Union is that so much space has to be given to what the Bolsheviks *said*, their quarrels, rationalisations, promises, theories, that the basic nastiness of what was going on in those early years is lost to view.

What in fact was going on was that an opportunist revolutionary demagogue of genius with the temperament of a dictator and the morals of a card-sharper, V. I. Lenin, within months of seizing power and proclaiming that the new Russia had no need for any police, had resurrected the Czarist Secret Police, the Okhrana, and called it the Vecheka, the All Russian Extraordinary Commission for Combating Counter-Revolution and Sabotage. Under the fanatical Pole, Felix Dzerzhinsky, urged on by Lenin in face of appalled opposition from the more innocent Bolsheviks, this child of the Revolution had, within three years, brought its strength up to two hundred and fifty thousand as against the fifteen thousand that the last Czar

266

had employed to keep order – but then the Okhrana had to hand over its prisoners for public trial; the Cheka had to do its own killing.

It was not simply that the terror instituted by Lenin was a pattern for the terror developed by Stalin. Arbitrary violence was in the blood. For example, Mr Leggett reminds us that the bloody war on the kulaks was started not by Stalin but by Lenin (when Lenin had gone, Trotsky wanted to renew it), who deliberately set the poorer peasants against the richer ones, encouraging them to cut each other's throats, as a calculated part of the business of destroying the villages as centres of conservatism; while the requisition squads which burnt and shot and looted in their search for hidden grain under Stalin had been invented ten years earlier by Lenin.

It was Lenin who set the tone – a tone already established in the almost insanely venomous polemics of his years of exile, the tone to become so familiar at the height of Stalin's purges, the tone which *Pravda* to this day uses to rally the workers of the world against the vile imperialists. Here he is telegraphing the Nizhni Novgorod (now Gorky) Soviet in August 1918, to instruct the comrades on the necessity for total ruthlessness as a pre-emptive move against a possible rising:

> You must exert every effort, form a troika of dictators . . .
> instantly introduce mass terror, shoot and transport hun-
> dreds of prostitutes who get the soldiers drunk, ex-officers,
> etc. Not a minute to be wasted . . . .

A little earlier in that summer we find him lashing the Petrograd comrades for dragging their feet in punishing the assassins of one of his commissars. Their offence was to '*obstruct* the *absolutely* correct revolutionary initiative of the masses,' who, he said, were demanding mass terror. (The italics are Lenin's own.)

It was the repeated advocacy of 'mass terror' by this frightful man which led directly to the sort of attitude expressed to perfection by the Red Army newspaper in September 1918 after the assassination of the Chekist Uritsky and an attempt on Lenin himself:

Without mercy, without sparing, we will kill our enemies in scores of hundreds. Let them be thousands, let them drown themselves in their own blood. For the blood of Lenin and Uritsky . . . let there be floods of blood of the bourgeois – more blood. As much as possible.

It was in this mood that the Cheka was established and nurtured by Lenin, and it was in this mood that Stalin in his turn picked up the ready-made instrument with the results we know.

Mr Leggett, as observed, is above all a scholar. He sticks to demonstrable facts. These are quite lurid enough in themselves, without going into their implications for the future (and our present).

Mr Leggett's gallery of Dzerzhinsky's deputies and chief lieutenants, so many of them Poles or Letts, is in itself an indictment of Lenin, who blessed their work: Peters, the brother of Peter the Painter of the Sydney Street siege, himself charged with the Houndsditch murders and lucky to get off; Latsis, another Lett – 'We are not waging war on individual persons. We are exterminating the Bourgeois as a class . . . . Do not look for evidence that the accused acted in word or deed against Soviet power. The first questions you ought to put are: To what class does he belong? What is his origin? What is his education or profession? And it is these questions that ought to determine the fate of the accused. In this lies the significance and essence of the Red Terror' – Kedrov, who went mad, perhaps in horror at the thought of his own crimes.

Others like them, the original knights of the Revolution, all driven by a burning sense of rectitude and the belief that they would succeed where God had failed in making a perfect world. Dzerzhinsky himself, self-consciously a man of steel, drove himself so hard that he broke down: one day at a New Year's party in the Kremlin he got wildly drunk and staggered about begging Lenin and other comrades to shoot him dead: 'I have spilt so much blood that I no longer have any right to live. You must shoot me now!'

This is a book that was needed, a complete study of the Cheka, with its major personalities in place, its emergence until it controlled the national stage and everything on it, its routine activities, its special operations, its organisation, its ethos. It would have been enough if Mr Leggett had done no more. But he does much more. To follow the story as he tells it is to understand the inevitability of the Russian tragedy once Lenin and his Bolsheviks had filched the revolution from the doomed unfortunates who had made it.